R 6/18

DATE DUE

PRINTED IN U.S.A.

The Alphabet Effect

A Media Ecology Understanding of the Making of Western Civilization

The Hampton Press Communication Series
MEDIA ECOLOGY
Lance Strate, supervisory editor

Mediating the Muse: A Communications Approach to Music,
  Media, and Cultural Change
  Robert Albrecht

Online Connections: Internet Interpersonal Relationships
  Susan B. Barnes

Bookends: The Changing Media Environment of the American
  Classroom
  Margaret Cassidy

Walter Ong's Contribution to Cultural Studies:
  The Phenomenology of the Word and I-Thou Communication
  Thomas J. Farrell

The Power of Metaphor in the Age of Electronic Media
  Raymond Gozzi, Jr.

An Ong Reader
  Walter Ong, Thomas J. Farrell, and Paul A. Soukup (eds.)

No Safety in Numbers: How the Computer Quantified Everything
  and Made People Risk Aversive
  Henry J. Perkinson

The Media Symplex: A the Edge of Meaning in the Age of Chaos
  Frank Zingrone

forthcoming

Interpretations of Culture, Technology and Communication:
  The Media Ecology Tradition
  Casey Man Kong Lum (ed.)

Cybermedia and the Ecology of Digital Media
  Lance Strate and Susan B. Barnes (eds.)

The Legacy of McLuhan
  Lance Strate and Edward Wachtel (eds.)

The Alphabet Effect

A Media Ecology Understanding of the Making of Western Civilization

Robert K. Logan
University of Toronto

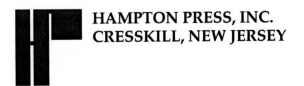
HAMPTON PRESS, INC.
CRESSKILL, NEW JERSEY

Printed in the United States of America

Library of Congress Cataloging-in-Publication Data

Logan, Robert K., 1939-
   The alphabet effect : a media ecology understanding of the making of Western civiliza-
tion / Robert K. Logan.
        p. cm. -- (The Hampton Press communication series. Media ecology)
   Includes bibliographical references and indexes.
   ISBN 1-57273-522-8 (cloth) -- ISBN 1-57273-523-6 (pbk.)
     1. Alphabet--History. 2. Writing--History. 3. Civilization--History. I. Title. II. Series.

P211.L7298 2004
411--dc22   2004051516

Hampton Press, Inc.
23 Broadway
Cresskill, New Jersey 07626

This book is dedicated to Maria Lelensky Logan
with thanks for her support and understanding

Contents

Preface

It is a rare privilege for an author to write a second edition of a book, especially one that focuses on a subject as ancient as the phonetic alphabet. Yet it is a tribute to the phonetic alphabet that it continues to play an important role in the evolution of information technology, which has led to so many new developments since the alphabet effect was first published 18 years ago. Almost all the new developments center around the use of microcomputers, which first appeared in the late 1970s, and the emergence of the Internet, e-mail, and the World Wide Web as major cultural forces beginning in 1994 with the release of the first commercial Web browser, Netscape. This book updates those developments and the role played by alphabetic literacy in their phenomenal transformation of our culture.

No book is ever finished: Once a book is in print, the author continues to make discoveries related to his or her original theme. I welcome this opportunity to return to my original work to update it and add new insights that have come to me since the book first appeared and to take advantage of the scholarship that continues in this fascinating field, such as Leonard Shlain's book, *The Alphabet Versus the Goddess*. As a result, this edition is richer and, hence, longer than the book that appeared 18 years ago. One of the principal additions is a fuller treatment of the non-alphabetic writing systems (Chinese, Japanese, Egyptian, Runic, Oghamic, and Mayan) and the inclusion of an important omission—namely, a treatment of the invention and use of the Korean alphabet, which is also a totally phonetic alphabet and should have been included in the first edition.

In the 18 years since the appearance of the first edition of this book, I have engaged in a number of research projects (Logan, 1995, 2000) influenced by the alphabet effect. I have taken the opportunity in the second edition of this book to briefly report on these projects as a way to illustrate how the alphabet effect continued to impact on human communications beyond the original hypothesis that I first developed with McLuhan in 1977 (McLuhan & Logan, 1977).

I wish to acknowledge all of those who made this book possible. First to my father Nathan, who taught me about the practical side of communication, and to my mentor Marshall McLuhan, who showed me the many levels of communications and who coauthored the principal ideas presented in this book. I wish to thank my editor, Lance Strate, who has been a great supporter of mine in this project and many others. I also wish to thank my publisher Barbara Bernstein, and her able staff at Hampton Press for all of their help and forbearance. Finally, I wish to acknowledge the assistance of my wife, Maria, for creating the happy environment in which I could work on this project.

1

Alphabet the Mother
of
Invention

The alphabet was the most significant of the boons conferred upon
mankind by Phoenicia. It is generally considered the greatest invention ever made by man.

(Hitti, 1961, p. 102)

We live in an age of rapid technological change in which we feel the
underpinnings of our society and culture are constantly being uprooted.
This might explain the present concern for roots that grips contemporary thought. This book is about roots too—those of Western civilization, which we trace back to our unique writing system, the phonetic
alphabet. As we explore the history of ideas, we discover that many of
the seminal ideas in Western science, mathematics, jurisprudence, politics, economics, social organization, and religion are intrinsically linked
with the phonetic alphabet. The magic of the phonetic alphabet is that it
is more than a writing system; it is also a system for organizing information. Of all mankind's inventions, with the possible exception of writing
itself, nothing has proved more useful or led to more innovations than
the alphabet. It is one of the most valuable possessions in all of Western
culture, yet we are blind to its effects and take its existence for granted.
It has influenced the development of our thought patterns, social institu-

1

tions, and our sense of ourselves. The alphabet, as we discovered, has contributed to the development of codified law, monotheism, abstract science, deductive logic, and individualism, each a unique contribution of Western thought. Through the printing press, it has reinforced or encouraged many of the key historical events of modern Europe including the Renaissance, the Reformation, the Industrial Revolution, the rise of democracy, mass education, nationalism, and capitalism. Marshall McLuhan (1962) summed up this idea in a succinct manner when he wrote in the Gutenberg Galaxy, "By the meaningless sign linked to the meaningless sound we have built the shape and meaning of Western man" (p. 65). The purpose of this book is to understand exactly what McLuhan meant by that pithy statement.

The alphabet is one of the first things that children learn once they are able to speak. It is the first thing that is taught in school because it is the gateway to learning and knowledge. The twenty-six letters of the English (or Roman) alphabet are the keys not only to reading and writing but also to a whole philosophy of organizing information. We use the letters of the alphabet to order the words in our dictionaries, the articles in our encyclopedias, the books in our libraries, and the files on our computers. These systematic approaches to coordinating information based on the medium of the alphabet have suggested other forms of classification and codification that are part and parcel of Western science, law, engineering, economics, and social organization.

Not only has the alphabet performed admirably as a tool for literacy, it has also served as a model for classification. It has played an instrumental role in the development of the logical style of analysis that is characteristic of the Western way of thinking. Learning how to read and write with the alphabet has brought us more than literacy and a model for classification. It has provided us with a conceptual framework for analysis and has restructured our perceptions of reality. All of these effects take place independent of what we read. The information that is coded is not important; it is the act of coding that has been so influential and acted as a springboard for new ideas. Other writing systems exist, but none has provided such fertile ground for abstract ideas nor such an efficient tool for organizing information.

THE ALPHABET AS PHONETIC CODE

The phonetic alphabet is a unique system of writing in which a small number of letters or visual signs (22–40) are used to represent the basic sounds or phonemes of a spoken language. The letters are used to code the sounds of each word phonetically.

The first alphabet was invented over 3,500 years ago in the Near East by the Canaanites, a Semitic people, and contained only 22 letters. It became the model for hundreds of other phonetic alphabets including English, French, Latin, Greek, Latvian, Russian, Romanian, Arabic, Turkish, Persian, Sanskrit, Korean, Hebrew, and Swahili. Each of these phonetic alphabets is descended from the first Canaanite alphabet through a complicated process of borrowing and adaptation. The English alphabet is derived from the Roman alphabet, which in turn can be traced back through the Etruscan, Greek, and Phoenician alphabets.

The letters of today's European alphabets and their sound values correspond to those of that first Semitic alphabet with some additions (see chap. 2, this volume). The original alphabet invented by the Canaanites contained only consonants. The Greeks, however, improved on the Semitic alphabet by adding vowels. They also added a small number of new consonants to represent special sounds in their spoken language. In fact, each of the cultures that adopted an alphabetic writing system invariably added new letters to represent the unique sounds of their spoken language.

The order of the letters of modern alphabets is more or less the same as that of the original one. Even the names and shapes of the letters are in many cases recognizable from their original ancestors. For example, our letter B evolved from the Greek letter beta, β, which in turn is derived from beit, ℶ, which in the original Canaanite meant "a house" and was drawn as a box, ☐. The English letter B still stands for the same "b" sound, and the uppercase form, B, still looks a bit like its original except now the house is not so square and it has two rooms. This letter, whether as b, beta, or beit, has always been the second letter of the alphabet.

Not only have the order, name, and shape of the letters remained the same for thousands of years, but so too has the sound value of the letters. The "b" sounds, represented in English or French with b, in Greek by β, in Hebrew by ℶ, and in Canaanite by ☐, are not exactly identical; each has its own unique flavor, but they are easily recognizable from one speaking group to another. It is possible to render the approximate pronunciation of a foreign language we do not understand if it is written with the Roman alphabet. This is the power of the alphabet—namely, its ability to phonetically code the spoken word independent of the language being transcribed.

The alphabet is not the only form of writing. Because the alphabet seems to us such a natural way to write, we tend to believe that all writing systems are alphabetic. This is not true. There are two other widely used systems of writing. One is logographic writing, in which each spoken word is represented by its own unique visual sign, which denotes or depicts the word symbolically (ideograms) or pictorially (pictograms). It is the oldest form of writing, dating back to 3100 B.C. when the Sumerians first developed their writing system. It is still employed in modern Chinese writing.

A third form of writing is the syllabic system, in which each individual syllable in the spoken language is phonetically coded with its own unique sign so that each of the following syllables would have its own sign or character: ba, be, bi, bo, and bu. The first use of syllabic signs was by the Sumerians, whose later writing system was a mixture of syllabic signs and ideographic characters. The first purely syllabic code was that of the Akkadians, who took over the Sumerian writing system and tailored it to their needs. An example of a modern day syllabic code is the Japanese writing system, which employs two different codes—one a pure syllabary and the other a mixture of syllabic signs and Chinese characters. Syllabaries lie somewhere between logographic and alphabetic writing systems. Alphabets code each individual phoneme, whereas syllabaries code each individual syllable, and logographic systems depict an entire word with one sign. The phonetic alphabet is the most recent of the three writing systems. It is also the most economical, with the fewest number of signs, and hence is the most abstract. It is these properties of the alphabet that have influenced the development of Western culture and contributed to what we call the alphabet effect.

Because the alphabet is so much a part of our information environment, however, we often take its existence for granted and are blind to its effects, much as fish are unaware of the water in which they swim. The alphabet effect is a subliminal phenomenon. Of all the writing systems, the phonetic alphabet permits the most economical transcription of speech into a written code. The phonetic alphabet introduced a double level of abstraction in writing. Words are divided into the meaningless phonemic (sound) elements of which they are composed and then these meaningless phonemic elements are represented visually with equally meaningless signs—namely, the letters of the alphabet. This encourages abstraction, analysis (because each word is broken down into its basic phonemes), coding (because spoken words are coded by visual signs), and decoding (because those visual signs are transformed back to spoken sounds through reading). There is more to using the alphabet than just learning how to read and write. Using the alphabet, as we will soon discover, also entails the ability to: (a) analyze, (b) code and decode, (c) convert auditory signals or sounds into visual signs, (d) think deductively, (e) classify information, and (f) order words through the process of alphabetization. Each of these skill sets was essential to the development of the Western or European mode of thought. These skills are the hidden lessons of the alphabet that are not contained (or at least not contained to the same degree) in learning the Chinese writing system or a number of other nonalphabetic writing systems as well. These are the features of the use of the phonetic alphabet that give rise to the alphabet effect.

The extra lessons of alphabetic literacy explain why North American schoolchildren take just as long to learn to read and write as Chinese children despite that they have to learn only 26 letters compared with the 1,000 basic characters required to read Chinese. In both China and North America, children begin school at age 5 and have learned how to read and write, more or less, by the time they are 8 years old. Western children take the same time because, along with reading and writing, they are learning many other things (Rappaport, 1976). What they learn are the intellectual by-products of the alphabet, such as abstraction, analysis, rationality, and classification, which form the essence of the alphabet effect and the basis for Western abstract scientific and logical thinking. The use of the phonetic alphabet helps explain why Western and Chinese thinking are so different (abstract and theoretical for the West versus concrete and practical for the East).

THE ORIGINAL HYPOTHESIS

This study of the alphabet effect emerges from and is based on a tradition (known originally as the Toronto School of Communications) established by Harold Innis (1971, 1972) and Marshall McLuhan (1962, 1964) at the University of Toronto. It began in the early 1950s when they explored the ways in which media of communication, including the alphabet, have shaped and influenced human culture and its various social institutions. In particular, they showed that the use of the phonetic alphabet and the coding it encouraged led the Greeks to deductive logic and abstract theoretical science (see chap. 6, this volume). It is also worth noting that the tradition that began as the Toronto School of Communication has a much geographic broader base and operates under the more descriptive moniker of media ecology.

My own interest in understanding the alphabet effect arose from my research with McLuhan and my earlier attempts to understand the origins of abstract science in the West. The earliest form of science as it was practiced in ancient China, Egypt, and Mesopotamia was strictly phenomenological and concerned with practical questions. It was based exclusively on observation and not on any particular theoretical foundation. Joseph Needham (1956, 1979), the China scholar, nevertheless argued that the Chinese contributed to the development of abstract science in the West because of their many practical inventions and the transfer of technology from East to West. His assertion leads naturally to this question: Why did abstract theoretical science not begin in China, but rather in the West?

In an attempt to answer this question, I once suggested that monotheism and codified law, two features of Western culture absent in China, led to a notion of universal law, which influenced the development of abstract science in ancient Greece. When I first shared this hypothesis with McLuhan, he agreed with me, but pointed out that I had failed to take into account the phonetic alphabet, another feature of Western culture not found in China, which had also contributed to the development of Western science. Realizing that our independent explanations complemented and reinforced each other, we combined them in a paper entitled, "Alphabet, Mother of Invention" (McLuhan & Logan, 1977) to develop the following hypothesis.

Western thought patterns are highly abstract compared with Eastern. There developed in the West, and only in the West, a group of innovations that constitute the basis of Western thought. These include (in addition to the alphabet) codified law, monotheism, abstract theoretical science, formal logic, and individualism. All of these innovations, including the alphabet, arose within the narrow geographic zone between the Tigris-Euphrates river system and the Aegean Sea and within the narrow time frame between 2000 B.C. and 500 B.C. We do not consider this to be an accident. Although not suggesting a direct causal connection between the alphabet and the other innovations, we would claim, however, that the phonetic alphabet (or phonetic syllabaries) played a particularly dynamic role within this constellation of events and provided the ground or framework for the mutual development of these innovations.

The effects of the alphabet and the abstract, logical, systematic thought that it encouraged explain why science began in the West and not the East despite the much greater technological sophistication of the Chinese, the inventors of metallurgy, irrigation systems, animal harnesses, paper, ink, printing, movable type, gunpowder, rockets, porcelain, and silk. Credit must also be given to monotheism and codified law for the role they played in developing the notion of universality—an essential building block of science. Almost all of the early scientists—Thales, Anaximenes, Anaximander, Anaxagoras and Heraclitus, were both lawmakers in their community and monotheistically inclined. They each believed that a unifying principle ruled the universe.

Phonetic writing was essential to the intellectual development in the West. No such development occurred in the East. The remainder of this book is devoted to articulating this hypothesis, which McLuhan and I formulated in our original article. The hypothesis, however, is extended to include the influence of the alphabet on the development of Western civilization after its first flowering in ancient Greece. To do this, we review the history of Western ideas from the invention of writing in Sumer 5,000 years ago to the most recent applications of computer technology. We trace the role that the phonetic alphabet has played directly and indirectly (through science, logic, codified law, and monotheism) in the development of Western civilization.

First, we review the history of writing and learn how the alphabet was first invented. We then compare European and Chinese culture, showing how the differences in the two writing systems account for the many contrasts in these two civilizations. After this we will examine the historic accomplishments of various societies, studying the way in which the alphabet influenced the development of their thought and cultural patterns. Beginning with Mesopotamia, we examine in turn the following cultures: Hebrew, Greek, Roman, Arab, Medieval, Renaissance, Industrial, and Post-Industrial. We show how each of these cultures was influenced by the alphabet effect and in turn developed its own unique application of alphabetic literacy.

A central theme in this study is the notion that a medium of communication is not merely a passive conduit for the transmission of information, but rather an active force, "a living vortex of power," which creates new social patterns and perceptual realities. Innis (1971) wrote that, "a medium of communication has an important influence on the dissemination of knowledge over space and over time and it becomes necessary to study its characteristics in order to appraise its influence in its cultural setting" (p. 33). Once the dominant media and technologies of a culture are known, one knows "the cause and shaping force of the entire structure [and] what the pattern of any culture [has] to be, both psychically and socially" (Innis, 1972, p. xii). A person who is literate has a different worldview than one who receives information exclusively through oral communication. The alphabet, independent of the spoken languages it transcribes or the information it makes available, has its own intrinsic impacts. These effects have changed the nature of Western civilization so that it differs both from nonliterate cultures and from those societies whose system of writing is nonalphabetic, such as Chinese or Japanese.

Because media effects are so important, one cannot understand historical processes and cultural development solely in terms of what information has been communicated. One must also understand the way in which that information was mediated. In other words, one must also examine the effects of media independent of the messages they transmit. Marshall McLuhan expressed this idea with his famous adage, "the medium is the message," which forms an integral part of the philosophy of the Toronto School of Communication. Like most good aphorisms,

McLuhan's famous dictum cannot be taken literally. It is not that the medium is literally the message, but rather that, independent of its content or messages, a medium has its own intrinsic effects on our perceptions which are its unique message. "The message of any medium or technology is the change of scale or pace or pattern that it introduces into human affairs." McLuhan (1964) cited the way the railway created "totally new kinds of cities and new kinds of work" (p. 8). What McLuhan wrote about the railroad applies with equal force to the medium of alphabetic writing. "The medium is the message" because it is the "medium that shapes and controls the scale and form of human association and action" (McLuhan, 1964, p. 9). The effects of a medium impose a new environment and set of sensibilities on its users, and it is only by studying both the medium as a message and the messages that the medium transmits that a full appreciation of cultural and historical processes can emerge.

THREE COMMUNICATION AGES

Building on the ideas of Innis, McLuhan divided human history into three distinct periods based on the modes of sensibilities their media made available to them. The first era is that of oral communication; it stretches from the time humankind first acquired speech to the beginnings of literacy 5,000 years ago. The second era is the age of literacy; it includes the period from the invention of writing to the discovery of electricity and its use in the form of the telegraph. The age of writing is further subdivided into three distinct periods, the first beginning with the advent of written symbols based on pictograms and ideograms, the second with the invention of the phonetic alphabet, and the last with the emergence of the movable type printing press. The third communication era, that of the electric flow of information, covers the period from the first use of the telegraph in 1844 to the present. Although Innis and McLuhan never made a clear distinction between electric (mass media such as telegraph, telephone, radio, and TV) and electronic (computing) communications, we do in this study. The focus of this book is the study of the phonetic alphabet, but we also examine the origin of writing and show how it led to the development of the phonetic alphabet. We then study the use of the alphabet and its contribution to the development of the printing press and finally its impact on the electronic flow of information, especially the way in which it shaped the use of computers and the Internet.

2

The Origin
of
Writing

To study the origin of the alphabet by the Canaanites somewhere in the middle of the second millennium B.C., we must first examine how writing was invented by the Sumerians some 1,500 years earlier around 3100 B.C. Writing systems developed independently in four other cultures— namely, Egypt, China, the Harappa or Mohenjo–Daro people of the Indus valley, and Meso-America (Diringer, 1948; Driver, 1976; Gelb, 1963; Naveh, 1982). Their invention followed a different set of circumstances than those in Sumer. All other writing systems of the world, including the phonetic alphabet, have been derived either directly or indirectly from contact with one of these five writing systems through borrowing and modification. The Meso-American writing system, only 400 years old at the time the conquistadors arrived in the 16th century, is thought to have never evolved beyond its original pictographic/ideographic stage. The Harappa–Mohenjo–Daro system, still undeciphered, apparently evolved into a mixed system of pictograms and syllabic signs before its demise. Like the Meso-American, it represents a dead end. The writing systems of modern India do not derive from the Harappa culture, but rather from the Aramaic alphabet—a direct descendant of the original Proto–Canaanite Semitic alphabet that evolved under the influence of the Egyptian writing system. The Chinese writing system, basically unchanged from its original form, is still purely logographic. A number of the Oriental writing systems derived from Chinese (such as Japanese) use a mixture of Chinese characters and syllabic signs. The one exception is the Korean writing system, which is based primarily on a phonetic alphabet invented in 1443, but which still makes use of Chinese characters.

The Egyptian writing system underwent the most dramatic changes, evolving first syllabic elements and then 24 uniconsonantal signs that functioned as an alphabet for rendering proper names and a small number of words. The system of uniconsonantal signs served as a model for the Proto–Canaanite alphabet, which eventually led to the totally phonetic Greek alphabet from which all European alphabets are derived. Although Sumerian and Egyptian writing represent two independent systems, it is possible that as a result of commercial and diplomatic contacts the idea of writing was transferred from the Sumerians to the Egyptians. Similar speculative arguments have been made to suggest that the Chinese also borrowed the idea of writing, but developed their own unique system.

For now we turn our attention to the invention of writing in Mesopotamia, which grew out of earlier notational schemes of tallies and clay accounting tokens. Ironically, writing did not evolve from storytelling or the need to preserve oral tales and legends, but out of the need to enumerate and make records of commercial transactions. Written records began with quantitative rather than qualitative data. "Writing was not a deliberate invention, but the incidental by-product of a strong sense of private property" (Speises, 1960). This should not be surprising, because quantitative information is far more difficult to remember than verbal information. It is much easier to remember a story with a narrative and various characters or personalities than a set of numbers.

TALLIES

Before we can actually begin our study of the Sumerian invention of writing, we must turn the calendar back thousands of years to the first forms of human notation, which were tallies in the form of notches etched on animal bones to record quantitative data (Breasted, 1926). Other forms of tallying have been found including notched sticks, knotted strings, and counting objects in the form of pebbles, grains, twigs, or shells. All of these notational devices recorded the number of items, but provided no qualitative information about the nature of the items. The first form of human notation was therefore mathematical and not literary.

Tallies are based on the principle of one-to-one correspondence in which each item being enumerated is matched by a mark or counter depending on the system (Schmandt-Besserat, 1984a). The number of identical marks or counters used for the tally was equal to the number of items being enumerated, such as the number of sheep in a flock, the number of animals killed in a hunt, or the number of full moons since the last meeting of two clans. The major limitation of tallies is that they record only the quantitative feature of the set of objects being enumerated, leaving the identification of the objects to context or to the memory of the enumerator. Therefore, tallies are qualitatively nonspecific. They can satisfy only simple, low-technology cultures where only a few obvious items of daily life require accounting. For example, they cannot be used to tally a complex set of commercial products.

As primitive as they were, tallies produced an impact on the human mind at the cognitive level. They represent the first use of visual symbols to store, manipulate, and display information. In turn, this fostered abstract thought processes as items of daily life came to be dealt with through the means of an abstract notation. Three deer, for instance, could be represented by three abstract marks. Tallies segmented reality. As a substitute for the deer, the marks isolated the deer from their context and abstracted them for scrutiny. Tallies also encouraged objectivity by separating the information from the knower, while displaying that information for all to use. Tallies replaced verbal communication with objective nonverbal data removed and abstracted from their original context. Tallies created a new reality and set the stage for counting, mathematics, accounting, and, more important for our story—writing.

ACCOUNTING TOKENS

The next step in the development of notational technologies were clay accounting tokens. Denise Schmandt–Besserat's (1978) exhaustive study of tokens revealed that these clay artifacts, 2 to 3 centimeters long, were used for the enumeration and accounting of agricultural staples. Their use began in the prehistoric Middle East, circa 8000 B.C., at the beginning of the agricultural age, which also had its roots in the Middle East. Each uniquely shaped token designated some measure of an agricultural commodity or product. The system, which started with 24 kinds of tokens, grew to 190 different types of tokens by 3300 B.C., just before the advent of writing and abstract numerals in Sumer. The shapes included spheres, disks, cones, tetrahedrons, biconoids, ovoids, cylinders, and triangles, which were further differentiated with incisions and punched marks. The tokens designated agricultural products and commodities such as measures of grains (a ban [6 liters] or a bariga [36 liters] of grain, of which there were three varieties: barley, wheat, and emmer); jars of oil; containers of foodstuffs such as butter, berries, or dates; livestock, primarily sheep and goats differentiated by age, sex, and breed; wool, cloth, and different types of garments; measures of land expressed in terms of the amount of seed required to sow it; and service or labor expressed in the time units of days, weeks, and months.

Tokens and tallies share many characteristics. This suggests that the token system may have evolved from pebbles. Both tokens and tallies are palpable symbols that are easy to manipulate and are used in one-to-one correspondence with the objects being enumerated. Both fragment reality in that they abstract data from the context in which they are generated and from linguistic discourse and hence are not dependent on any particular spoken language. This helps explain the wide distribution of tokens throughout the ancient Middle East among people who spoke different dialects and languages. This is similar to today's use of Arabic numerals, whose use spans many different cultures and linguistic groups.

Despite their similarities, tokens differed from pebbles and other tallies in significant ways. Tokens were not randomly collected objects put to the secondary use of counting. They were man-made artifacts prepared specifically for the purpose of accounting. Compared with a series of more or less identical counters such as grains or pebbles, tokens were molded into distinctive shapes that were easy to recognize and simple enough to be systematically reproduced. Compared with unspecific tallies, each token shape stood for a specific commodity. In other words, tokens communicated both quantitative and qualitative information (Schmandt-Besserat, 1987).

Tokens functioned as metaphors, translating words for economic concepts into a tactile medium. This was a radical change in data processing. Compared with a group of pebbles that could not be understood out of context, the tokens became a reliable tool for data storage. Their meaning could be understood and translated unambiguously into speech by anyone initiated into the system. The tokens were a tool for data manipulation. Like tallies, they made possible the processing and retrieval of large amounts of data, but tokens had yet another advantage. They also permitted a new dimension, that of diversification, which allowed many different commodities to be dealt with at once. As new commodities requiring enumeration arose, a newly shaped token could be created. The elements of an inventory consisting of different types of commodities could be manipulated simultaneously. As with tallies, the data could be easily laid out and displayed, and hence grasped both visually and physically. Tokens, however, could be organized and reorganized into different piles or more sophisticated patterns according to any number of possible categories, which facilitated and enhanced classification. In a certain sense, the token system is the forerunner of the abacus as well as spreadsheet analysis.

Tokens also had the potential to act as a means of communication. Although tallies could be used only as personal memory aids for items known to the enumerator alone, tokens were universal and systematized. A token came to represent the same product to individuals of entirely different communities speaking different languages and separated by great distances. The main drawback was that the system became cumbersome. Although it was open and complete and could be expanded at will to convey new meanings, the creation of new shapes and markings was bound to reach a stage of saturation or overburdening. This created the need for a new form of data processing, which eventually led to the invention of writing and abstract numerals.

THE COGNITIVE IMPACT OF THE TOKEN SYSTEM

The token system changed the way people stored, manipulated, displayed, and communicated information and, in particular, the way people counted. Tokens were a new tool for counting and computing. The unique feature of the counters was that they specifically designated the object being enumerated by the coding of qualitative information through a three-dimensional shape. Each token with its unique shape was used to enumerate one object or commodity and no other. For example, ovoids could count only jars of oil. In other words, tokens merged the representation of the qualitative and quantitative features of a commodity. There was no token representing the abstract unit of one. There were only tokens representing one unit or one measure of a specific commodity. When counting with tokens, it was not possible to separate the nature of the item counted from that of the quantity. Abstract counting was not possible with the token system; tokens did not represent abstract numbers.

In fact, there exists no evidence for the use of abstract numbers at the time tokens first appeared, nor during the time of their major use and development from 8000 B.C. to 3100 B.C. Schmandt-Besserat's (1984a, 1987) analysis of notched bone (Marshack, 1964) led her to the conclusion that these tallying devices were used exclusively in a non-mathematical, one-to-one correspondence mode. There does not seem to be the grouping of notches into sets corresponding to cardinal numbers such as 2, 3, 5, or 10. Analysis of the use of tokens has yielded a similar result—namely, that tokens were used to enumerate in one-to-one correspondence like tallies with the added feature that their distinctive shape qualitatively designated the specific commodity being enumerated. Evidence for the way in which tokens were used comes from groups of tokens representing specific transactions found stored and bundled in clay envelopes. The analysis of these assemblages of tokens indicates that each enumeration of a product was tied to multiple repetitive occurrences of the tokens designating that product. That is, the tokens were used in one-to-one correspondence: n ovoids were used to designate n jars of oil. In contrast, n jars of oil are never represented as a set of n tokens, each representing the abstract unit one tied to the ovoid token for a jar of oil. The syntax of the tokens is such that they never functioned as adjectives modifying a noun. The syntactical structure of an abstract number, such as three, acting as an adjective modifying a noun (or a noun phrase) such as a jar of oil in the phrase three jars of oil does not appear before writing.

Given the lack of evidence for the use of abstract numbers with tallies and tokens, Schmandt-Besserat (1984a, 1987) postulated that tokens reflect a stage in the evolution of counting, before abstract numbers were used, known as concrete counting. Many historians of mathematics view the evolution of counting as having taken place in three main stages:

1. One-to-one correspondence with no precise concepts of numbers.
2. Concrete counting with the use of special numerical expressions for counting different specific classes of items.
3. Abstract counting with abstract numbers that are universally applicable.

Schmandt-Besserat's (1984a, 1987) analysis of the archaeological data supports the claims of historians of mathematics and suggests that the use of tallies represented counting in a one-to-one correspondence with no specific concept of number. Tallies and tokens permitted people to count larger quantities of items than the vocabulary of enumeration that was available to them in their spoken language. Tokens acted as concrete numbers. As we have seen, they had meaning only as units of the commodity they designated and enumerated, and not as abstract absolute quantities. Concrete numbers, such as a brace of partridge or a yoke of oxen, like tokens cannot be used to designate two as an abstract number and then be used to enumerate other objects. A brace of sandals is meaningless; instead one must refer to them as a pair of sandals—that is, as a concrete number or as two sandals, where two operates as an abstract number. The invention of tokens made it possible for enumeration to become specific and to develop concrete counting.

The dominant technologies of a culture, whether they are informational, mechanical, or economic, are interrelated and follow a similar pattern of evolution, reinforcing each other until a new level of technological innovation or breakthrough arises and new social patterns emerge.

The history of information processing in the Middle East during the period 15,000 to 3,000 B.C. is one of major breakthroughs followed by long periods of stability. The breakthroughs—tallies, tokens, and writing—may be viewed as break boundaries between radically different economic and social systems. The tally system was in use for thousands of years by hunting and gathering societies. It remained static, not undergoing any significant morphological or functional changes as long as hunting and gathering was the economic base of the culture. It is not a coincidence that the token system—a major elaboration and significant modification of the tally system and a breakthrough in information processing—emerged around 8000 B.C. just as agriculture emerged as the economic base for a new form of society.

The token system became a stable technology of information processing for the next 5,000 years until another major shift in economic life occurred—namely, the urbanization of Sumer at Uruk between 3350 B.C. and 3100 B.C. (Kramer, 1956). With urbanization, tokens began to evolve new forms and applications. Clay tokens were used to record the payment of tributes and taxes to those who maintained and administered the irrigation system on which all agriculture depended. Tokens became an administrative tool that allowed political and economic control of the agricultural countryside by urban centers of commerce and trade. Cognitive breakthroughs and advances associated with these innovations resulted in a chain reaction in which new information-processing techniques arose, including abstract numeration, logographic writing, and phonetic coding.

The new advances in the technology of information, such as tallies, tokens, abstract numerals, and writing, did not occur in isolation. Rather, new information forms emerged as changes took place in the socioeconomic environment. The cognitive foundations of the previous level of information technology served as a starting point for satisfying the new information demands of a changed environment. For example, the tally system was transformed into the token system by the demands for new accounting procedures required by the new agricultural lifestyle. Similarly, urban life brought with it pressures for a more complex accounting system as the number of items to be enumerated and the number of social interactions to be taken into account dramatically increased. These demands manifested themselves in a spurt of creative activity in which the simple token system was articulated and expanded and new structures were added, which eventually led to the invention of writing and abstract numbers. The use of tokens not only set the stage for writing, but for alphabetic writing, in the sense that the token system involved the repeated use of a small number of identically shaped tokens just as alphabetic writing makes use of identically shaped letters.

An overview of this complex process of innovation, described next can be obtained from Table 2.1, which shows the stages through which the use of tokens passed and the cognitive process associated with them.

TABLE 2.1

Breakpoints in the History of Information Processing With Tallies and Tokens

Time Frame	Morphology	Associated Cognitive Advance or New Communication Capability
15,000-8,000 B.C.	Tallies Notched sticks, etched bones, pebbles, shells	Enumeration: One-to-one correspondence
8000-3400 B.C.	Simple tokens Three-dimensional clay objects	Concrete counting and numbers Record keeping and data storage Information or data processing Primitive sign and symbol capability Classification-control-centralization
3400-3250 B.C. (Urbanization at Uruk)	Complex tokens Greater variety of clay objects ● Multiplication of shapes ● Incisions and punctuations ● Perforations	Sign and symbol articulation-metaphor Abstracting classes through common shapes, but differentiating subjects Complex classification Complex data processing and record keeping Specialization

TABLE 2.1 *(Continued)*

Breakpoints in the History of Information Processing With Tallies and Tokens

Time Frame	Morphology	Associated Cognitive Advance or New Communication Capability
3250-3150 B.C.	Token-impressed envelopes	Abstracting three-dimension artifacts into two-dimention signs
	Clay containers of tokens whose outside surface has been impressed with the tokens that are contained inside.	Primitive set theory or chunking of data More abstract symbolization—visual metaphor
3150-3100 B.C.	Impressed tablets	Translation of tactile into visual Greater abstract symbolization
	Two-dimensional clay tablets on which token forms have been impressed.	The token is no longer physically present Ability to work in a totally two-dimensional medium
3100 B.C.	Incised tablets	Advent of writing and abstract numerals
	Two-dimensional clay tablets on which: • signs have been incised that replicate the shapes of tokens, • ban and bariga token have been impressed, • new incised signs have been added.	Logographic writing Abstract numerals Phonetic writing

18

COMPLEX TOKENS, ENVELOPES, AND IMPRESSED LOGOGRAMS

Changes in the way quantitative information was processed can be attributed to changes in the socioeconomic system of its users. The token system during the long purely agricultural period from 8000 B.C. to 3350 B.C. remained remarkably stable with the appearance of a limited number of plain or simple tokens corresponding to basic agricultural commodities of the time, such as wheat and sheep. Between 3350 B.C. and 3100 B.C., the token system underwent a metamorphosis that can be attributed to the pressures of urbanization. With the rise of urban life and, in particular, the monumental temple complexes such as Eanna at Uruk, the largest economic institution of its time, there suddenly appears in the ruins, along with "other administrative material such as seals and sealings" (Schmandt-Besserat, 1988a), complex tokens representing a number of finished manufactured products, no doubt produced in the urban workshops of Uruk and other population centers. The great majority of tokens from this period are found in the temple precincts, indicating that they were associated with a coercive taxation and redistribution system of a strong central government. This interpretation of the token findings is reinforced by Sumerian reliefs of the period showing citizens delivering their goods to the temple (Kramer, 1956).

Another important development in the token system occurs with the appearance of clay envelopes, which functioned as containers to hold a number of plain tokens. It is presumed that the envelopes were used to consolidate all of the tokens employed in a single transaction. The surfaces of the envelopes were marked with the seals of the individuals involved in the transaction, and hence the envelope served as a receipt or contract (Schmandt-Besserat, 1984b). However, the envelopes had the disadvantage of masking their contents because of the opacity of their clay surfaces. This problem was overcome by impressing the tokens to be contained in the envelope onto the wet surface of the envelope. This technique revealed the contents without the necessity of breaking the envelope, and it also had the unexpected and certainly unplanned side effect of creating the first two-dimensional logograms (Schmandt-Besserat, 1987).

A logogram is a two-dimensional visual sign abstractly representing the written form of a single word. Egyptian hieroglyphics and Chinese characters are examples of logograms. Two different types of logograms can be distinguished: pictograms, which represent the words they designate pictorially; and ideograms, which represent the ideas of the words they designate. A logogram can also simply represent the word symbolically. The system of writing that makes use of logograms is called logographic writing.

The purpose of the token impression was to reveal the content of an envelope, not to substitute token impressions for tokens. Yet this is precisely what happened. Approximately 50 years later, it was realized that the actual tokens contained within an envelope were totally redundant and their use was dropped. The curved envelopes quickly evolved into flat two-dimensional tablets with the impressions of tokens on their upper surfaces. The evolution of envelopes into tablets represented a major breakthrough in information processing. The flat tablet became the prototype of all two-dimensional writing surfaces, including the pages of a book and the CRT video display of a computer.

It is important to note that the impressed logogram, semantically, was no different from a three-dimensional token. The logograms were two-dimensional negative imprints of the three-dimensional tokens. They were immediately recognizable to the users of the token system because they shared the same outline and bore the same markings as the actual tokens. In fact, the first tablets are not true writing, but merely the permanent records of an accounting system based on tokens in which the tokens were actually discarded once their imprints were made. From the point of view of function or informational content, impressed logograms on clay tablets operated exactly the same way as the three-dimensional token system. The medium changed, however, and the way that information was displayed changed radically from a collection of palpable three-dimensional clay objects to abstract symbols arrayed in two-dimensional patterns on the flat surface of a clay tablet. The shift from three-dimensional artifacts to logograms in the form of negative images impressed on two-dimensional surfaces triggered a chain reaction that resulted in the invention of logographic writing, phonetic coding, and abstract numerals. It also represented a shift away from the use of the tactile sensorium as represented by the three-dimensional tokens to the more abstract visual sensorium of the two-dimensional shapes on a planar surface.

PREPARING THE WAY
FOR NUMERALS AND WRITING

The manufacture and manipulation of tokens and impressed signs promoted the development of hand–eye coordination and fine motor skills essential for writing. More important, tallies, and especially tokens, introduced the visual bias that characterizes written notation. Tokens stressed the importance of uniformity—the same kind of uniformity needed for an alphabetic writing system. Tokens were the first class of artifacts whose uniformity of shape was key to their function. Tokens were used as repeatable symbols in much the same way that numerals and the letters of the alphabet are. The visual bias created by the use of uniform and repeatable tokens increased when the tokens were used to imprint the outer surfaces of clay envelopes and, later, the impressed tablets. The pattern of token markings arranged in neatly spaced lines within a two-dimensional array permitted the user (or reader) to encompass the whole field of data in a single glance.

Tallies, tokens, and impressed signs also paved the way for writing and abstract numerals on the cognitive level. Each of these methods of record keeping can be regarded as phases in the development of abstract notation. Impressed token markings increased the level of abstraction. The two-dimensional format of the impressed tablets was more abstract than the three-dimensional tokens in that the negative impression of the tokens could not be grasped in the hand and manipulated like three-dimensional tokens. The loss of volume, concreteness, and tactility removed the symbols one step further from the physical three-dimensional reality for which they stood. The display of information within a two-dimensional array, however, permitted the user to see the information in a new light. By being able to observe more data at a single glance, the user of the tablet system began to think more globally about the data. More abstract patterns of classifying and analyzing the data became possible. If the medium is the message, then the message of the two-dimensional display of information on tablets was that of abstraction, classification, analysis, uniformity, repeatability, and the power of the visual.

I believe that the development of tallies, tokens, impressed signs, numerals, and writing were phases in the development of metaphorical (visual) thinking; the earlier notational forms created a perceptual and cognitive environment conducive to the invention of writing and eventually the phonetic alphabet. To summarize how tallies, tokens, and impressed signs led to numerals and writing, let me iterate the many features that abstract numbers and writing shared with the previous record-keeping devices (tallies, tokens, impressed envelopes, and impressed tablets).

Each system employed metaphors and symbols, and hence abstracted information, by fragmenting reality from its representation in a sign system, thus creating an artificial medium for the expression and notation of ideas in which the basic elements were easily manipulated. Each system consisted of uniform elements, which were used in a repeatable fashion within the context of a linear two-dimensional array (truer of later stages of the token system), and thus produced a visual bias that required good hand-eye coordination for their creation and use. The application of these systems promoted objectivity, and hence standardized uniform measures and a system of economic and political control.

THE ADVENT OF WRITING AND ABSTRACT NUMERALS

Once tokens were used to produce two-dimensional impressed signs, a series of rapid but fundamental changes took place that transformed the token-based notational system for concrete numbers. There emerged two notational systems—one for abstract numerals and one for written words. Abstract numerals were built out of the two impressed token signs for the small and large measure of wheat, the ban, which came to represent the number 1 and the bariga, which represented 10. The second notational system was a full-fledged writing system for transcribing the words of spoken language into visual signs incised on the clay surface of a tablet with the sharp end of a stylus. The shapes of the original impressed token signs were imitated in the new incised format and formed the first vocabulary or lexicon of the new written language. Words other than those for commercial commodities emerged based on the principle of representing words pictographically or ideographically. Paradoxically, the first incised signs did not represent the words pictorially, but represented the shape that the accounting token corresponding to that word made when impressed into a clay tablet. Writing began as an extremely abstract symbol system.

The transformation that took place circa 3100 B.C. was far more than a change of form from impressed tokens to incised signs. It was a change of concept. Instead of signs that fused qualitative and quantitative information, there were two separate types of notation: one verbal and one numerical. Incised signs were used to transcribe spoken words or qualitative information (i.e., that is, rendering spoken language in a written form). The two former impressed logograms—ban and bariga—were used to express abstract numbers. With the emergence of two notational forms, a qualitative one with written words and a quantitative one with abstract numerals, the language of the written word and the language of mathematics emerged as two separate, distinct systems for recording information. The transformation that led from impressed logograms to incised pictographic writing and abstract numerals involved the following five major changes.

1. The transition from token impressions to incised signs: The two-dimensional impressions of tokens onto clay tablets inspired the emergence of a new form of signs. The new incised signs took the form of small designs traced with the

sharp end of a reed stylus on the surface of a clay tablet while the clay was still wet. The designs mimicked the shape and form of the token impressions. The stylus was pressed lightly onto the clay surface to produce the number of short strokes necessary to draw a sign. Circa 3100 B.C., the practice of imprinting the clay tokens was dropped completely, with the exception of the two signs for the two grain measures that continued to be impressed.

How did this technique for creating signs arise? One possible motivation for the use of incised signs rather than impressed tokens is that the former technique allowed the creation of new signs for words that had no corresponding token. Still another reason is that there could be no confusion with the old notational system. The sign for a ban of wheat repeated twice followed by a jar of oil sign can only be read as two jars of oil if the jar of oil sign is incised. If the jar of oil sign had been impressed, however, the three signs could possibly have been misinterpreted as a tablet from the old system and read as two bans of wheat and a jar of oil. By using incised signs for the words and impressed signs for the numbers, the new tablets could never be confused with the older tablets consisting of impressed signs only.

The transition between impressed and incised signs was rapid—a matter of only 50 years or two generations. The commodities signs produced by impressing the corresponding token into the clay were now rendered with a stylus by sketching the token's outline and repeating its markings. Each of the incised logograms in this new written language became a visual metaphor or pictographic symbol of the former tokens. The critical empirical evidence supporting this hypothesis for the invention of writing is the existence of a one-to-one morphological correspondence between the first pictographs representing the most usual Sumerian commodities, such as grain, livestock, oil, and textiles, and the three-dimensional tokens used to represent these goods before writing.

2. An increase in the repertory of signs—pictography and ideography. The representation of tokens by an incised sign on the tablets led to the idea that any concept could be conveyed by an incised sign. In other words, the use of the stylus led to the invention of new pictographic and ideographic signs completely unrelated to the tokens and designating new concepts unrelated to agricultural commodities.

3. New semantic and syntactic values of the symbol system: Not only did the incised signs differ from the impressed logograms morphologically, but also semantically and syntactically. The impressed logogram for a sheep carried the meaning of one sheep and functioned as a modified noun (i.e., a concrete number) in which both quality and number were denoted. In contrast, the incised logogram was, a more abstract symbol that denoted an unmodified noun and hence stood for a sheep. A separate symbol was required to denote the number of sheep even if it was only one.

4. Signs to express sounds—phonetic writing. Pictography was unable to satisfy one particular need of the Sumerian scribes: It could not render an individual's name. It was beyond the capability of pictograms or ideograms to represent each individual by a miniature portrait. Sumerian ingenuity provided the solution. Names were expressed phonetically. Logograms, used to write an individual's name, were read phonetically as the sound of the word they represented in Sumerian. The sign for oil was read as the sound "i" (long e), and the sign for arrow was read "ti." When associated together in rebus fashion as the Sumerians would have done it, the two signs spell "E.T."—the name of the cinema hero from outer space. This development eventually led to the phonetic alphabet and the alphabet effect.

5. Signs to express plurality—numerals. The first written numerals representing abstract numbers appeared at exactly the same time as incised logographic writing (Schmandt-Besserat, 1984a). The actual signs to represent numerals were made by impressing different combinations of the cone and sphere tokens representing, respectively, the small and large measure of wheat, ban, and bariga. These numerals still retained the visual metaphor of the one-to-one correspondence with a pile of pebbles. The number 2 was represented by the impression of two cones (or two wedges) and the number 3 by three cones (or three wedges). The new element of abstraction in notation was the use of a new sign, the circle (i.e., the impression of the sphere), for the number 10. This created an economy of notation because 23, for example, could be represented as 2 circles and 3 wedges instead of 23 wedges. This system was more efficient than the older system of tallying. It was an early and primitive predecessor of the system of Roman numerals, which would represent 23, for instance, as two Xs and three Is or XXIII. The two

impressed logograms used to represent the abstract numbers 1 and 10 still retained their function as concrete numbers for grain. It was left to the scribe to decide, according to the context, whether the wedge was the numeral 1 or a ban of grain, and whether a circle was the numeral 10 or a bariga of grain.

THE BIFURCATIONS OF IMPRESSED LOGOGRAMS

As we have seen, both logographic writing and the notation for abstract numbers arose 5,000 years ago from clay accounting tokens, which in turn first made their appearance 10,000 years ago. The token system underwent a linear sequence of development and enrichment from 8000 B.C. to 3100 B.C., which comprise the following steps or stages:

1. plain tokens;
2. complex tokens;
3. tokens in clay envelopes;
4. impressed logographs on clay envelopes containing tokens; and
5. impressed logographs on clay tablets.

None of these changes represents a bifurcation, but they do represent either an increase in the variety and number of tokens or a morphological change of the tokens—that is, a change in their physical form. The meaning or function of a three-dimensional token circa 8000 B.C. or an impressed logogram created by pressing a token into wet clay circa 3100 B.C. were the same. During the five steps, neither writing nor abstract numerals emerged. The next development in notational technology was profound and followed shortly after the introduction of the two-dimensional clay tablet. The impressed logograms on clay tablets not only underwent semantic and morphological variations, but were subject to a series of Prigogenian bifurcations discussed next.

The two logograms for the small and large measure of grain, the ban and the bariga, remained unchanged morphologically. They continued to serve as concrete counters for the two measures of grain, but they also took on a second semantic function: They came to represent the abstract numbers 1 and 10, respectively. At the same time that this transition took place, incised logograms also came into being. All of the existing impressed logograms other than the ban and bariga logograms ceased to function as concrete counters; they changed both morphologically and semantically. Each impressed logogram—with the exception of the two grain signs—was replaced by incised signs that graphically resembled the older impressed logograms they were replacing. In addition to this morphological change, the signs also changed semantically. They no longer functioned as concrete numbers, but as logograms designating single spoken words or phrases. For example, the impressed sign that had designated one sheep was replaced by an incised sign that was read simply as sheep. In addition to the transformation of the old impressed signs into incised signs, other incised signs began to appear, designating concepts that had not been part of the original token vocabulary consisting of approximately 190 agricultural commodities and manufactured goods.

Not long after their introduction some 50 years later, incised signs took on a second semantic function. As well as ideographically or pictographically coding a single word, they were also used to phonetically code those phonemes and words that had the same pronunciation as the word they represented ideographically or pictographically. The incised sign for an arrow—ti—also represented its homonym, life, also pronounced "ti."

The sudden explosion of semantic function in 3100 B.C. marks the beginning of literacy and numeracy. To understand the interplay of the cognitive elements that contributed to this development, we require a more sophisticated model. The work of Ilya Prigogene and his theories of bifurcation and social amplification illuminate this process, which took place in Sumer 5,000 years ago.

At this point in our discussion, we need to divert the flow of ideas on the development of writing and talk about Prigogene's theories of complexity. From his studies of chemical systems, Prigogene developed the notion that out of the chaos of a system there spontaneously arises a new level of order as a bifurcation from an older form of organization giving rise to a new form of organization. A bifurcation, as the etymology of the word suggests, is the splitting of a stream of development into two branches. With a bifurcation the older form of organization remains, but a new form of organization rises that evolves from the older form retaining some of its properties unchanged, transforming other elements into new structures, and suppressing other elements so that they appear only as vestigial reminders of earlier structures with little or no structural role. For example, biological evolution can be thought of as a series of bifurcations. The evolution of language represents another example. Earlier spoken language communication between hominids consisted of hand signals, facial gestures, body language, and nonverbal vocalizations. All of these elements have been incorporated into spoken language and still play an important role in communications. Some scholars claim that 90% of the communication of spoken language is still nonverbal, and the way things are said is more important than what is actually said. When spoken language evolved into a transcribed form of language, the vestigial elements of speech—namely, vocalization, gesture, hand signal, and body language—were abstracted away, and written communication became purely conceptual based on the literal meaning of the words. With mathematics and science, further abstractions took place with all of the ambiguities of verbal language being removed so as to create instruments for numerical calculations and analysis, respectively. Our hypothesis is that the emergence of writing and mathematics represents an evolution of spoken language that can be modeled in terms of Prigogenian bifurcations. Hence, new levels of order emerge from the chaos of the information loads that developed when speech could no longer handle the complexity of large-scale agricultural activity in the city-states of Sumer circa 3100 B.C.

The emergence of the complex notational structures of the numerals and writing that suddenly appear in 3100 B.C. can be described as a series of bifurcations involving the two-dimensional concrete counter logograms whose impression was made by pressing the original three-dimensional tokens from which they were derived into a wet clay tablet. The emergence of abstract numerals and writing can be described in terms of the following three separate bifurcations:

Bifurcation 1: the split of two-dimensional impressed logographic signs into two morphologically and semantically distinct sets of signs—the incised signs and impressed signs in which incised signs are used exclusively for verbal notation or writing and impressed signs used exclusively for accounting and numerical notation;

Bifurcation 2: the split of the impressed logograms for the ban and bariga into two semantic functions—the old one as concrete numbers for small and large measures of grain and the new one as the abstract numbers for 1 and 10, respectively; and

Bifurcation 3: the split of the semantic function of the incised signs, in which they are used not only to code spoken words ideographically or pictographically, but also phonetically.

It is impossible from the archaeological data (Schmandt-Besserat, 1979, 1988b) to give the exact dates of these bifurcations. Logic dictates that Bifurcation 3 must have occurred sometime after Bifurcation 1 because the incised signs would have been established as logograms designating a word with a particular sound before they could have been used to phonetically code the homonyms of that word. Empirical evidence supports this conclusion because fewer examples of the phonetic use of the incised signs are found compared with the more concrete use of the signs as logograms.

The relative timing of Bifurcations 1 and 2 can be determined by a process of elimination and a linguistic analysis of the archaeological data. Because it is only the relative timing of Bifurcations 1 and 2 that is in doubt, there are only three logical possibilities as illustrated in Table 2.2: (a) Bifurcation 1 occurs before Bifurcation 2, (b) Bifurcation 1 occurs at the same time as Bifurcation 2, or (c) Bifurcation 1 occurs after Bifurcation 2.

The fact that impressed logograms functioning as abstract numbers do not appear before the existence of incised signs, and when they do appear are always used to modify an incised sign, indicates that Bifurcation 2 did not occur before Bifurcation 1. There are no cases where the ban and bariga signs are used to modify an impressed token logogram such as the jar of oil or the sheep sign.

However, the absence of any tablets in which incised signs are repeated many times to function as concrete numbers in the way tokens or impressed-token logograms functioned indicates that Bifurcation 1 did not occur before Bifurcation 2. This leaves only one possible conclusion: Bifurcations 1 and 2 occurred at precisely the same time, and hence model B in Table 2.2 best explains the data. It would seem that the emergence of abstract numerals and ideographic writing were tied to each other and arose at the same point in history.

Each of the three bifurcations represents the birth of a new form of semantic or numerical expression in which a new abstract branch splits off from an older, more concrete one. Bifurcation 1 represents the emergence of true writing using an ideographic or pictographic coding scheme in which each word is uniquely represented by a visual sign— that is, the written form of the word. Bifurcation 1 also involved the splitting of abstract logograms, each designating a single word, from impressed logograms or concrete numbers that designated both a quantity and quality. The incised logogram abstracts away from the impressed logogram the sense of number, leaving a purely qualitative system of notation. Hence, the beginning of true writing is born, which is capable of coding a spoken language into written signs.

Bifurcation 2 represents the emergence of a notation for abstract numbers, which eventually evolved into our present system of Hindu–Arabic numerals. It also involved the splitting of abstract numbers from concrete numbers, and hence the creation of a purely quantitative notation in which the quantity being notated is totally independent of the nature (or quality) of the objects being enumerated.

TABLE 2.2

Bifurcations of Tokens

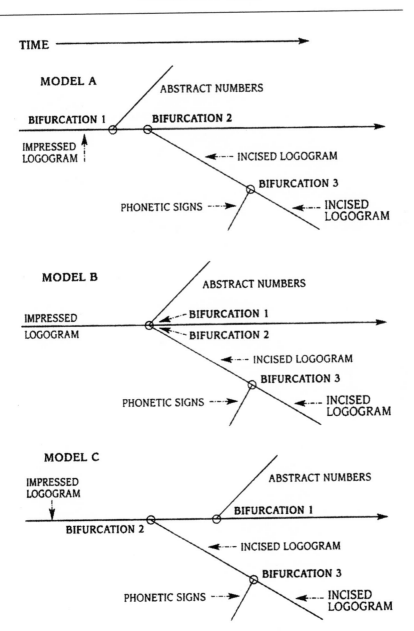

Bifurcation 3 took place within the confines of verbal writing and represents the separation of logographic and phonetic coding. These two systems of coding, which emerged within 50 years of the beginning of true writing, also exhausted all of the known possible techniques for coding spoken language into written signs. (Exceptions such as the Morse code or the electronic binary coding of information with computers represent a form of coding in which written language and not spoken language is coded.)

Bifurcations 1 and 2, which occurred at the same moment in history, represent the original split between the quantitative and qualitative modes of notation and analysis that exists today. Bifurcations 1 and 2 reversed the 5,000-year-old trend that had been established with tokens of combining quantitative and qualitative description and analysis. The separation permitted a specialization of notations, and therefore techniques of analysis that led to many other advances. This split also had an impact at the subliminal level and set the pattern of information processing. It contributed to a cognitive style of analysis in which the quantitative and qualitative are carefully distinguished and treated separately. The Western characteristic of specialization had its roots in Bifurcations 1 and 2, and thus began some 5,000 years ago.

In addition to specialization, the three bifurcations led to other Western characteristics of abstract thought including the phonetic alphabet. Compared with those of the East, Western thought patterns are abstract and deductive rather than concrete and analogical. As shown, each of the bifurcations involves a transition from a less abstract to a more abstract notational element (see Table 2.3):

Bifurcation 1: from token impressions to ideographic writing,

Bifurcation 2: from concrete to abstract numbers, and

Bifurcation 3: from ideographic to phonetic coding.

The concrete counters, whether tokens or impressed logograms, coded information by analogy: quantitatively by one-to-one correspondence and qualitatively by pictographic symbols. Abstract numbers and phonetic signs code information using logical algorithms and promoted the abstract logical thought of Western civilization, which was the heir to the token system. With this in mind, one can date and place the origin of Western thought to circa 3100 B.C., when in Sumer abstract numerals, ideographic writing, and phonetic coding emerged, setting the pattern for all subsequent intellectual developments that were derived from these systems of notation (Logan, 1986a; McLuhan & Logan, 1977). Thus, the roots of the alphabet effect can be traced back to the time before the actual invention of the alphabet.

TABLE 2.3

Bifurcations of Token Signs

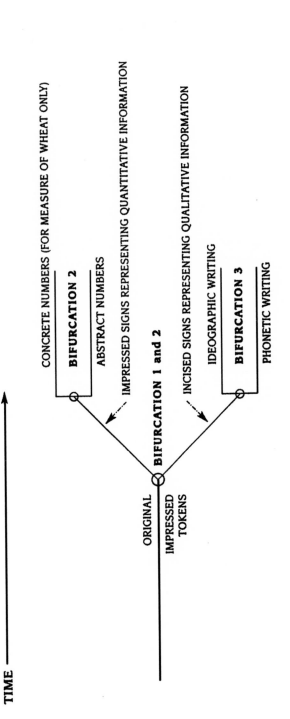

THE BEGINNING OF
TRUE WRITING IN MESOPOTAMIA

It is the transition from the impressed tablets with a vocabulary of 200 token signs to the incised tablets with a proliferation of pictographic signs, created with the use of a stylus, that marks the advent of writing—mankind's greatest breakthrough in data processing. The new incised signs were used to communicate new forms of information. For the first time in the history of humankind, the full spoken language could now be rendered in terms of written visual signs. The Sumerian writing system was originally a primarily ideographic or pictographic system in which each and every word was represented by its own unique logogram incised on a clay tablet. The Sumerians then developed the cuneiform writing system in which the ideograms or pictograms became abstracted and were made by impressing wet clay with wedge-shaped reeds instead of incising the signs with the end of a sharpened stylus. The word *cuneiform* is derived from the Latin *cuneus*, meaning "wedge." Because of the fast-drying nature of the clay, the original pictograms became highly stylized to speed up the process of writing. After the clay was impressed, the tablets were baked to form permanent records, some of which have survived to this day.

As the Sumerian writing system evolved, the logograms were used phonetically as well as pictographically or ideographically. The Sumerian words for arrow and life are both pronounced "ti." As an example, let us consider the following pictograph for the word arrow, †. This pictograph can also be used phonetically by adding a determinative sign, ' , so that the sign † no longer indicates arrow, but rather the word that sounds like arrow ("ti")—namely, life also pronounced "ti." This device was extended to polysyllabic words as well. Let "4" and "C" be pictograms for the English words four and sea. Let us use the determinative sign, ', to indicate that the pictograms should be treated as phonograms. The symbols "4C," which would be read as four seas, become 4'C' and are read as the polysyllabic word foresee. It was in this way that the Sumerians created their phonetic syllabary. They used over 600 signs, phonographically, to represent the syllables of their spoken language. This new technique represented a new and higher level of abstraction because now smaller phonetic units—namely, syllables—were being recognized and manipulated independently.

The Sumerians were conquered by the Semitic-speaking Akkadians who eventually founded the Babylonian empire. The Semitic language of the Akkadians was completely different from the non-Semitic language of the Sumerians. Hence, when the Akkadians took over the Sumerian writing system, they converted it to their language's needs.

An ideogram for a given Sumerian word was no longer pronounced as it would have been in Sumerian. Instead, the pronunciation of the equivalent Akkadian word was read. The cuneiform symbol for the Sumerian word ka, meaning "mouth," was read as the Akkadian word pum, also meaning "mouth." The symbol, however, could also be used phonographically, with the proper determinative, as an element of the phonetic syllabary, in which case it retained its original Sumerian sound value and was pronounced "ka" and not the Akkadian "pum." Because of the two languages, the Akkadians were forced to use the syllabic signs in a more abstract manner than did the Sumerians. Not long after adopting the Sumerian system, the Akkadian Babylonians reduced the number of syllabic signs to 60 and used these signs phonetically. They still retained the use of their ideographic or pictographic signs, however, and hence made use of a mixed system of signs. The reduction of the number of syllabic signs from the 800 used in the late Sumerian period (Oppenheim, 1964) to 60 at the time of Hammurabi represents a bifurcation to a systematic syllabary, which was accompanied by other reforms in the system of weights and measures. The information overload, which stimulated the emergence of a new level of order, was the transition in Mesopotamia from independent city states to an empire that incorporated cultures with different languages. The governance of this new geopolitical entity required a simplification of the notation system used to administer a far-flung empire.

The Akkadian–Babylonian syllabic system had some of the features of our alphabetic system, but lacked its ability to provide a unique spelling of a word. The syllabic sign consisted of a consonant and a vowel in which either one might precede the other. Let us illustrate how the system worked by representing the word level using a syllabary containing the syllabic elements le, el, ve, and ev. The word level could be rendered le-ve-el or le-ev-el, and hence does not have a unique spelling as it does when it is rendered alphabetically in terms of the letters l, e, and v.

3

The Origin of the Phonetic Alphabet: The Invention of the Mother of Invention

EGYPTIAN WRITING

To examine the invention of the phonetic alphabet by Semitic tribesman of the Sinai, we must first study Egyptian writing or *hieroglyphics*. The name hieroglyphics is derived from the ancient Greek for "sacred carvings" because hieroglyphics were first carved on stone. The Egyptians later began to write on papyrus with brush and ink. The Egyptian writing system first appeared about 3000 B.C., only 200 years after the emergence of the Sumerian writing system. At the time of the first appearance of Egyptian hieroglyphics, there was a great deal of contact and trade between the Egyptians and Sumerians. Therefore, it has been suggested that perhaps the Egyptians picked up the idea of writing from the Sumerians and developed their own system.

The Sumerian writing system slowly evolved from the token system and was used at first for accounting purposes. There was no such incubation period with Egyptian hieroglyphics. This led Fischer (1989) to speculate that, "since the hieroglyphic system does not seem to have undergone a long period of incubation, it may well have been conceived by a single individual" (p. 66). Like the Sumerian writing system, the original pictograms were used phonetically from the beginning.

The Egyptians actually developed two parallel writing systems: the hieroglyphic system, which was used for formal writing on stelea and monuments; and hieratics, a cursive script written on papyrus with brush and ink and used by scribes for practical matters requiring a written record. Unlike the Sumerian–Akkadian writing system, and their own hieratic system the hieroglyphics were extremely representational throughout their existence (Fischer, 1989). In both the hieroglyphic and hieratic systems, the pictographic signs were used phonetically through the addition of a determinitive sign in a manner similar to the Sumerian–Akkadian system.

The Egyptians also developed uniconsonantal signs that allowed them to represent all the sounds of their spoken language. They also created biconsonantal and triconsonantal signs. These phonetic signs could have operated as a phonetic alphabet but the Egyptians being conservative restricted their use to only a few applications:

1. the rendering of foreign proper names,
2. "grammatical adjuncts such as suffix-pronouns",
3. prepositions ("nearly half of the simple prepositions"),
4. "some of the commonest words" such as "name, know, be healthy, thing, and say." (Fischer, 1989, pp. 63–64)

The Egyptians never made great use of their consonant-only alphabet. Their writing system contained approximately 400 signs, which were a mixture of pictograms, syllabics signs, and unionsonantal, biconsonantal, and triconsonantal signs. Perhaps those in power did not want to simplify their writing system, because a complex system allowed the priestly class to maintain its monopoly on reading and learning. The idea of using a small number of consonants as an alphabet was not lost to civilization, however. The Seirites, a Semitic tribe living in the Sinai who mined copper and traded with the Egyptians, borrowed the idea. They were the first people to write in a purely alphabetic manner.

THE ADVENT OF THE ALPHABET

Alphabetic writing first surfaced in the Sinai and Canaan in the first half of the second millennium B.C. This alphabet, known as Proto–Sinaitic script, was first discovered (Flinders Petrie, 1906) in 1905 at the Serabit el Khadem temple in the Sinai. Other inscriptions have been found in or near copper mines in the Sinai and are thought to be left by the Seirites, who worked these copper mines. Referred to in the Bible as the Kenites or the Midianites, these are the people with whom Moses sojourned in the desert of Sinai when he was forced into exile from Egypt. It has been conjectured (Gardiner, 1961; Sprengling, 1931) that the Seirites borrowed the idea of alphabetic writing from the Egyptians. Because of the complexity of the Egyptian writing system, the uneducated Seirites chose to borrow the simplest aspect of the Egyptian system—namely, that involving the uniconsonantal signs. One piece of evidence to support this hypothesis is that, for both the Egyptian hieroglyphics and the Semitic alphabet, the vowels are not notated, whereas the Mesopotamian writing systems notated the vowels.

With the emergence of each new level of notation, we have attributed the transition as due to the necessity to deal with a new level of complexity due to some form of information overload. In the case of the Semitic tribesmen who wanted to develop a writing system for their spoken language, the Egyptian system represented a level of complexity they could not handle because they had not been educated in the Egyptian scribal tradition, and the hieroglyphic system was kept purposively complex because the scribal class wanted to maintain their monopoly of knowledge and the privileges that accompanied that competency. The uniconsonantal system that the Canaanites borrowed from the Egyptians to make their proto-Canaanite alphabet was the result of a bifurcation from the purely hieroglyphic system to one that included uniconsonantal signs. The impetus for developing this system for the Egyptians was that they discovered that they were unable to transcribe foreign proper names with the logographic system. The uniconsonantal signs therefore emerged to deal with this complexity that the use of their writing system entailed.

In both systems, the signs operate according to a phonetic acrostic principle, whereby each sign represents an object, and the sound value of the sign is the same as the first consonant of the name of the object depicted. Words are spelled out phonetically using the names as a rebus. For example, *cat* would be spelled by picturing a can, an apple, and a table in sequence. Some of the signs in the Egyptian and Seirite systems were similar. The original Seirite alphabet began with 27 or 28 letters, but was quickly simplified down to 22 signs (Cross, 1989). Each letter had its own Semitic name and sound value. As with the Egyptian uniconsonantal signs, the Proto–Sinaitic alphabet consisted solely of consonants. The vowels and vocalization of speech were not indicated and had to be filled-in by the reader.

The first two letters of the Semitic alphabet are aleph and bet, the Semitic words *aleph* for ox and *bayit* for *house*. These letters were originally denoted by ⵀ and ▢, which visually represented, in an abstract manner, an oxhead and a house, respectively. These two letters gave rise to

the first two letters of the Greek alphabet, alpha and beta, from which
the term *alphabet* is derived, and to a and b, the first two letters of the
Roman and English alphabets. Other letters of our alphabet that derive
from the original Semitic alphabet are (Bernal, 1990; Cross, 1989; Naveh,
1982; Ouaknin, 1999):

Roman Alphabet	Greek Letter	Originally From the Semitic Letter
a	alpha	*aleph* for *ox*
b	beta	*bayit* for house
c (originally g)	gamma	*gimmel* for *camel*
d	delta	*daleth* for *door*, originally *dag* for *fish*
e	epsilon	*heh* for *man at prayer*
f	digamma	*vav* for *nail* or *hook*
h	eta	*het* for *barrier*
I	iota	*yod* for *hand*
k	kappa	*kaf* for *palm of the hand*
l	lambda	*lamed* for *ox goad*
m	mu	mem for water (*mayim*)
n	nu	*nun* for *snake* (*nachal*)
o	omicron	*ayin* for *eye*
p	pi	*peh* for *mouth*
q	koppa	*kof* for *ape*
r	rho	*rosh* for *head*
s	sigma	*shin* for *tooth*
t	tau	*tav* for *mark* (two crossed sticks)
u, v	upsilon	*vav* for *nail* or *hook*
x	xi	*samek* for *ladder*
z	zeta	*zayin* for *weapon* or *conflict*

The invention of the alphabet by the Seirites has been challenged by more recent finds of alphabetic inscriptions in Palestine—namely at Shechem, Gezer, and Lachish (Albright, 1966). These inscriptions seem to belong to the 16th and 17th centuries B.C., which makes them 100 to 200 years older than the Sinai inscriptions, which are dated to circa 1500 B.C. The number of signs found in these three early sites in Palestine is quite limited—a total of 15 signs altogether—representing even fewer letters. That these signs are earlier forms of the Sinai inscriptions is evident from the extreme pictorial way in which they are drawn. The Sinai inscriptions have already developed some form of abstraction. To conclude on the basis of this scant evidence that the writing system began in Palestine rather than Sinai is probably premature. It is possible that still earlier forms of the alphabet will surface. Nevertheless, this extant evidence led the renowned epigraphist Joseph Naveh (1982) to conclude that, "although the Proto-Sinaitic inscriptions form a relatively large group, they are an integral part of the corpus of the early alphabetic inscriptions called Proto–Canaanitic" (p. 27). We conform to Naveh's convention and refer to both the Canaanite and Sinaitic scripts as the Proto-Canaanite, leaving open the formal question of their origin.

This thesis does not necessarily rule out the connection between the Canaanite alphabet and Egyptian writing suggested earlier. The Canaanites were also in close contact with the Egyptians, as indicated by the Amarna, letters of the 14th century B.C., in which the rulers of Canaan corresponded with the pharaohs of Egypt—namely, Amenhotep and Akhenaton. In fact, Naveh (1982) also acknowledged this possibility: "The Proto-Canaanite script . . . was invented circa 1700 B.C. by Canaanites who had some knowledge of Egyptian writing" (p. 42).

A third set of early alphabetic inscriptions, found in 1928 at Ras Shamra on the Mediterranean coast of North Syria, helped decipher the Proto–Canaanite scripts. This was the Ugaritic cuneiform alphabet dated to the 14th or 13th century B.C. (Cross, 1967). This system differs markedly from the other alphabets in two major ways: It contains 30 uniconsonantal letters rather than 22, and it is written in clay using the cuneiform technique of Akkadian–Babylonian writing. The cuneiform alphabet never evolved beyond its form at Ras Shamra. Its major historical interest is the help it rendered in deciphering earlier texts.

THE SPREAD OF THE ALPHABET

The alphabet proved to be such an efficient system for transcribing a spoken language that it spread from one culture to another, where it was modified each time to suit the different sounds of the local language.

New letters were sometimes added to represent a new sound or an old letter was modified to represent a variation of an old sound. The Proto–Canaanite alphabet evolved into the Phoenician and Proto–Arabic alphabets, which in turn led to still other descendants—the grandchildren and great grandchildren of the original alphabet. The Proto–Arabic alphabet, which broke away from the Proto–Canaanite alphabet about 1300 B.C., added additional consonantal signs and evolved into the early scripts of the Arabian peninsula and Ethiopia.

The Phoenician alphabet, gave rise directly to two other West Semitic alphabets: the early Hebrew alphabet and the Aramaic alphabet. Hebrew and Aramaic are languages closely related to Phoenician. At first Hebrew and Aramaic were written with the Phoenician alphabet, although this created an artificial circumstance for Aramaic because of the richness of its sounds. The Hebrew and Aramaic scripts soon developed their own national character, beginning in 850 B.C. for Hebrew and 750 B.C. for Aramaic. Despite that these languages had a richer range of sounds, they both stuck with the original 22 letters of the Phoenician alphabet.

The Aramaic script gave rise to many more alphabets. Aramaic became the official language and script of the Neo-Assyrian Empire and later the Persian Empire (before the Arabic script developed). As a result, the Aramaic alphabet spread to Central Asia and the Indian subcontinent. After the fall of the Persian Empire, the people of these regions developed their own alphabetic writing systems based on the Aramaic alphabet, but applied to Indo-European languages. Thus, the alphabets of India, Afghanistan, and Turkestan are derived from Aramaic.

The Aramaic script also gave rise to a number of others in the Middle East. These included the Palmyrene script extant from 44 B.C. to A.D. 272 and used in Manichean texts; the Syriac script extant from A.D. 200 to the present, which serves as the sacred script of the "Assyrian" Christian Church; and the Nabatean script extant from 150 B.C. to the sixth century A.D., which led directly to classical Arabic. The Arabic script in turn gave rise to the contemporary Persian script. The alphabetic order of Arabic deviates from the original Canaanite order probably because new letters had to be introduced to represent the richer sound system of Arabic, and the letters were regrouped according to similarities of sounds (Naveh, 1982). The "old order was retained, however, when the letters were used as numerals." Many (22 out of 28) of the Arabic letters have four different forms: "isolated, final, initial and medial" (Bellamy, 1989, p. 92).

The Phoenician alphabet was transformed by the Greeks and used to render their Indo-European tongue. The Greek alphabet then evolved to become the basis of all the other European alphabets. The Phoenician alphabet was unable to survive the ravages of time. Its use spread to Phoenicia's western colonies, principally to Carthage, where it was known as Punic. After the destruction of Carthage in 146 B.C., the script survived in certain northwest African areas in a form known as Neo-Punic and then suddenly disappeared somewhere in the early third century A.D.

The Proto–Canaanite alphabet began as phonetic pictograms used to spell out words as a rebus. The reason they must be identified as pictograms, despite that they are used phonetically and as a rebus, is that they take their sound value and name from the object they depict. For example, *aleph* is represented visually by an oxhead, *beit* by a house, and *ayin* by an eye.

In the first stages of the alphabet, the letters retained their pictorial character, and their position or orientation was not fixed nor was the direction in which they were written. Sometimes the order was horizontal (right to left or left to right), sometimes vertical (up or down), or even boustrophedon. *Boustrophedon,* from the Greek word signifying "turning like oxen in plowing," is a style in which the script goes horizontally in one direction and then reverses direction in the next line like an ox plowing a field. The Proto–Arabic script was also pictographic and had no set direction of writing.

> Horizontal boustrophidal writing was very common in the Old South Arabic monumental scripts. . . . Given the lengths of South Arabic monumental inscriptions which covered huge walls, the use of boustrophedon was virtually inevitable; the reader had to walk several yards in order to read a line, but he could read the next line when he retraced his steps and thus he could continue walking and reading." (Naveh, 1982, p. 49)

As the proto-alphabetic scripts were used more and more, they became more cursive and abstract and less pictographic (Naveh, 1982). "The twenty-two letters of the later Proto-Canaanite dropped all pictographic features. From the mid-eleventh century onward, we deal with stabilized, linear letters written in right-to-left, horizontal lines—this is the Phoenician script; its less developed ancestor is termed Proto-Canaanite" (Naveh, 1982, p. 53). The fixing of the direction of Phoenician from right to left resulted in this direction for all those alphabetic scripts directly descended from it, including Hebrew, and both ancient and modern Arabic, which descended from Nabatean, and Aramaic.

The Ethiopic script, which descended from the South Arabic scripts, which in turn descended from Proto–Canaanite, does not read from right to left, but left to right. Greek, which also reads from left to right, is therefore probably descended from Proto–Canaanite rather than

Phoenician. The alphabetic order of the letters became fixed for the first time with the Ugaritic script of the 14th to 13th centuries. With rare exception, all alphabetic scripts follow the same order, indicating their common origin.

THE INTRODUCTION OF
VOWELS IN ALPHABETIC WRITING

The first proto-alphabetic scripts, such as the Egyptian hieroglyphic script, had no provisions for vowels or vocalization. Reading a script correctly was a matter of good guesswork guided by context. The Phoenician alphabet never evolved any provision for vocalization nor was a separation between words indicated. Both Hebrew and Aramaic made a separation between words and added vowels where necessary. This was achieved through *mater lectionis*, which in Latin means "mother of reading," whereby the aspirant consonants are used to render vowels, at first at the ends of words, but later also in medial positions (Naveh, 1982). Vowels were added explicitly to the Hebrew script during the Middle Ages sometime between the 7th and 9th centuries through the device of adding dots and dashes below the letters or, in some instances by adding a dot beside the top of a letter.

The lack of vowels or vocalization, although a shortcoming of Semitic alphabets, is not as serious a problem for a Semitic language as it is for an Indo-European language because the roots of Semitic words are given by their consonants, usually three in number. The internal vowels are used to indicate "details, such as the parts of speech, the voice, the mood, the tense" (Diringer, 1948, p. 217). The English words *sang, sing, song,* and *sung* illustrate this use of internal vowels. The ambiguity caused by the lack of vowels is resolved either through context or, in the case of Aramaic or Hebrew, through *mater lectionis* as indicated earlier. The Hebrew name *David*, if rendered only in terms of its consonants, would be spelled DWD. To indicate the "i" sound in David, the letter yod is used so that David is rendered as DWYD (Gelb, 1963).

The Greeks developed their totally phonetic alphabet by modifying the Semitic alphabet they borrowed from the Phoenicians. Legend credits Cadmus with having made this gift to the Greeks. His name is thought to be derived from the Semitic word *kedem*, meaning "east." "Herodotus calls the alphabet kadmeia grammata and grammata phoinikeia, 'Cadmean characters' and 'Phoenician characters' " (Cross, 1989, p. 78). The Greeks borrowed the names, values, order, and shapes of the Phoenician alphabet. They modified it, however, by converting the five unstressed aspirant consonants (aleph, hey, yod, ayin, and vav) into the vowels a, e, i, o, and u, respectively (see Table 3.1). In addition to these five vowels, the Greeks added two more completely independent vowels, eta, η, and omega, ω. The Greeks also added three new consonants, theta, θ, phi, φ, and psi, ψ, to represent sounds that occur in Greek, but not in any of the Semitic tongues.

TABLE 3.1

Vowels

English	Hebrew	Greek
a	aleph	alpha, α
e	hey	epsilon, ε
i	yod	iota, ι
o	ayin	omicron, o
u	vav	upsilon, υ

The explicit introduction of vowels into the Greek alphabet is another example of necessity serving as the mother of invention. It is almost impossible to render an Indo-European language like Greek unambiguously without vowels. Consider the difficulty we would have in English distinguishing between *bat, bait, bet, beat, bought, beet, bit, bite, boat, boot, but,* and *beauty* without vowels or rendering words like *idea, eye,* or *iodine.*

By introducing vowels explicitly, the Greeks created the most accurate and unambiguous phonetic writing system ever known to man. The phonetic alphabet permits a one-to-one correspondence between the spoken and written language. "The original Greek invention achieved the essential task of analysis and it has not been improved upon" (Havelock, 1963). The English alphabet, by rendering the 40 phonemes (20 consonants and 20 vowels) of the spoken language with only 26 elements, creates a host of ambiguities and hence represents a retrogression from the original Greek phonetic alphabet.

There are some scholars such as Gelb (1963) and Havelock (1963) who claim that, because of the lack of vowels, the Semitic alphabet is not truly an alphabet like the Greek and Roman scripts, but a syllabary in which each consonant represents the syllable consisting of that consonant and a nonindicated vowel. Ong (1982) disagreed with this assessment:

it appears somewhat awkward to think of the Hebrew letter beit (b) as a syllable when it in fact simply represents the phoneme [b], to which the reader has to add whatever vowel sound the word and context call for. Besides, when vowel points are used, they are added to the letters (above or below the line) just as vowels are added to our consonants. (pp. 89-90)

Although there is some validity to the notion that the Semitic alphabet is not a totally phonetic alphabet, one cannot deny that the Semitic alphabet represents a major breakthrough in the development of phonetic writing. The Semitic alphabet provided the vital link between Egyptian syllabic writing and the totally phonetic Greek alphabet, which contains both vowels and consonants explicitly.

Naveh (1982) pointed out, "Only in Greek and in its offshoots does each letter stand for either a consonant or a vowel" (p. 11). Although admitting that "the Greek system is more evolved than the Semitic one," Naveh could not accept Gelb's position. An alphabet is a system of writing with a limited number of signs (20–30) that have a fixed order, which, as Naveh reminded us, is basically the same for Greek, Latin, and Phoenician. The advantage of the Greek alphabet and all of its derivatives is that the reader does not have "to draw on non-textual" knowledge to read the script as is the case with the Semitic alphabets, where the reader must have prior knowledge of the word to read in the correct vowels (Ong, 1982). Which ever side of this controversy one wants to sit on no one can dispute Ong's conclusion: "The phonetic alphabet invented by ancient Semites and perfected by ancient Greeks, is by far the most adaptable of all writing systems in reducing sound to visible form" (pp. 91–92).

DATING THE TRANSFER OF THE PHONETIC ALPHABET FROM THE PHOENICIANS TO THE GREEKS

Naveh (1973, 1982) provided an even greater challenge to the scholars of Greek culture with his dating of the transfer of the Phoenician alphabet to the Greeks based on his studies of Semitic epigraphy. Naveh contended that the transfer occurred as early as 1100 B.C., whereas earlier scholars placed this event some 300 to 400 years later.

Based on the Cadmus myth, the similarity of early Greek and Phoenician letters, the identical order of the two alphabets, the similarity of the names *alpha* and *aleph* (or beta and beit), and the similarity of sound values of these corresponding letters, scholars are in unanimous agreement about the Phoenician origin of the Greek alphabet. Only the date is a source of disagreement. The earliest known Greek inscriptions are placed in the eighth century B.C., which is the date many scholars believed that the transfer of the Phoenician alphabet took place. Carpenter (1933) was the first to set this date. His technique was simple. Obviously the Greek alphabet must have branched off from the Semitic at the point where the chronologically contemporary resemblances are strongest. He chose the period between 732 and 710 B.C.; however, his idea of a borrowing at one fixed point in time is probably too simple.

Naveh accepted that the absence of evidence of a Greek alphabet before the eighth century B.C. argues strongly for its inception at this time. However, he pointed out a number of cases in Semitic epigraphy where no examples of known scripts have been uncovered for periods varying from 100 to 200 years. To support his argument, he pointed out that the earliest Greek alphabetic inscriptions were written in both horizontal directions and boustrophedon. In fact, the term *boustrophedon* is a Greek term coined to describe early alphabetic writing. He also pointed out that by the eighth century B.C., the time of the purported transfer, all the Semitic scripts with which the Greeks could have had possible contact had settled into a right to left horizontal pattern.

He considered it highly unlikely that the Greek alphabetic script first began right to left, then evolved into boustrophedon, and then eventually reversed directions. There is no known case where an alphabetic script was transferred from one culture to another and reversed directions. Ethiopic, which is written from left to right like Greek, was derived from Proto–Arabic, which split off from Proto–Canaanite when both were written in either direction. Phoenician eventually evolved a right to left script and Ethiopic a left to right script. This, claimed Naveh, is the likely pattern with Greek also. He contended that the transfer from Phoenician to Greek occurred when the Phoenician script was still in its Proto-Canaanite form and hence not yet settled in any direction. Greek and Phoenician then evolved into horizontal scripts written in opposite directions. Naveh placed this transfer at about 1050 B.C.

He provided additional evidence for this dating by comparing letters and showing that the Archaic Greek letters resemble the Proto–Canaanite letters of 1050 B.C. more than the Phoenician letters of the eighth century B.C. "The Greek letters are considerably less cursive than the eighth- or even ninth-century Phoenician letters" (Naveh, 1982, p. 178). He also pointed out that the Archaic Greek scripts show an enormous amount of local variation, whereas the eighth century B.C. Phoenician script had already evolved into a single national form. This local variation, which persisted until the fourth century B.C., when Ionian became the uniformly adopted Classical Greek script, argued for an earlier adoption than the eighth century B.C.

There is ample evidence of contacts between the Greeks and Canaanites as early as 1050 B.C. These include two 11th-century Canaanite inscriptions found at Nora in Sardinia and Teke near Knossos in Crete, plus evidence of a Greek settlement at Tell Sahas in Phoenicia as early as the late ninth century B.C. In the wake of recent inscriptions found at Qubur el-Walaydah and Izbet Sarta, Cross (1980) concluded, "These new data must be said to give added support to the thesis of Joseph Naveh for this high antiquity of the earliest use by the Greeks of the alphabet, and remove obstacles to dating their borrowing to the time of the transition from Old Canaanite to Linear Phoenician toward 1100 B.C."

We traced the history of the development of alphabetic writing in the West from its roots in the Proto–Canaanite alphabet of 22 uniconsonantal signs to the totally phonetic Greek alphabet complete with vowels. The Greek alphabet became the launching pad for all of the European alphabetic systems. The Greeks passed their alphabet to the Etruscans. The Etruscans together with a direct influence from the Greeks passed their alphabet onto the Romans (see chap. 8, this volume, for more details). The Romans through their conquests spread their alphabet throughout Europe. Eventually all of the countries of Europe, with the exception of those in Eastern Europe who converted to the Greek Orthodox religion, adopted the Roman alphabet with minor variations. The countries that then colonized different parts of the world brought the Roman alphabet to the Americas, Australia, Asia, and Africa. Examples include the Philippines colonized by the Spanish, Viet Nam colonized by the French, Indonesia colonized by the Dutch, and some 500 African languages (Man, 2000).

THE CYRILLIC ALPHABET

Around 800 A.D., after the schism between Rome and Constantinople, these two centers of Christianity sent out missionaries into the pagan world seeking to increase their political control of the remainder of Europe. The head of Byzantium in Constantinople, Michael III received a request from the king of Moravia (presently in the Czech Republic) for a teacher who could instruct his subjects in the faith in their own Slavonic language. At the time of this request, all religious texts were in one of only three languages: Hebrew, Greek, and Latin. Michael chose two brothers, Methodius and Constantine, known for their administrative skills and scholarship, respectively, to head the mission to Moravia and translate the Bible into Slavonic. The brothers had grown up in Macedonia so they were conversant in both Slavonic and Greek. To write in Slavonic, Constantine first invented an alphabet suitable for the language, which was based on a cursive form of the Greek alphabet and "which came to be called Glagolitic, from the Slavonic root for 'word' and to 'speak.' . . . The language fixed by the new alphabet, known as Old Church Slavonic, was then understood by all Slav speakers" (Man, 2000, p. 271). The new alphabet contained 40 letters and was well suited to the Slavonic language. His translation of the Gospels became the first version of the Gospels in a vernacular tongue in Europe (Man, 2000). When Constantine fell ill at the age of 52, he expressed the desire to die as a monk and, as was the custom, he was re-christened as Cyril. He eventually became canonized as Saint Cyril.

The Glagolitic alphabet that Constantine or St. Cyril created was then exported from Moravia to Bulgaria, where it was used extensively to train missionaries. The Bulgarians found the use of the Glagolitic alphabet difficult because they were not as familiar with the cursive form of Greek, but were used to the Greek capital letters. They modified the Glagolitic alphabet and renamed it in honor of St. Cyril as the Cyrillic alphabet. So the Cyrillic alphabet is not really an invention of St. Cyril, but is rather a modified form of his original invention of the Glagolitic alphabet (Man, 2000). The new Cyrillic alphabet was adopted by the Bulgarians, Russians, Ukrainians, Belo-Russians, Macedonians, and Serbs. Basically all the Slavic nations that eventually became Eastern Orthodox adopted the Cyrillic alphabet. In contrast, those Slavic nations such as Poland and Croatia, which became Roman Catholic, adopted the Roman (or Latin) alphabet. Ironically the Czechs, which included the Moravians, also became Roman Catholic and adopted the Roman alphabet. The Romanians who practice for the most part an Orthodox form of Christianity originally adopted the Cyrillic alphabet, but sometime during the 19th century they opted to use the Roman alphabet in deference to the fact that their spoken language is a Romance language. The Soviets under the leadership of Stalin forced the use of the Cyrillic alphabet on the Islamic people throughout Soviet Central Asia, where it is in use for 50 different languages (Man, 2000). The Cyrillic alphabet, which was also adopted by the Mongolians for political reasons to show their solidarity with the Soviets, survives there to this day.

THE RUNIC AND OGHAM ALPHABETS

Before bringing this discussion to a close, we briefly mention the runic and ogham alphabets. Runes were used in Northern Europe from about the 3rd to the 16th centuries A.D. Their exact origins are somewhat mysterious, but it is clear that they were derived from one or more of the

Italo–Greco alphabets of the Mediterranean region, such as the Greek, Latin, or Etruscan ones. One theory maintains that runes were an invention of the Goths, who borrowed many of their letters from the Etruscans. Another proposal is that runes arose from the contact of the Goths with a Greek colony on the shores of the Crimean Sea.

Runes, as the etymology of the name implies, was a secret writing system used for religious and mystical purposes. The runic alphabet was suppressed by the Church for this reason. "Runes were never a purely utilitarian script; right from their adoption into Germanic usage they served for the casting of lots, divination and other rites" (Elliott, 1959, pp. 1–2). Runes were also used for making inscriptions on weapons, sepulcher stones, caskets, coins, and jewelry. There have also been manuscripts inscribed with runes that have been found.

A number of varieties of runes evolved in the course of their history of which the three main branches were Anglo-Saxon, Scandinavian, and Germanic. The number of letters were approximately the same as in the Roman-based European alphabets. What distinguished the alphabet was the order of the letters, which was markedly different from the original Canaanite alphabet. The runic alphabet did not have a fixed direction; inscriptions have been found that run from left to right, right to left, and, as in the case of the Kylver stone, in both directions (Elliott, 1959).

The original Germanic runic alphabet contained 24 letters. The Anglo-Saxon runic alphabets used in England expanded in some cases to 33 letters, but the Scandinavian runic alphabet suffered a reduction in the number of letters to 16. Although it is true that a number of the runic signs were derived from north Italic alpine alphabets, it is also clear that some of the runic signs were part of pagan lore and were in use before the contact of the Germanic tribes with the north Italic writing systems. Elliott (1959) suggested that some of the signs find their "origin in the Indo-European sun-cult . . . the sun motif which lies at their root is apparent in many variations of circles, semi-circles, swastikas, and the like, but there also occur pictorial representations of men and animals, parts of the human body, and various implements such as axes, arrows, and ships" (p. 64). Elliott suggested that runes represent an amalgamation of alphabetic script and the pagan symbols.

The Celts of the British Isle also created an alphabet that shared some of the characteristics of runes. Oghams were used by the Celtic priests—druids—to transmit their secret lore and mark boundary stones or grave markers. Their system of writing corresponds roughly to the same time period as runes, but no definitive relationship between the two writing systems has been discovered. Like runes, oghams is an alphabetic system with each letter representing a basic phoneme of their spoken language. Ogham letters are thought to have derived from the

Roman alphabet despite that the order of the letters like runes does not correspond to the order of the Roman alphabet. Also, the letters are formed by one to five parallel straight lines like notches or strokes on a tally stick oriented in different directions with respect to the direction of writing. The letters are grouped in five groupings of five letters each and have therefore been surmised to have originated as a form of finger spelling (Lehmann, 1989).

4

Non-Western
Writing Systems

THE CHINESE WRITING SYSTEMS

Before turning to the study of the effects of alphabetic writing on the West and comparing its effects to those of nonalphabetic cultures, we pause to reflect on those factors that might have hindered the development of alphabetic writing in the Orient with the sole exception of the Korean alphabet, which was invented in 1443. In this chapter, we confine our analysis to the Chinese, Korean, Japanese, and Meso-American writing systems, omitting a number of other writing systems. The examples we have chosen are enough for us to understand the contrast between alphabetic and nonalphabetic writing systems, which is the focus of our study. I leave the description of these writing systems to others and stay focused on my topic.

Writing in the Orient began in China during the Shang dynasty and dates back to 1200 B.C. The first inscriptions were made on turtle shells and animal bones and were used for the purpose of divination (Keightley, 1989). This earliest form of writing underwent an evolution in which the following stages emerged:

1. The Ta Chuan (greater seal) inscriptions found on bronze vessels from the 12th to the 8th centuries.

2. The Hsiao Chuan (lesser seal) inscriptions engraved on wood, ceramic, or bronze "by which administrators . . . would sign their documents and letters. The characters looked carved, the strokes being unmodulated, of uniform width, and rather mechanical and geometric" (Keightley, 1989).

3. Li shu (clerkly script), dating from the 3rd century A.D. on, "was characterized by its rapid, flowing strokes that were suited to the needs of the clerks" of the imperial bureaucracy. The script developed slowly over time, with some of its elements dating back to the time of Confucius in the sixth century B.C. (Keightley, 1989).

The Chinese writing system began with pictograms. "The simplest —and presumably, the earliest—graphs were pictures of men, body parts, animals, the sun and the moon, falling rain, vessels and so on" (Keightley, 1989, p. 188). The next stage, as was the case with all other writing systems, was that these pictorial symbols were used to represent a word with the same sound as the original word depicted by the pictogram. "The Chinese used this principle of borrowing the sound of one word to help write another extensively, but in many cases they did not signal what they were doing" (Keightley, 1989, p. 189). With time, however, they resolved this ambiguity by combining the phonetic symbol with a second symbol, a semantic classifier, which operated as an "ideograph for it indicated the idea, not the word" (Keightley, 1989, p. 190). A word is therefore represented by two symbols; one provides the sound of the word, and the other provides the idea of the word or category to which the word belongs.

Keightley (1989) provided the example of how "the graph for lai, a growing grain, was distinguished from the homophonic lai, 'to come', by the addition of a semantic classifier meaning 'grass' or 'vegetation'." This technique of compound graphs known as *hsieh-sheng* (corresponding in sound) is used to represent a large percentage of Chinese words. Some words, however, like the word for bright, which combines the symbol for the sun and the moon, are nonphonetic and purely ideographic. To read and write Chinese, therefore, it is necessary to memorize the sound and meaning of a large number (numbering in the thousands) of simple graphs and to use the information they provide to decode (or code) the word being (or to be) depicted. This differs from an alphabetic system, where less than 30 symbols have to be memorized or a syllabary where 60 to 90 symbols must be learned.

The method of rendering Chinese words uses a number of techniques, some a single graph that is pictographic (at least originally), but in the large majority of cases through the use of a compound graph. The compound graphs usually contain a phonetic element and a semantic qualifier to resolve the ambiguity of the highly homophonic nature of Chinese. However, some compounds, like *bright* are purely ideographic. Other examples include *good* represented by the graph for a woman and the graph for a child or *security* depicted by the graph of a woman shown under the graph for a roof. The words for *above* and *below* show the relationship graphically. There is a lack of agreement as to whether Chinese writing is pictographic, ideographic, or logographic (de Francis, 1989). For the purposes of this discussion, the important point is that the Chinese writing system is only partially phonetic and requires the memorization of a large number of visual signs for the purposes of reading and writing. "An eminent Chinese linguist (Chao, 1976, p. 92) has suggested that English is 75% phonetic, Chinese only 25%" (de Francis, 1989, p. 51). In alphabetic writing systems such as English, there are often ambiguities between the written signal and the spoken word being denoted. With the exception of totally phonetic languages such as Finnish, there are also ambiguities of pronunciation. George Bernard Shaw's famous example (Stubbs, 1980) of using *ghoti* to render the spoken word *fish*—taking "gh" from enough, "o" from women, and "ti" from nation—dramatically demonstrates the pronunciation ambiguities of the English alphabet. These ambiguities make spelling many words in English a challenge, but they do not obviate the alphabet effect.

We have referred to the Finnish alphabet as totally phonetic, but this is only partially true. No alphabet can be perfectly phonemic, because it must be read by people who speak different dialects and, hence, have different pronunciations of the language being transcribed by the alphabetic script.

Naturally all languages are phonetic in the sense that they depict spoken language in terms of visual signs, but Chinese writing cannot be decoded by resorting to phonetics alone, and therefore it cannot give rise to the same effects as an alphabetic writing system. de Francis (1989) cited research that reveals, "that if one has memorized the pronunciation of 895 phonetic elements singled out by Soothill, it is possible in 66% of the cases to guess the pronunciation of any given character one is likely to encounter in reading a modern text" (p. 111). Not only are Chinese characters difficult to write and a challenge to read, they "are extremely clumsy and time-consuming when it comes to indexing written materials, and there can be little doubt that in many other ways they retard Chinese progress" (de Francis, 1989, p. 243). Unlike alphabetic writing, Chinese writing does not promote classification, analysis, or abstraction—an opinion shared by sinologists Alfred Bloom (1951), who wrote *The Linguistic Shaping of Thought: A Study of the Impact of Language on Thinking in China*, and Chad Hansen (1982), author of *Language and Thought in Ancient China*.

Although the Chinese writing system has phonetic elements to it, it still requires a tremendous amount of memorization to read and write. "The K'anghsi dictionary of Chinese in AD 1716 lists 40,545 characters. No Chinese or Sinologist knows them all, or ever did. Few Chinese who write can write all of the spoken Chinese words that they can understand. To become significantly learned in the Chinese writing system normally takes some twenty years. Such a script is basically time-consuming and elitist" (Ong, 1982, p. 57).

Although the Chinese writing system might not be the best suited for scientific activities, they were nevertheless the source and inspiration of a high culture that had a strong, almost defining influence on all the East Asian cultures. As Keightley (1989) pointed out, "the seminal and overriding importance of Chinese script in the general history of East Asia (was) the cultural dominance that imperial China exerted over Korea, Japan and much of Southeast Asia" (p. 171).

The characters were things of great visual beauty that inspired a great deal of poetic expression. "A man absorbed with writing was absorbed not just with words but with symbols and through the act of writing with the brush, with a form of painting . . . the way in which something was written could be as important as its content" (Keightley, 1989, p. 171).

Another interesting feature of Chinese writing is that people speaking different dialects of Chinese, that are not mutually understandable when spoken can communicate with each through writing and can read the same text translating it into their respective dialects. Because Chinese writing has evolved so little from its origins, contemporary Chinese are able to read texts that are 3,000 or more years old. The way in which readers of Chinese characters who speak different dialects can understand the characters, despite that they pronounce them differently, is easily understood if one considers Arabic numerals such as 1, 2, and 3, which are pronounced differently depending on the spoken language of the reader but are mutually understood across all language barriers.

One of the puzzles of the Chinese writing system is that it "never advanced to what was, in other cultures, the next and seemingly natural step, the development of a syllabary in which graphs were used purely for writing sounds rather than writing words (even though) the potential was clearly there" (Keightley, 1989, p. 192). As Keightley pointed out, the Japanese used "the Chinese logographs to invent their own kana syllabary in the ninth and tenth centuries A.D." (p. 192). Keightley attributed the lack of this development to two factors: (a) the writing system they created was so firmly established and well liked because of its elegance and beauty there was no motivation to simplify it; and (b) unlike the case with the Mesopotamian system, where two dissimilar languages (Sumerian and Akkadian) were rendered by the same script, Chinese did not have such a stimulus.

I find the first argument cogent but not the second given the large number of Chinese dialects. I suggest that perhaps two other factors were also in play. The first factor is the conservative nature of Chinese culture with its emphasis on preserving its traditions. The second factor is the nature of the spoken language, which is tonal and consists of monosyllabic words and, hence, contains a large number of homophones. There are no prefixes or suffixes, only single-syllable words. This severely limits the number of possible sound combinations for forming words. Tone and redundancy are employed to accommodate the rich vocabulary of Chinese. Compound words are created by combining simple single-syllable words the way *houseboy* or *ice cream* are formed in English. The use of tone or pitch also increases the number of possible word combinations. The four tones of Mandarin and five of Cantonese increase the number of basic sounds to 1,380 and 1,868, respectively. It is only through redundancy, however, that these limited number of sounds are able to accommodate the large Chinese vocabulary. Virtually every Chinese word is a homonym, with an average of 10 different words for each sound. There are 2,365 different Mandarin words, each with its own unique pictogram or character, that are all pronounced *shih*. Part of the redundancy is resolved by tone and context and part by using two words with similar meaning side by side, like the English expression of native Chinese speakers—"look see"—which is a literal translation from the Chinese.

Because of the tremendous phonetic redundancy of their words, there was little or no motivation until the advent of computers for the Chinese to develop a phonetic writing system, let alone an alphabetic one. In fact there are good reasons to retain their pictograms. Chinese characters, with their unique representation of each word, reduce the redundancy of the spoken language, making it easier to read. Redundant combinations like look-see are no longer needed, because the character for *look* or *see* cannot be mistaken for its homonyms. The other advantage of the logographic nature of Chinese writing is that it enables "those who speak mutually unintelligible idioms to converse together, using the pencil instead of the tongue" (Clodd, 1913). This property of Chinese writing has helped Beijing exercise hegemony for many centuries over the vast geographical zone that comprises China.

THE KOREAN WRITING SYSTEMS

Not only did China exert a geopolitical influence over the territory it ruled, it also exerted a cultural influence over all of the East Asian nations. We begin the study of the impact of the Chinese writing system with the Koreans, who became acquainted with the Chinese writing system in the fifth century B.C. and developed their own writing system in northern Korea in the second century A.D. (de Francis, 1989). The early Korean writing system, hanmun (Chinese writing), made use of Chinese characters. Korean names and places were rendered by utilizing the phonetic value of the Chinese characters. Three systems of writing emerged from these early efforts to create a Korean writing system *idu* (clerk reading) and *hyangch'al* (local letters) and *kugyo"l* (oral formulae) (Kim-Renaud, 1997). In idu many words were borrowed directly from the Chinese language, represented with Chinese characters but pronounced in a Korean manner with the result that many Sino-Korean words created in this manner are part of modern Korean (Yi, 1975). The hyangch'al attempted to use the phonetic values of the Chinese characters to represent Korean words. This system never really took off and was confined to its use to write poetry.

Perhaps because none of the early Korean writing systems was satisfactory the Koreans created their own indigenous alphabetic writing system in 1443 under the leadership and efforts of their king. King Sejong, who was a scholar, wanted to create a writing system that would be easy to learn so as to create the condition for universal literacy among his subjects. Promulgated in 1446 with the name *Hunmin cho"ng'u"m* (Correct Sound for the Instruction of the People), this alphabet now goes by the name of *han'gu"l* (Great Script). "The Korean alphabet does not consist of symbols that are arbitrarily selected to signify specific sounds, as is the case with nearly all other alphabets, but there is an iconic relationship between the letters and the sounds they represent" (Kim-Renaud, 1997, p. 3). The shape of the letters are meant to represent the configuration of the speech organ, which includes the lip, tongue, teeth (molar and incisor), and larynx, when the phoneme associated with the letter is enunciated.

> In the basic letters representing the five basic series of sounds, the so-called molar (k) and lingual (n) are constructed differently from the labial (m), the incisor (s), and laryngeal consonants. The latter three depict the shape of the speech organ involved. In contrast, the molar and the lingual letters graphically depict not the organ alone but the articulatory gesture . . . for the molar the root of the tongue blocking the throat; lingual shows the tip of the tongue touching the upper palate. (Ahn, 1997, p. 93)

The pictographic representation of the speech organ is a unique feature of the Korean alphabet and represents a great achievement on the part of King Sejong and the scholars who assisted him in creating this writing system.

"Another characteristic of the Korean alphabet is that it is not written in a linear, sequential fashion as are most alphabetic systems: Rather the letters are put together into a syllable block" (Ahn, 1997, p. 4). The syllable block was divided into an initial, medial (vowels), and final part. The use of an alphabet to render syllable blocks is still another unique feature of the Korean writing system. There are 28 letters in the Korean alphabet: 17 are used to represent the initial part of a syllable, and 11 represent the medial part (Ahn, 1997).

Although the hang'ul writing system has no need for the use of Chinese characters, as is demonstrated by the writing system used currently in North Korea, Koreans tended to use a certain number of Chinese characters in their written expression. This was due to the great prestige that the Chinese writing system had throughout the Orient in general and specifically in Korea. The number of Chinese characters used in Korean writing has steadily declined with time, but they can still be found in the written texts used in South Korea.

> The alphabet was used only for unscholarly, practical, vulgarian purposes. "Serious" writers continued to use the Chinese character writing in which they had so laboriously trained themselves. Serious literature was elitist and wanted to be known as elitist. Only in the twentieth century, with the greater democratization of Korea, did the alphabet achieve its present (still less than total) ascendancy. (Ong, 1982, pp. 92-93)

This observation by Ong perhaps explains why Korean culture did not experience the alphabet effect despite that its writing system contained a perfectly phonetic alphabet. As pointed out to me by the editor of this series, Lance Strate, perhaps the uniqueness of the Korean writing system helped Korea maintain its unique cultural heritage and independence despite being geographically squeezed between two giant nations—China and Japan.

THE JAPANESE WRITING SYSTEM

The Japanese did not become acquainted with Chinese writing until 400 A.D. They were in part aided by the Koreans who had a longer and closer contact with the Chinese, but it was the Japanese interest in Buddhism, which began in the middle of the sixth century, that brought them in contact with a large body of Chinese writing. The Japanese like the Korean before them used Chinese characters to represent words but gave them a Japanese pronunciation. At first they used the Chinese word order, but later they used the writing system in which they used the Japanese word order. The Japanese referred to the Chinese characters as *kanji*, but when they used the characters phonetically to represent the sounds of Japanese they called them *kana*. The use of *kana* increased as the Japanese used the Chinese characters phonetically to write texts in their own language (de Francis, 1989). The use of the Chinese characters phonetically initially caused some difficulties because characters were borrowed from different parts of China where there were tremendous differences in pronunciation. In the ninth century A.D., two syllabaries emerged that resolved these ambiguities. They were *hiragana* (easy kana) used for informal writing and *katakana* (side kana) used for formal writing and official documents. Hiragana is the system used for everyday writing today, with katakana serving the role of italics in our writing system. The hiragana syllabary, which once numbered almost 300 symbols, eventually evolved into the modern system with only 46 symbols.

In the actual Japanese writing system, a mixture of kanji and kana symbols are used, making for a difficult and complex writing system. The main stem of a word is often rendered in kanji and the grammatical case endings in kana. In the popular press, the practice has developed to attach small kana symbols called *furigana* to each kanji symbol to make sure the reader can decipher the Chinese characters. Sansom (1928), an authority on Japanese writing, commented: "One hesitates for a epithet to describe a writing system which is so complex that it needs another writing system to explain it . . . as a practical instrument it is surely without inferiors" (p. 44). Others including Lance Strate have suggested that Perhaps the phonetic nature of the Japanese writing system contributed to Japan's industrialization, militarization, market economy, and, within recent years, democracy.

MESO-AMERICAN WRITING SYSTEMS

To complete our survey of writing systems, we quickly review the writing systems of Meso-America, Mexico, and Central America. Of the 13 different writing systems that have been identified so far, the most advanced was that of the Lowland Classical Mayans, which according to Lounsbury (1989), "qualifies as writing in the fullest sense," (i.e., it graphically represented complete sentences). Although the writing system has not been fully deciphered, it seems to be a hieroglyphic system that contains some phonetic elements. The system is extremely old, dating back to approximately 30 B.C. The most interesting feature of the writing system was its notation of numbers, which included a symbol for zero and a place number system for representing numerals.

5

A Comparison of the Chinese and the Western Alphabetic Writing Systems and their Impact on Cultural Patterns

---

THE IMPACT OF WRITING
ON THOUGHT AND CULTURE

There is widespread agreement among scholars that spoken language has had the single greatest influence of all factors on man's thought processes and is responsible for its origin. Second only to the impact of speech on thought has been writing (Breasted, 1926). Harold Innis (1971, 1972) was one of the first scholars to study the way in which writing affected man's thinking patterns.

> The art of writing provided man with a transpersonal memory. Men were given an artificially extended and verifiable memory of objects and events not present to sight or recollection. Individuals applied their minds to symbols rather than things and went beyond the world of concrete experience into the world of conceptual relations created within an enlarged time and space universe. The time world was extended beyond the range of remembered things and the space

59

world beyond the range of known places. Writing enormously enhanced a capacity for abstract thinking which had been evident in the growth of language in the oral tradition. Names in themselves were abstractions. Man's activities and powers were roughly extended in proportion to the increased use and perfection of written records. (Innis, 1972, p. 10)

Walter Ong (1982) expressed a similar sentiment: "Without writing, the literate mind would not and could not think as it does, not only when engaged in writing but normally even when it is composing its thoughts in oral form. More than any other single invention, writing has transformed human consciousness."

If writing has had the impact that Innis and Ong suggested, the particular form a writing system assumes should play a crucial role in shaping the thoughts of its users. Not only should one expect a major difference in the thought patterns of literate and preliterate people, but one should also expect comparable differences in the thought patterns of societies whose writing systems differ significantly, as pointed out by Innis (1971, 1972), McLuhan (1962, 1964), and Foucault (1973). Differences in modes of communication according to our hypothesis result in differences in thought patterns and social forms.

COMPARING CHINESE AND ALPHABETIC WRITING SYSTEMS

Chinese and Western alphabetic literacy represent two completely different forms of writing. The alphabet is used phonetically to visually represent the sound of a word. In alphabetic writing, a word is broken down into its basic phonemes, which are then individually represented visually with the 20 to 30 letters of the alphabet. The Chinese writing system requires the memorization of literally thousands of characters. About 1% of Chinese words are represented pictographically with a single character. The majority of words are represented by two characters. One character provides an indication of the pronunciation of the word. The other character acts as a classifier and represents the semantic category to which the word belongs and, as a consequence, resolves the ambiguity due to the fact that Chinese spoken language is highly homophonic. Chinese reading and writing entails a great deal of memorization and the use of pictographic and ideographic elements; as a consequence, it is less abstract than alphabetic writing. It is harder to order or classify Chinese words because it is not a purely phonetic writing system as is the case with alphabetic writing, where words can be ordered precisely using the alphabet. It is our hypothesis that differences in Eastern and Western thought patterns are due in part to the vast differences in their respective writing systems.

COMPARING CHINESE
AND WESTERN CULTURAL SYSTEMS

We attempt to show in this chapter that the absence of Western-style abstractions and classification schemes in Chinese culture is related to the differences in writing systems. This study was originally an attempt to understand why science began in the West despite the superiority of Chinese technology, a point we illustrate later. Most of the technology used in Europe before the Industrial Revolution actually originated in China, and yet we have the curious historical fact that modern abstract science began in Europe.

Despite that I clearly stated in the first edition of this book that Chinese culture evolved in a different direction than European culture (this "is not to suggest that Chinese culture is inferior [to European culture]; quite the opposite is true"), some critics have accused me of being Eurocentric. Nothing could be further from the truth given my great admiration of this nation's accomplishments. I wrote then, that "Chinese culture has created its own triumphs in arts, technology, philosophy, and religious thought, which have not been rivaled by any other culture." One example is the fact that it is one of the oldest continuous cultures in existence today having made major contributions in all aspects of culture, including governance, law, science, mathematics, medicine, technology, religion, philosophy, literature, the graphic arts, music, and architecture.

I hope that I have made it clear that there is no way one can look on Chinese culture as being any less successful or sophisticated than European culture. It is a fact, however, that Chinese thinking is considerably more concrete and practical and less abstract than Western thought, which has been one of the factors that allowed it to contribute as much to world culture as it has and will allow it to contribute in the future. Chinese logic is based on analogy and induction rather than matching and deduction as is the case with the alphabetic cultures of the West. Chinese mathematics is more algebraic than geometric. Chinese technological inventiveness is unparalleled by that of any culture, yet China never exploited its technology in a systematic manner as was done in the West during the Industrial Revolution. The Chinese created an elaborate legal system, but not a codified one. They developed their own unique way of dealing with space and time, but one that is not Cartesian. They were deeply spiritual and mystical thinkers, yet they were not monotheists.

It is my thesis that these differences are in part due to the differences in writing systems: logographic writing versus alphabetic (or purely phonetic) writing. Table 5.1 lists characteristics of these two worlds. Although this table is simplistic, it is useful because it allows us to see the overall patterns of Eastern and Western thought at a glance.

The characteristics listed in each column are not necessarily the exclusive property of that culture, but rather represent the directions in which that culture has evolved. There are aspects of Western culture that are traditional rather than progressive or more inductive than deductive. By the same token, the East has at times been rational or abstract rather

TABLE 5.1

Comparison of Chinese and Western Cultural Patterns

China	Europe
Logograms	Alphabet
Right-brain oriented	Left-brain oriented
Nonlinear	Linear
Acoustical	Visual
Analogical	Logic
Inductive	Deductive
Concrete	Abstract
Mystical	Causal
Intuitive	Rational
Generalist	Specialized
Decentralized	Centralized
Local	Universal
Integrative	Fragmented
Space oriented	Time oriented
Traditional	Progressive
Cyclic time	Continuous time
Algebraic	Geometric
Concrete science	Abstract science
Order and pattern	Natural law
Craft	Technology
Invention	Exploitation
Technique	System
Customs-mores (Confucius)	Codified law
Harmony of nature (Tao)	Monotheism
Relativity	Absolutism

than intuitive or concrete. As we explore Chinese law, science, technology, logic, and philosophy, however, we see how the characteristics of the first column predominate over those of the second column. Later in this study, we see that with the coming of electricity, the characteristics of the two cultures begin to merge.

CHINESE LAW

The role of law and attitudes toward it are quite different in Eastern and Western civilizations. Law in the West, for example, tends to take on a much greater importance than it does in the East (Escarra, 1936). Another major difference is that Western law is codified, whereas Chinese law is based on custom and mores as pointed out by the great China scholar Needham (1979):

> The Chinese early acquired a great distaste for precisely formulated abstract codified law from the abortive tyranny of the politicians belonging to the School of Legalists during the period of transition from feudalism to bureaucration. Then when the bureaucratic system was finally set up, the old conceptions of natural law in the form of accepted customs and good mores proved more suitable than any others for Chinese society in its typical form. (pp. 36–37)

There is no doubt that China's bad experience with the Legalists probably contributed to the rejection of codified law. There were also many bad experiences with codified law and tyrants in the West as well, yet somehow codified law survived in the West. Why? I believe it was the nature of the writing system.

The Chinese developed two concepts of law: *fa* and *li* (Needham, 1979). The proponents of *fa*, the Legalists, believed in formalistic law. The thinkers associated with *li* were Confucians and adhered to the body of ancient customs, such as filial piety. Neither the concept *fa* nor *li*, however, applied to nonhuman nature. This helps explain why the Chinese never developed the concept of scientific laws as laws of nature. Within the realm of law, no analogy was made between the world of nature and the world of human behavior (Needham, 1979). The lack of formal law in China had another lingering effect on the development of science—namely, the lack of standard weights and measures in China until modern times (Needham, 1956). "Their very aversion from codification was one of the factors which made the Chinese intellectual climate uncongenial to the development of systematized scientific thought" (Needham, 1956, p. 204).

CHINESE SCIENCE

What makes the lack of theoretical science in China so puzzling is the high level of technological progress achieved there. The list of significant scientific and technological advances made by the Chinese long before their development in the West includes the equine harness, iron and steel metallurgy, gunpowder, paper, the drive belt, the chain drive, the standard method of converting rotary to rectilinear motion, and the segmental arch bridge (Needham, 1979). To this must be added irrigation systems, ink, printing, movable type, metal-barrel cannons, rockets, porcelain, silk, magnetism, the magnetic compass, stirrups, the wheelbarrow, Cardan suspension, deep drilling, the Pascal triangle, poundlocks on canals, fore-and-aft sailing, watertight compartments, the sternpost rudder, the paddle-wheel boat, quantitative cartography, immunization techniques (variolation), astronomical observations of novae and supernovae, seismographs, acoustics, and the systematic exploration of the chemical and pharmaceutical properties of a great variety of substances.

Having carefully documented through years of historical research the contribution of Chinese science and its influence on the West, Needham (1979) posed the following question: "Why, then, did modern science, as opposed to ancient and medieval science, develop only in the Western world?" (p. 11). The crucial term in the question posed by Needham, modern science, really means abstract theoretical science based on experimentation and empirical observation, which began in Europe during the Renaissance.

Abstract theoretical science is thus a peculiar outgrowth of Western culture and is little more than 350 years old. Nonabstract practical science as it occurs in China and the remainder of the world is a universal activity pursued by all cultures as part of their strategy for survival. In *The Savage Mind*, Lévi-Strauss (1960) gave numerous examples of elaborate classification schemes of preliterate cultures based on their empirical observations and demonstrating their rudimentary concrete scientific thinking.

China created what was probably the most sophisticated form of nonabstract science the world has known. Yet technological sophistication by itself does not guarantee the development of abstract theoretical science. Other factors (social, economic, and cultural), obviously present in the West and not the East, must have played a crucial role.

Before delving into the impact of the Chinese writing system, let us first review the fundamental elements of Chinese science. According to classical Chinese thought, the universe consists of five elements: earth, water, fire, metal, and wood. The five elements are ruled by the two fundamental universal and complementary forces of yin and yang, which represent, respectively, the following pairs of opposites: cold and warm, female and male, contraction and expansion, collection and dispersion, negative and positive. The five elements and the two forces of yin and yang form a blend of opposites in which a unity emerges more through harmony than through the fiat of preordained laws (Needham, 1956). Chinese science always had a mystical and mysterious aspect to it. Those thinkers who were most rational—the Confucians and Logicians—had little interest in nature. The Taoists who were interested in nature were mystics who mistrusted reason and logic. Chinese science was colored by the Taoist attitude toward nature, which is summarized by the following passage from the Huoi Nan Tzu book: "The Tao of Heaven operates mysteriously and secretly; it has no fixed slope; it follows no definite rules; it is so great that you can never come to the end of it; it is so deep that you can never fathom it" (p. 1.6).

It is not difficult to understand how the Taoist mystical attitude toward nature might preclude the development of abstract science. However, we are still left with the question of why those who were rational, such as the Confucists and the Logicians, were not interested in nature and why those who were interested in nature, such as the Taoists, were mystical. In other words, why wasn't there a group in China that was both rational and interested in science and nature? Eberhard (1957) offered an explanation: "Science had only one function, namely, to serve the government and not its own curiosity. All innovations were looked upon as acts of defiance and revolution." The difficulty with the explanation provided by Eberhard is that it applies to the West as well. Western scientists faced the same problems in Europe. The work of Copernicus was openly contested and then suppressed by the Church, yet the Copernican revolution succeeded.

Fung (1922) offered a philosophical explanation for the lack of theoretical science: "Chinese philosophers loved the certainty of perception, not that of conception, and therefore, they would not and did not translate their concrete vision into the form of science" (p. 137). The Chinese thinker was content to live in harmony with nature with no need to subdue it or have power over it as is the case in the West. Fung claims that this philosophical disposition provided no motivation to the Chinese to turn from their internal reflective state to the external active stance that the West adopted to develop scientific thinking. Her explanation is similar to that of Latourette (1964), who claimed that Chinese thinkers were more interested in controlling their minds than nature, whereas in the West it was the opposite.

The philosophical and ethical considerations cited by Fung (1922) and Latourette (1964) as well as the political and bureaucratic issues brought forward by Eberhard (1957) are valid and provide critical background information against which one must consider the question of why abstract science did not develop in China. The central question that must still be addressed, however, is why the intellectual climate in China was not conducive to "science for science's sake," abstract laws, the "study of the process of thinking (logic)," or the translation of a "concrete vision into the form of science."

THE INFLUENCE OF WRITING SYSTEMS

Needham (1979) suggests where to look for the answer to this question:

> The cause for the breakthrough [in science] occurring in Europe was connected with the special social, intellectual and economic conditions prevailing there at the Renaissance, and can never be explained by any deficiencies either of the Chinese mind or of the Chinese intellectual and philosophical tradition. (p. 19)

Needham, however, missed one of the key cultural factors that differentiates East and West—namely, the difference in their writing systems:

> My view is that in Chinese civilization there were factors inhibitory to the growth of modern science, while in Western civilization, the factors were favorable. . . . Had the environmental conditions been reversed as between Euro-America and China, all else would have been reversed too—all the great names in the heroic age of science, Galileo, Malpighi, Versalius, Harvey, Boyle, would have been Chinese and not Western names; and in order to enter today fully into the heritage of science, Westerners would have to learn the logographic script just as the Chinese now have to learn alphabetic languages because the bulk of modern scientific literatures is written in them. (p. 152)

I totally agree with the first part of Needham's remark—that there were in China "factors inhibitory to the growth of modern science." I disagree with the second part because it is my contention that one of the "inhibitory factors to the growth of modern science," ironically enough, was the Chinese logographic script. It is my belief that the first scientific literature, whether Oriental or Occidental, was destined to be written in an alphabetic script because the alphabet creates the environmental conditions under which abstract theoretical science flourishes.

It would be simplistic to suggest that it was the relative impact of the alphabet and logographic writing alone that explains the emergence of abstract science in Europe and not China. However, this factor cannot be ignored as Needham (1979) suggested:

> There is a commonly received idea that the ideographic language has a powerful inhibiting factor to the development of modern science in China. We believe, however, that this influence is generally grossly overrated. It has proved possible in the course of our work to draw up large glossaries of technical terms used in ancient and medieval times for all kinds of things and ideas in science and its applications. (p. 38)

Needham's assertion that an adequate vocabulary existed for expressing scientific ideas in Chinese is correct, but he failed to understand or take into account the subliminal or hidden effects of rendering scientific words in a logographic script. An examination of the etymologies of the most important Chinese scientific words that he provided in his magnum opus, *Science and Civilization in China*, illustrates our point (Needham, 1956). Table 5.2 provides a list of Chinese scientific terms along with their English meaning; romanization, modern, and ancient Chinese character rendition; and an interpretation of the ancient Chinese character that indicates the etymology of the word. An examination of the table reveals that even the most abstract scientific term must be rendered in a concrete form when it is written. This, undoubtedly, has had a subliminal effect on Chinese scientific thinking.

It is not just the concrete nature of Chinese characters, but the difficulty in classifying them that makes them less conducive to abstract scientific thinking than an alphabetic script. The alphabet, as we show in later chapters, is a natural tool for classifying and served as a paradigm for codified law, scientific classification, and standardized weights and measures. The relationship of science and classification is something that the Chinese recognized despite the difficulty that their characters pose to this activity: *kho hsiieh*, the traditional and current Chinese term for *science*, means "classification knowledge." The European term for *science* has a similar meaning. Derived from the Latin word *scientia* from *scire*, "to know," *science* is defined in *Webster's New World Dictionary* as "systematized knowledge derived from observation, study, etc."

To understand which of the two types of script—the alphabet or Chinese characters—is best suited to classification, one need only compare Western and Chinese dictionaries. The ordering of words in Western dictionaries is always alphabetical. The situation in the Chinese languages is much more complicated because of the logographic and only partial phonetic nature of their written characters. Chinese dictio-

TABLE 5.2

The Etymology of Chinese Characters Representing Scientific Terms

Scientific Term	Chinese Character	Romanization	Old Chinese Symbol	Description of the Character
begin	始	shih		A drawing of a woman and a fetus
stop	止	chih		A foot
sun	日	jih		A pictogram depicting the sun
bright	明	ming		The pictograms of the sun and moon together
light	光	kuang		A human figure holding a torch
snow	雪	hsueh		A pictogram of a snowflake
life, birth	生	sêng		A plant growing out of the ground
water	水	shui		A pictogram depicting water
fire	火	huo		A pictogram depicting a flame
earth	土	thu		A pictogram showing a phallus altar to the earth god
law	則	tsê		A hand carving a written code
count	算	suan		Bamboo counting rods

68

naries can be organized on various principles. "The characters are classified according to their initial and final sounds, in others according to radicals and in still others by subject" (Latourette, 1964, p. 650). Even without a basic phonetic writing system, the Chinese attempted to classify their words phonetically, but their writing system discouraged this effort and, as a result, classification never reached the level of abstraction that it did in the West. This despite that there exist special words in the spoken and written language that classify words so as to avoid the ambiguities of the many homophones found in Chinese (B. Kalgren, 1962, p. 24).

The failure to achieve standardized measures and weights might also be due in part to a writing system in which the characters (or at least the radicals) are composed of unique, nonrepeatable, nonstandardized components. The alphabetic writing system consists of standardized, repeatable elements from which written words are composed. This system therefore provides a model for standardized components and hence the standardized weights and measures that contributed to the development of Western science.

The linking together of standardized repeatable elements to form words also enables the alphabet to serve as a paradigm for deductive logic in which ideas or statements are linked together to form arguments. This is not the case with Chinese writing and might partially explain why the Chinese never developed Western-style logic. Their thinkers favored dialectical forms rather than deductive ones (Needhan, 1956), and their reasoning tends to be inductive rather than deductive. It is not logical, but rather analogical, much as Chinese characters are analogs of the words they represent.

The linear, sequential mode of building a system that the alphabet encouraged and Chinese characters discouraged also influenced industrial development in the East and West. Despite their technological progress, the Chinese never linked their inventions together to create the assembly-line production characteristic of the Western Industrial Revolution.

The Chinese writing system also reinforced the conservative nature of the Chinese spirit. Because the Chinese characters can be read by people speaking different dialects of Chinese, they have a unifying and preserving effect on the culture (Paul, 1890). This encouraged and reinforced the Chinese reverence for their past and their traditions while dampening their enthusiasm for scientific and technological innovation.

The lack of abstraction in the writing system reflects itself throughout Chinese thought and discourages the development of the abstract notions of codified law, monotheism, abstract science, and deductive logic. We see that once a culture begins to develop along concrete lines, this tendency is reinforced in all areas. The lack of abstract writing discouraged the development of monotheism, codified law, and deductive logic, all of which in turn made the development of abstract science more difficult. Having explored the limitation logographic writing placed on the development of abstract Chinese thought, we now examine in the following chapters the way in which phonetic writing or the alphabet created the conditions for codified law, monotheism, abstract science, deductive logic, the printing press, and the Industrial Revolution.

THE ALPHABET VERSUS THE GODDESS

The focus of this study is the way in which the phonetic alphabet has influenced the development of Western civilization in contrast to the way in which Oriental civilization has developed. Earlier I outlined the principal differences of these two great cultures attributing left-brain patterns to the West and right-brain patterns to the Orient. Since the appearance of the first edition of my book, Leonard Shlain's (1998) book *The Alphabet Versus the Goddess: The Conflict Between Word and Image* has appeared. He also studied the impact of alphabetic writing, but with a different focus. "While McLuhan, Logan and others have explored the effects that alphabetic literacy has had upon Western history, I wish to narrow the focus to a single question: how did the invention of the alphabet affect the balance of power between men and women?" (Shlain, 1998, p. 2).

Shlain's hypothesis, like mine, made use of the split-brain hypothesis, but he took a different tack than mine by associating the left brain with alphabetic writing and the masculine way of thinking and the right brain with imagery and the female way of thinking. He wrote, "I hypothesized that when a critical mass of people within a society acquire literacy, especially alphabetic literacy, left hemisphere modes of thought are reinforced at the expense of right hemisphere ones, which manifest as a decline in the status of images, women's rights, and goddess worship" (Shlain, 1998, p. viii). Having established his hypothesis, Shlain then went on to gather historical data to support his contention that, "the demise of the goddess, the plunge in woman's status, and the advent of harsh patriarchy and misogyny occurred around the time people were learning how to read and write" alphabetic texts (p. viii).

Table 5.2, which outlines the differences between Eastern and Western cultural patterns, is quite similar to Shlain's characterization of the differences in the mental processes of men and women. He wrote, "I propose that a holistic, simultaneous, synthetic, and concrete view of the world are the essential characteristics of a feminine outlook; linear, sequential, reductionist, and abstract thinking defines the masculine" (Shlain, 1998, p. 1). My list for Eastern cultural patterns like Shlain's for the feminine includes the qualities concrete, integrative (read holistic), and inventive (read synthetic). My list for Western cultural patterns like Shlain's for the masculine includes the qualities abstract and linear. My two omissions sequential and reductionist are precisely that—omissions because they describe Western thought patterns just as accurately as they describe the masculine outlook.

Another parallel between my work and that of Shlain is that I compare the alphabetic writing system to Oriental writing systems in which the characters are iconic, whereas Shlain compared alphabetic culture to preliterate iconic or imagery based culture. This is why I believe that his ground-breaking work, which I greatly admire, complements mine. It is for this reason that I have provided the reader with a brief summary of the main ideas of the Alphabet Versus the Goddess. This review, however-er, is no substitute for reading Shlain's book in full, which I strongly rec-ommend to the reader, once they have finished this one, of course.

6

The Development of Phonetic Writing and Codified Law in Mesopotamia

EARLY POLITICAL AND CULTURAL HISTORY OF MESOPOTAMIA

Writing systems, as discovered in the last chapter, play an important role in the evolution of a culture and its thought patterns. The Chinese ideogram retraces the meaning of a word graphically, whereas, in the West the sound of a word is analyzed and reconstructed alphabetically. Phonetic writing has changed the character of its user's thought patterns. Through its impact on Babylonian, Hebrew, and Greek society, it helped create the conditions for abstract and rational thinking and prepared the ground for the development of codified law, monotheism, abstract science, and deductive logic. This process began in ancient Iraq or Mesopotamia, where urban agriculture-based civilization first evolved and where writing was used for the first time in the history of humankind.

The first city-states to form in Mesopotamia, such as Lagash, Nippur, Ur, Uruk, and Eridu, were populated by the Sumerians

(Albright, 1957, p. 146). They settled the southern basin of the Tigris–Euphrates river system just before it empties into the Persian Gulf in what historians believe to be the setting of the biblical Garden of Eden (Welland, 1972). Each city-state was ruled by a governor who also functioned as the high priest of the local god. The autocratic forms of government that arose in Sumer were in response to the need to maintain the irrigation systems of canals and dams that supported the agricultural economy.

The wealth that the irrigation-based farming created permitted the first flowering of urban civilization. The writing system was used as a tool to develop and promote commerce, government, diplomacy, religion, morality, justice, and the literary arts. The Sumerians built elaborate cities and temple structures from sun-baked mud bricks. Their towering temple structures or ziggurats (which Herodotus reported to be eight stories high) were the basis for the Hebrew legend concerning the Tower of Babel. According to Genesis, the Lord punished the builders of the Tower of Babel for their arrogance by confounding "their language, that they may not understand one another's speech." The Sumerians, who spoke a non-Semitic tongue, were in fact invaded in the second half of the third millennium B.C. by Semitic-speaking tribesmen whose language indeed confounded them.

One of these groups, who settled in Akkad under the leadership of Sargon, conquered the principal city-states of Sumer and succeeded in uniting the diverse regions of Mesopotamia into a single empire. The Akkadians conquered the Sumerians militarily, imposed their language, but adopted Sumerian culture including their arts, sciences, and religion. Akkadian, the language of the invaders, so dominated Mesopotamian life that Sumerian soon ceased to be spoken and became a dead language by the time of Hammurabi (Albright, 1957).

Although the Akkadians were strongly influenced by the Sumerians and adopted most elements of their culture, they also introduced a number of new ideas of their own reflecting their attitudes toward government, economics, and religion. Their kings became progressively more authoritarian and absolute to the point that Naram-Sin, the grandson of Sargon, had himself declared a god during his own lifetime. Instead of a network of independent city-states, an imperial empire evolved in which vassal states were ruled by the emperor-king.

The Akkadians also introduced major changes in the economic system. The theocratic communalism of Sumer gave way to a quasicapitalistic economy in trade and commerce, which augmented agricultural activities. These activities gave rise to a new social class of the bourgeoisie consisting of farmers, shopkeepers, and minor officials that came to be known as *muskenum*.

In addition to these social, economic, and political changes, the Akkadians also brought to Mesopotamia a more profound conception of God. In place of allegiance to local gods who ruled the city-state in which they were resident, the universal worship of Marduk arose throughout the empire over which the Akkadians exercised political control. The Sumerian pantheon survived, but played a minor role compared with the imperial role played by Marduk (Albright, 1957).

THE DEVELOPMENT OF WRITING AND CIVILIZATION

Sumer is the birthplace of both writing and civilization, two aspects of human culture that historically have always been interrelated. Writing promotes a relationship among standardization, abstraction, and symbolism—one of the fundamental characteristics of a civilized culture (Albright, 1957).

The writing system that developed in Sumer quickly spread to other cultures in the Near East, including the Hittites (the Anatolians), the Elamites (the Persians), and the Cretans. We have noted that, aside from Mesopotamia, writing developed independently in only four other cultures—namely, Egypt, the Indus Valley, China, and Mesoamerica. As in Sumer, each of these societies was urbanized and had evolved an economy based on agriculture. A third common factor in each of these cultures was an extensive use of canals and irrigation systems.

Despite the small size of the sample, one is tempted to speculate that there exists a possible relationship between writing and irrigation systems. Perhaps the linear form of organization that canals and irrigation systems require creates an environment conducive to the development of writing, another system with a linear organization. Alternatively, possibly the organizational requirements needed for a system of irrigation channels and dams give rise to a direct need for writing.

> In order to dig canals and build dams, and especially in order to maintain the vital irrigating system after it had been finished, a coordinated state organization was imperatively necessary. Without supervision and compulsory labour the canals silted up, the dams broke, and the increasingly necessary dikes burst. (Albright, 1957, p. 146)

One of the tools that arose and permitted the coordinated state organization was writing:

> The Sumerian writing owes its origin to the needs arising from pub-
> lic economy and administration. With the rise in productivity of the
> country, resulting from state-controlled canalization and irrigation
> systems, the accumulated agricultural surplus made its way to the
> depots and granaries of the cities, necessitating keeping accounts of
> goods coming to the cities, as well as of manufactured products
> leaving the cities for the country. (Gelb, 1963, p. 62)

Mankind's first writing system appeared in Sumer around 3000 B.C.
(Driver, 1976; Kramer, 1959) and consisted basically of pictographic
signs etched in clay (Schmandt-Besserat, 1981a, 1982b). The first written
signs found at Level IV of Uruk are highly irregular, indicating the pecu-
liarities of individual scribes. The lack of standardization persists to the
Shuruppak period, 2600–2500 B.C. (Driver, 1976). The etching on the
clay surface, however, was shortly replaced by the cuneiform system of
impressing the clay tablets with the wedge-shaped stylus. The purely
pictographic nature of the original signs became more stylized and
abstract. This permitted the standardization of signs. Once signs were
drawn approximately the same by everybody, universal literacy was
possible (Driver, 1976). The other development that promoted increased
abstraction of writing was phonetization and the emergence of syllabic
signs.

Syllabic signs were used phonetically to render words. The
Sumerians were the first to initiate this technique, but they exploited it
only superficially. The real development in this direction occurred, paradoxically, when the Akkadians attempted to render their Semitic language using the Sumerian writing system that was originally designed
for a non-Semitic language (Driver, 1976).

It should be remembered that the Akkadians used the same
cuneiform signs to render both the Sumerian language and their own
Semitic tongue. They retained the sacred texts of the Sumerians for religious purposes in much the same way that the Italians retained Latin
texts and used the Roman alphabet to transcribe both Italian and Latin.
The application of a single script to a dual purpose—namely, to ideographic and syllabic writing, and to two totally different languages—
resulted in almost every sign ultimately becoming a polyphone (i.e., had
many different pronunciations and meanings), to the great confusion of
the reader.

One sign depicting the rising sun came to represent over 70 words
and 12 different syllables (Driver, 1976). The ambiguity introduced by
this multiple use of signs caused confusion and reader error. Context
helped resolve some of the ambiguity, but finally two devices were
invented to reduce the confusion. One was the determinative sign and
the other was the phonetic complement.

The determinative sign was an ideographic sign added to another ideogram to indicate to what general class of objects or concepts that ideogram belonged. Determinative signs denoted deities, animals, plants, fishes, rivers, cities, material, or gender, among other things. The determinative sign was not pronounced; it acted purely as a classifier.

The phonetic complement, in contrast, was a syllabic sign that determined which of the many phonetic values of the ideographic sign under consideration was intended by indicating what consonant the word began with. The phonetic complement, like the determinative sign, was not read, but was a silent visual sign to resolve ambiguity.

The determinative sign and phonetic complement were two devices developed strictly for resolving the ambiguities of reading. As we see later, they played an additional role in the development of Babylonian thinking by providing a model for classification. These two devices provided temporary relief and served as transitory strategies for resolving ambiguities during the period when the same signs were being used not only for two languages, but also for a mixed system of ideographic and syllabic signs. The ultimate strategy for resolving ambiguities was to use signs in a purely phonetic way to denote syllables and drop ideographic signs altogether with a few minor exceptions. Another way to resolve the ambiguity was to use the signs for one language only.

Both of these developments occurred. After the conquest of Sumer by the Akkadians, Sumerian was still used for certain ritual and religious practices, but Akkadian became the *lingua franca*. This pattern of language use was interrupted for a period of approximately 100 years when Sumerian became the official language once again and Sumerian culture experienced a renaissance and a final flowering. During this period, Sumerian texts were translated into Akkadian, and bilingual dictionaries were compiled. When the Akkadians regained political control of Mesopotamia, the process of translating suddenly came to a halt and Sumerian became a dead language (Oppenheim, 1964). The language was used only by religious officials as is the case with Latin today. Sumerian texts were maintained in libraries, but no active scholarship or new literature developed in the Sumerian tongue once the Ur III dynasty was overthrown in 2004 B.C.

By the time of Hammurabi in the 18th century B.C., the Akkadian tongue enjoyed total domination in the affairs of his empire. As the Akkadians came to dominate the political and cultural life of Mesopotamia, they also shifted their style of writing into an increasingly phonetic mode of operation in which fewer and fewer word signs were used. Word signs never disappeared, but they became less important.

With the transition to a greater use of phonetic writing, the Babylonian writing system became simpler, but the transition to a purely phonetic system or an alphabetic system never occurred in Mesopotamia. "At no time did any of the Mesopotamian syllabaries contain signs for all the possible syllables existing in the languages for which they were used. The principle of economy aiming at the expression of linguistic forms by the smallest number of possible signs, resulted in various economizing measures" (Gelb, 1963, p. 69). There was no such thing as a standard Mesopotamian syllabary, but rather at different times and in different areas a particular syllabary was in use. The Mesopotamian syllabary systems consisted of signs that usually represented monosyllables ending in a vowel or consonant. The writing system used for the Hammurabi Law Code can be resolved into 83 vowels and uniconsonantal syllabic signs of the form a, i, e, o, ba, bi, be, bu, ab, ib, ub, da, di, du, ad, id, and ud (Gelb, 1963, pp. 108–115).

The economic and simplified writing system used in the time of Hammurabi represents a major reform of the writing system, which in earlier times had been much more complicated. "It is estimated that the earliest Sumerian writing (Uruk IV-II) consisted of close to 2000 different signs, while in the later Fara period the number is only 800" (Gelb, 1963, pp. 221–222). The reform of the writing system and the reduction in the number of signs had an important impact on cultural development during Hammurabi's time, as we shall see once we examine the uses to which writing was put.

WRITING AND CIVILIZATION IN MESOPOTAMIA

The use of writing completely transformed the nature of Mesopotamian culture and created the conditions for civilization and the other trappings of urban life. Writing created a pattern of cultural development that was to repeat itself throughout history.

> There is no need to urge that the introduction of writing was the factor which was responsible for the birth of original civilizations. It seems rather that all the factors—geographic, social, economic—leading towards a full civilization simultaneously created a complex of conditions which could not function properly without writing. Or, to put it in other words, writing exists only in a civilization and a civilization cannot exist without writing. (Gelb, 1963, pp. 221–222)

The first uses of writing in Sumer were modest and confined to economics and administration among a population of "priests, scribes, architects, artists, overseers, merchants, factory workers, soldiers and peasants and their religious rulers or war leaders" (Roux, 1980, p. 76).

Once the art of writing had been mastered for economic and administrative purposes, it was then used for literary, religious, and historical purposes. Stories, fables, and literary creations about gods, heroes, kings, and even animals were composed and recorded. A wisdom literature developed as proverbs and inspiring sayings was collected and cataloged.

In addition to these religious, philosophical, and cultural texts, there also appeared practical collections of information. Among these were a collection of tablets that Kramer termed the *world's first farmer's almanac* because they guided a farmer through his annual agricultural activities. The almanac begins with the line: "In days of yore a farmer gave [these] instructions to his son" (Kramer, 1959, pp. 65–66).

Another collection of practical information is the world's oldest medical handbook, a clay tablet recovered from Nippur, which had been prepared by an anonymous Babylonian physician who collected more than a dozen of his favorite remedies. The tablet revealed that Mesopotamian pharmacology had made considerable progress and was acquainted with "quite a number of rather elaborate chemical operations and procedures" (Kramer, 1959, pp. 60-62).

Other collections of practical information were prepared for scribes and those studying to become scribes. Schools for scribes, called *tablethouses* were attached to the most important temple schools. Young people were taught how to read and write (Driver, 1976). Students were taught the forms, conventions, and principles of writing to ensure that the system could be universally understood (Gelb, 1963). These requirements of standardization eventually contributed to the development of scientific and legal thinking in Mesopotamia.

Grammar lists were prepared to make the student aware of different grammatical classifications and constructions. Word lists were compiled to teach the scribes the different pictographs and syllabic signs. Later when Akkadian scribes were trained to translate Sumerian words into Akkadian and back again, dictionaries were prepared as well as other scribal tools. Lexical tables have been found in which ideograms are listed with their names, pronunciation, and Sumerian and Akkadian word values or meanings.

> There are lists of gods with their names in both languages, their titles or functions or temples, lists of countries and towns with their names in both languages, and so on. Other series contain lists of purely Akkadian synonyms in two columns or glossaries of Hittite, Cassite, and even Hurrian or "Horite," words and phrases. (Driver, 1976, pp. 68–69)

It would appear that many of these school tablets were copied down by students through their teachers' dictations. The frequent variations of the spelling tends to confirm this supposition.

Although education was not universal in Mesopotamia, "a fair number of laymen could read if not write the cuneiform script" (Driver, 1976, p. 62). Because of the difficulties in learning how to read and the necessity for special training, however, literacy served as a barrier to deny most members of the society participation in certain decision-making activities. "The priests (who were also scientists, engineers and physicians) sustained their privileged position by carefully retaining a monopoly of knowledge, which being literate they alone could read, record and transmit" (Cottrell, 1965, p. 167).

For those who could read and write, literacy provided a strong stimulus to learning and scholarship, particularly in science and law—two fields in which abstraction and classification are so important. Writing, particularly with syllabic signs, provides a natural model or paradigm for both abstraction and classification. The mechanism whereby visual signs are coded as phonetic elements, which are then combined together to form a word, is an exercise in abstraction and logic that the human mind had not experienced until the development of phonetic writing. Classification schemes arose naturally out of the structures of a phonetic writing system. This was reinforced by the word lists and catalogs of tablet titles that were created to help organize the scribes' activities. The organization of libraries containing collections of tablets contributed to the development of classification and organizational methods and techniques. Each large city had a school for scribes to train the local youth, and each school had a library attached to it.

The influence of writing is reflected in the nature of Babylonian scholarship. Mesopotamian teachers "were keen observers of nature and the immediate world about them. The long lists of plants, animals, metals and stones which the professors compiled for pedagogic purposes imply a careful study of at least the more obvious characteristics of natural substances and living organisms" (Kramer, 1959, p. 136). The Babylonians' concern for classification extended also to their analysis of their own society, which they divided "into more than one hundred institutions, occupations, crafts, attitudes, and modes of action" (Kramer, 1959, p. 136).

In addition to serving as a paradigm for classification, the Babylonian syllabary also provided a model for standardization, universality, and abstraction. These notions were reflected not only in the development of codified law and observational science, but also in the arts and religion. Commenting on cylinder seals, W. F. Albright (1957) noted: "The design on these seals show that in the fourth quarter of the fourth millennium B.C. art had already passed far beyond any stage previously attained. Native skills, empirically developed by generations of artists and craftsmen, had reached the point where it became standardized and where canons of proportion were established" (p. 141).

Abstract thought could also be found in Babylonian religious and philosophical ideas. Many of the ideas that were to characterize Greek thought, such as the notion of fate or destiny, are found in Babylonian literature. Another indicator of the abstractness of Babylonian religious thought is that the gods, unlike their Egyptian counterparts, were not represented as animals (Albright, 1957, p. 176). Not only were the religious ideas in Babylon abstract, but they also began to evolve a universal message. This is partly due to the existence of an imperial empire, but is also a consequence of the paradigm of universality suggested by a national writing system. The spirit of universality is reflected in the following poem in praise of En-lil: "Unto En-lil do foreign lands raise their eyes (in adoration), Unto En-lil do foreign lands pay homage. The Four Quarters (of the earth) bloom like a garden for En-lil".

INTRODUCTION TO SCIENCE

Before the age of literacy, the thought patterns and social forms of society were coherent, cohesive, and integrated. With writing, a fragmentation of social and psychic patterns began, which reached its zenith in the mechanical forms of the assembly line characteristic of the Industrial Age. This was particularly true of education, where knowledge was divided into specialized disciplines or subjects, which were studied separately and taught by individuals who rarely communicated professionally with other scholars outside their own narrowly defined disciplines.

Writing encouraged this fragmentation right from the start of its use in Sumer. It inspired the organization of information into sundry categories and enumerations. "It has been suggested that writing was invented in Sumer to keep tallies and to make lists, and hence, was an outgrowth of mathematics" (Innis, 1972, p. 26). This observation is further supported by the etymology of the Semitic root for writing, *spr*, which also means to count and tell. One of the consequences of the closely linked arts of writing and enumeration was the creation of bureaucracies, which assisted and gave rise to theocratic governments. "The beginning of the principle 'divide and rule' was evident in recognition of the religions of Babylon and Egypt and encouragement of the religion of the Hebrews at Jerusalem" (Innis, 1957, p. 135). Priestly bureaucracies gave way to military bureaucracies, and the principle of divide and rule was expanded to the principle of divide and conquer. This led to centralized world states fragmented into individual provinces.

The written word not only created a new geopolitical environment, but, it also transformed learning. A division was created between the knower or author and that individual's written knowledge. The divorce between the author and his or her writing permitted the objectivity necessary for scientific thought. "The literate man or society develops the tremendous power of acting in any matter with considerable detachment from the feelings or emotional involvement that a non-literate man or society could experience" (McLuhan, 1964, p. 79). At the heart of the scientific method that writing encourages is the specialization and fragmentation of subjects that can eventually flip into tunnel vision.

The elements of universality, abstraction, and classification that became part and parcel of Babylonian thinking under the influence of phonetic writing subliminally promoted a spirit of scientific investigation, which manifested itself in the scribal schools. The major aim of the scribal school quite naturally was professional training to satisfy the economic and administrative needs of temple and palace bureaucracies.

> However, in the course of its growth and development, and particularly as a result of the ever widening curriculum, the school came to be the center of culture and learning in the Sumer. Within its walls flourished the scholar-scientist, the man who studied whatever theological, botanical, zoological, mineralogical, geographical, mathematical, grammatical, and linguistic knowledge was current in his day, and who in some cases added to the knowledge. (Kramer, 1959, p. 2)

The Age of Hammurabi marks the culmination of the regularization and reform of both the writing and legal systems in the form of the Hammurabic code. These developments were not coincidental. Both reforms promoted the paradigms of abstraction, classification, and universality and thus encouraged the development of scientific activities.

The two centuries following the Hammurabic era represent the first great scientific age of humankind, in which a new spirit of empiricism and scholarly interest in astronomy, magic, philology, lexicography, and mathematics emerged. In mathematics, a primitive place number system was invented as well as algorithms for arithmetic calculations. Mathematical tables were also created to simplify calculations. Achievements in algebra included the solution of quadratic equations by the method of false position. In astronomy lists of stars and constellations were compiled and the movements of the planets were charted.

The scholars of the Hammurabic era

> showed such taste and talent for collecting and systematizing all rec-
> ognized knowledge that Mesopotamian learning nearly stagnated
> for a thousand years thereafter. . . . We find a pervasive idea of order
> and system in the universe, resulting in large part from the tremen-
> dous effort devoted to the systematization of knowledge. (Albright,
> 1957, pp. 197–199)

The Mesopotamians' spirit of order and system is reflected in their cosmology or concept of the universe (Kramer, 1959, pp. 77–79). The Babylonian universe, *an-ki*, is divided into two major components: the heaven (an) and the earth (ki), which emerged from and remain fixed and immovable in a boundless sea, Nammu. Nammu acts as the first cause or prime mover of the universe. Between heaven and earth there moves Lil, a divine wind (also air, breath, or spirit) from which the luminous bodies (sun, moon, planets, and stars) arose. The order of creation is as follows: (a) the universe, an-ki (heaven-earth), emerges from the boundless sea Nammu; (b) it separates into heaven and earth; (c) Lil then arises between heaven and earth; (d) from which the heavenly bodies emerge; (e) followed finally by the creation of plants, animals, and human beings. The order of creation found in this cosmogony closely parallels the story of creation found in the BIble in the book of Genesis.

Mesopotamian cosmology and cosmogony, although polytheistic in nature, nevertheless evolved some rather abstract notions of the deities that created and controlled the universe. All the elements of the cosmos had been created by the four gods in control of heaven, earth, sea, and air. "Each of these anthropomorphic but superhuman beings was deemed to be in charge of a particular component of the universe and to guide its activities in accordance with established rules and regulations" (Kramer, 1959, pp. 77–79).

Although Mesopotamian cosmology contains mythic elements, the core of its world picture is based on empirical observations of the natural environment including the heavens. Systematic astronomical observations were not part of the Sumerian tradition, but were begun by the Akkadians, worshipers of the sun god Shamash. Their observations were somewhat crude (Neugebauer, 1952), and it was only with the flowering of the Assyrian empire in approximately 700 B.C. that accurate quantitative measurements were made. The earliest records of astronomical observations in Mesopotamia are those made during the reign of Ammi-saduqa of the appearances and disappearances of Venus. Tablets recording these observations have been used to date the chronology of the Hammurabic period (Neugebaner, 1952). Part of the motivation for these observations was what we could term *scientific* and *part astrological*, although the Babylonians made no distinction between science and astrology. Observations made for the purpose of divination served science as well, and paradoxically, vice versa.

Sumerian and Babylonian mathematical tables provide further evidence for the development of scientific thinking in Mesopotamia. These tables were combined with tables of weights and measures indicating that they were used in daily economic life (Neugebauer, 1969). The clear influence of writing and a notational system on the development and organization of mathematical skills is easily discernible from these tables. Economics proved to be a motivating factor for both writing and mathematics, which mutually reinforced one another's development.

The results were tables of multiplication, reciprocals, squares, square roots, cubes, cube roots, and sums of squares and cubes needed for solutions to algebraic equations and exponential functions. The sexagesimal number system 60 was developed in response to the Babylonians' concern for astronomy. The parallel between the approximately 360-day year and the 360-degree circle are obvious.

Tables of quadratic and cubic functions were prepared for civil-engineering projects of dam building, canal dredging, and the construction of attack ramps to breach the ramparts of besieged walled cities. Certain Babylonian mathematical tablets indicate that astronomy, banking, engineering, and mathematics were practiced in a systematic and scientific manner. Two types of tablets were prepared. In one set, only problems are given, but each tablet contains problems related to the other and carefully arranged beginning with the simplest cases. The second set of tablets contains both problems and their solutions worked out step by step (Neugebauer, 1969). The achievement of Babylonian mathematics, which has been likened to that of the Renaissance, is all the more remarkable when one considers the short period in which it developed and flowered: all within 200 hundred years or so of the major reforms in the writing system.

The existence of these tablets illustrates two important impacts of writing on science. The first is the impulse to organize information in an orderly and systematic manner. The ordering of individual words that the use of syllabic signs creates in the thought patterns of their users inspires a similar ordering of the contents of their writings. That this was critical for the development of science is beautifully illustrated by the Babylonian mathematical texts created as aids to various scientific and engineering activities.

The second impact of writing is the ability to preserve the accomplishments of one age so that they can form the basis of a later development. Little if no progress was made in Babylonian mathematics from the time of the Hammurabic explosion of knowledge to the Assyrian empire of 700 B.C. Yet the tablets preserved the knowledge that an earlier age had created, and they served as the foundation for the Assyrian development.

The mathematical and scientific achievements of the Mesopotamian civilization just reviewed are certainly worthy of our respect and admiration. We must be careful, however, not to jump to the conclusion that this culture had solidly embarked on the road of scientific thinking because of the progress in astronomy, mathematics, and engineering that has been described. The reader must bear in mind that the same practitioners of this rudimentary form of science were also engaged in astrology, the reading of animal entrails, the interpretation of omens, and other forms of superstition. The early forms of science as practiced in Babylon are not a scaled down or less advanced version of science as we know it today, but rather a mixture of logic, superstition, myth, tradition, confusion, error, and common sense. No distinction was made between religious and scientific thinking. "Medicine grew out of magic, and in many cases was indistinguishable from it" (Cottrell, 1965, pp. 169–171). What is important about Babylonian science from a historical point of view was its influence on future generations, Hebrews, Greeks, Arabs, and eventually on Renaissance Europe.

The Babylonians made use of a logical mode of thought complete with abstract notions and elements of classification (Albright, 1957, p. 198). Their approach was wholly empirical, however, unlike the theoretical and more analytic style of Greek science, which, according to Kramer (1959), required "the influence of the first fully phonetic alphabet" (pp. 35–36). For example, the Sumerians compiled grammatical lists and were aware of grammatical classifications, yet they never formulated any explicit rules of grammar. In the field of science, lists were also compiled but no principles or laws were ever enunciated. In the field of law, a legal code was developed but never a theory of jurisprudence (Kramer, 1959).

CODIFIED LAW

One of the major contributions of Mesopotamian culture was the codification of law, which led to our abstract notions of justice in the West and influenced the formulation of both Hebrew scriptural morality and Roman law. Sumerian literature is filled with examples of gods and earthly rulers who are defenders of the downtrodden and upholders of justice.

One example of this spirit is found in a Sumerian hymn found at Nippur. It sings the praises of the goddess Nanshe, who is described as she "who cares for the widow, who seeks out justice for the poorest. The queen brings the refugee to her lap, finds shelter for the weak" (Kramer, 1959, p. 106).

Another example is Uru-ka-gina, the King of Lagash, "who reestablished the righteous laws of Nin-girsu" (Kramer, 1959, pp. 35–36) and "freed the citizens of Lagash from usury, monopoly, hunger, theft and assault; he established their freedom" (Roux, 1980, p. 133). A votive inscription lists the many injustices that existed in the previous regime, explains how Uru-ka-gina was able to bring an end to these practices, and then describes in great detail how these injustices are to be corrected by listing the exact fees to be paid for services rendered to the public (Kramer, 1963, pp. 317-318). These inscriptions from Uru-ka-gina's regime, with their explicit statements of acceptable tariffs, served as a forerunner of the later legal codes, which also set acceptable rates for the services of a wagon driver or boatman or the price for products such as barley and sesame oil.

The Sumero–Akkadian concern for justice was reflected in the legal codes. The most famous legal code and the first to be discovered in modern times (at Susa in 1901) was that of Hammurabi, who ruled Babylon from 1792 to 1750 B.C. This code is still the most complete that has been recovered from ancient Mesopotamia, but it is not the oldest.

The oldest known legal code, dating back to 2100 B.C., is that of Ur-Nammu, described as "the king who observed the just laws of the sun-god." It consists of a prologue and a collection of at least 29 laws (Finkelstein, 1969). Five of the 29 laws concern payment of fines as compensation for injuries caused in scuffles. "If a man to a man with a ges-phu-instrument (copper knife) the nose has cut off, 2/3 of a silver mina he shall pay" (Finkelstein, 1969, p. 87). This type of law represents a reform, by our standards, of the more primitive eye-for-an-eye principle, which ironically reappears in later Babylonian codes and in the Old Testament. The principle of making restitution through fines as compensation for wrong doing such as perjury, property damage, deflowering, and divorce is found in 12 other laws in addition to the 5 dealing with injuries due to fighting. In addition to the laws (Finkelstein, 1969) for compensation, there are also laws concerning marriage and divorce (Laws 4–12) and slavery (Laws 14, 21–23). The laws tend to be grouped according to categories, showing the first signs of codification.

The Bilalama code dates back to the city of Eshnunna in the later part of the 20th century B.C. No prologue or epilogue was found, and only 59 of the 61 laws recovered were decipherable. The laws are codified in a somewhat systematic manner like the earlier Ur-Nammu code. They deal with prices, tariffs, sales, deposits, valuation of damages sustained, family affairs, marriage, divorce, slavery, and theft (Gadd, 1965). This code also contains the principle of compensation for injuries.

A contemporary of Bilalama, Attakhushu, King of Elam (Persia), also established a legal code in the market of his capital. The *stele*, referred to as a "stake of righteousness," was surmounted by an image of the sun god and listed the fair prices for products to be bought and sold in the market (Kramer, 1955).

The last of the pre-Hammurabic legal codes extant is that of Lipit-Ishtar, who ruled the city-state of Isin from 1934 to 1924 B.C. This code (Finkelstein, 1969), written in Sumerian, consists of a prologue, an epilogue, and 38 laws of which the first 3 and the last are difficult to determine. The remainder are codified in the following manner: "hiring of boats (laws 4 and 5); real estate, particularly orchards (7-11); slaves and perhaps servants (12-33); rented oxen (34-37)" (Kramer, 1955, pp. 159–161).

The classical legal code of Hammurabi, which we shortly examine, marks the beginning of the widespread use of legal codes throughout all of Mesopotamia. Hammurabic legal codes remained in force as the basis of government throughout the history of Mesopotamia down to the last Chaldean dynasty (sixth century B.C.). Copies of the original Code of Hammurabi were made throughout this period of 1,200 years, and some of the laws even survived the demise of Mesopotamian civilization and found their way into Islamic law (Welland, 1972). Hammurabi, descended from the Amorite invaders, inherited his father's tiny kingdom centered at Babylon in 1792 B.C. Through a series of piecemeal conquests and alliances over 38 years, Hammurabi conquered all of Mesopotamia from Persia to Syria and assumed the title of Mighty King of the Four Quarters of the World (Roux, 1960, p. 189).

While he was increasing the amount of territory under his control, Hammurabi was securing his conquered lands through a series of political, administrative, social, and religious measures and reforms. Among these reforms was that of the writing system, in which he set a pattern for uniformity, regularization, and standardization. He created a central regime that was able to exercise control, yet he also gave a measure of self-rule through local assemblies of elders. While preserving local customs and traditions, he was nevertheless able to create a uniformity throughout his empire. A spirit of freedom and order coexisted in which the arts, science, religion, literature, and commerce flourished. It was a time of high civilization—the highest the world had known to that date.

At the foundation of this ordered kingdom or empire was a code of law that was most likely a collection of precedents from actual rulings by the king as well as laws from previous codes. These laws were based on the set of principles that constituted the Akkadian and particularly Hammurabi's sense of justice or mesarum. The code, which was carved on stelae and placed in temples, consisted, like the earlier codes, of: (a) a prologue in which the deeds of the king are described; (b) the body of the law, which contained at least 282 individual laws; and (c) an epilogue that threatened divine punishment to any who defaced the code. It is interesting to note that the language of the prologue is more archaic and literary than is that of the body of the laws (Albright, 1957, p. 43).

As to the purpose of the code, other than its ostensible goal of bringing justice to Sumer and Akkad, we can only speculate. The Hammurabic law represents a major expansion of the earlier codes we have examined and probably addresses additional concerns. This is not to underplay the ethical side of the Hammurabic code, however, which goes far beyond any of its predecessors in this regard. Yet the reforms introduced by Hammurabi have wider scope and deeper implications. There is another agenda at work in this code, hinted at in the prologue written in Akkadian where Hammurabi stated, "I established law and justice 'in the language of the land'" (Meek). It was in Hammurabi's reign that the Akkadianization of Mesopotamia, which began with Sargon and was interrupted by the Sumerian renaissance, was finally completed.

Hammurabi also had the task of coordinating and uniting a vast multicultural, multiracial, and multilingual society consisting of previously semi-independent walled cities that had constantly warred against each other. To rule such an empire, coordinate its economic and agricultural activities, and command the loyalty of its diverse geopolitical entities, he had to appease each element of the society and satisfy them that they were being treated fairly and equally with all the rest. As a wise leader, Hammurabi utilized both justice and the appearance of justice to pacify his subjects and ensure their cooperation. The codification and public proclamation of laws contributed to both of these processes and continued the Sumero–Akkadian tradition of justice. Writing out the rules of the game and posting them in each city-state ensured uniformity of measures, commodity prices, professional fees, and transport tariffs throughout the empire. "On the economic side, as on the administrative, the motive of law-giving at this period seems not to be reform but the need of forging a single government out of different elements" (Kramer, 1955, pp. 18–19). Hammurabi set a pattern—one that was to be repeated by future administrators of large empires. Therefore, codified law represents a bifurcation from a set of local laws to govern a city state to one that could govern and administer an empire consisting of diverse cultures.

The Hammurabic code, which introduced many new ideas, still retains a number of the basic categories and actual laws of earlier codes. However, it contains many more laws—namely, 282—and shows a much greater degree of systematic codification no doubt due to the

TABLE 6.1

The Hammurabic Code

Category	Law Number
Perjury	1–5
Theft	6–25
Feudal obligations, land and the military	26–41
Feudal obligations, land and civilians	42–71
Housing	72–87
Lending and borrowing	88–126
Marriage	127–172
Children	173–195
Injuries—compensation and punishment	196–214
Liabilities:	
Physicians	215–223
Veterinarians	224–225
Branders	226–227
Builders	228–233
Boatmen	234–240
Oxen	241–256
Tariffs and liabilities for farmhands	257–267
Tariffs:	
Animals and wagons	268–272
Laborers	273–274
Boats	275–277
Slaves	278–282

improved and simpler writing that came into use during this period. Table 6.1 shows how the 282 laws of the Hammurabic code are organized.

Within these coarse categories, one can detect finer subcategories. There also seems to be a system to the way in which new topics are introduced. Law 195, which serves as the transition from the section on children to that concerning injuries, overlaps these two categories: "If a son has struck his father, they shall cut off his hands."

Additional evidence for the systemization of justice is found in the accounts of the judiciary, law courts, and trials discussed in the code and private letters. A separation of secular and religious courts took place during the time of Hammurabi, so that there emerged in addition to the temple officials, new judges who bore the name of king's judges (Kramer, 1955). This separation of church and state foreshadows a similar separation to take place years later in other highly literate empires (e.g., in Rome and the U.S. Constitution in the 18th century). Additional parallels can be drawn between the Hammurabic code and later Western law because of the new emphasis on the rights and freedoms of the individual, particularly that of holding private property (Bohl, 1946). The emergence of the individual in a literate society, which occurs for the first time in Babylon, recurs over and over again in each of the Western cultures where a phonetic form of literacy arises.

Although it is not possible to attribute a causal relationship between the advances in phonetic writing and the emergence of Mesopotamian science, mathematics, and codified law, their codevelopment is not coincidental. To continue our study of the alphabet effect, we must examine the next revolution in the introduction of phonetic writing in the West— namely, the advent of the Semitic phonetic alphabet. Our story now passes to the Israelites whose ancestors wandered from the Mesopotamian city of Ur sometime during or just after the reign of Hammurabi to settle in the land of milk and honey.

7

Alphabet, Monotheism and the Hebrews, the People of the Book

THE HEBREW SCRIPT

The appearance of the phonetic alphabet among the Semitic peoples in Canaan and Sinai in the middle of the second millennium B.C. marked the beginning of a new period of creativity that would take Western civilization beyond the Sumer–Babylonian cultural achievements of syllabic writing and codified law. The Proto–Canaanite (or Proto–Sinaitic) alphabet based on 22 uniconsonantal signs was adopted by a number of Semitic nations, including the Canaanites, Phoenicians, Midianites, Aramaeans, Nabateans, and Israelites or Hebrews. Of all the peoples whose writing systems directly descended from the Proto–Canaanite alphabet, the Hebrews were most influenced by the alphabet effect. They became the People of the Book, who expressed their culture almost exclusively through the written word and, hence, the alphabet.

An interesting feature of the Hebrew script is that as it evolved further and further away from Phoenician, it became more and more cursive. Almost all scripts evolve in two major forms—lapidary and cursive—corresponding to writing on stone and on papyrus (or parchment), respectively. The two forms influenced each other so that the divergence between them did not grow too great. Hebrew is unique in

91

that it did not develop a lapidary form, but grew progressively more cursive once it separated from Phoenician. The epigraphic evidence indicates that as early as the ninth century B.C., the Hebrews were not given to carving on stone or creating monumental stelae or offerings to gods.

Writing among the Hebrews was used for both commercial and literary purposes. All Israelites were encouraged to read to fulfill their religious duties, so that by the sixth or seventh century B.C. Hebrew society enjoyed a basic level of literacy. This is evidenced by the fact that seals denoting ownership were by this time purely literate, having shed all pictorial elements.

Because of the conservative nature of the use of the Hebrew script, its evolution was slow compared with that of Phoenician and Aramaic, and its evolution was abruptly interrupted by the destruction of the first Temple and the exile of the Hebrews in Babylon where Aramaic had become the dominant writing form. When the Hebrews returned from exile, they used Aramaic speech and writing for everyday affairs and Hebrew speech and writing for religious purposes. Slowly, however, they began to switch over to writing Hebrew in an Aramaic script, which by the time of the Diaspora had evolved into the square Hebrew now in use. The ancient Hebrew script came to a dead end in its evolution. It did not die, however, because it was preserved by the Samaritans, who live in the Palestinian town of Nablus (ancient Shechem) and use it to this day for their religious writings.

The Hebrews were the first people to create a nonmythological history of themselves. All other histories—those of Babylonians, Egyptians, Greeks—trace the origins of their people to the beginning of the universe. The story of the Hebrews as recorded in the Bible is more realistic. It begins with the departure of Abraham from his father, Terah, in the city of Ur of the Chaldees (Mesopotamia). Aside from its religious and metaphysical significance, the Bible is a fascinating, unique historical record that documents the transition of a people from an oral, traditional, and tribal society to a literate, highly organized nation engaged in international affairs.

THE CONTRIBUTION OF MOSES

The outstanding achievement of the Bible, however, is not its historicity, but its abstract theology. The Bible represents the first expression and articulation of the concept of the belief in one god. Monotheism, the cornerstone of all Western religion (Judaism, Christianity, and Islam), is a unique invention of the Israelites, and its formulation by Moses, we show, was influenced by his use of the phonetic alphabet. In fact, it is our hypothesis that the phonetic alphabet, monotheism, and codified law were introduced for the first time to the Israelites by Moses at Mount Sinai in the form of the Ten Commandments and that these three developments were self-supporting. Our hypothesis is supported by Ong's (1982) observation that, "writing makes possible the great introspective religious traditions such as Buddhism, Judaism, Christianity, and Islam. All of these have sacred texts" (p. 105).

Not only was the concept of monotheism a new idea for the Israelites, but so were the use of writing and codified law. Individual Israelites such as Moses were acquainted with Egyptian writing, but the general population—a nomadic people serving as slaves in Egypt—was nonliterate. Therefore, we have assumed that the introduction of monotheism, alphabetic writing, and codified law at Mount Sinai represented three separate innovations for the Hebrew nation.

The primary source of historical evidence on which we have constructed our hypothesis is the Bible, backed by archaeological and epigraphic material that support the historical basis of the Scriptures. The historical validity of the Bible has been confirmed by many scholars, including the material from the Patriarchal Age, that has been preserved by the oral tradition (Albright, 1957; Bright, 1959). "The historical background of the Torah is authentic. Although its history is legendary, it is grounded on a tradition that has a sound basis. The Torah correctly represents Israel as a young nation" (Kaufman, 1960, p. 200).

Only the earlier material—Genesis Chapters 1–11—containing the stories of the Creation and the Flood are not historical material, but are pure myth and folklore, parallels of which are found in Sumerian and Babylonian mythology (Kaufman, 1960, p. 208). The stories of the Patriarchs, Abraham, Isaac, and Jacob, however, have a basis in reality and have been shown to be consistent with other nonscriptural historical evidence (Bright, 1959). The Hebrew people during the Patriarchal Age were a band of seminomadic tribesmen driving their herds from one favorable pasturage to another. Their passage from northern Mesopotamia to Canaan appears to have been motivated more by religious factors than the need for new pasturage, as Genesis 12:1–2 suggests: "Now the Lord said unto Abram, Get thee out of thy country, and from thy kindred, and from thy father's house, unto the land that I will show thee: And I will make of thee a great nation."

THE ADVENT OF MONOTHEISM

The theism of the Patriarchs was not the same as the monotheism of Moses. The God of the Fathers—that is, the God of Abraham, the God of

Isaac, and the God of Jacob—although a more sophisticated concept than those of their contemporaries, does not rival the abstractness of the Yahweh of Moses.

One of the unique features of the Patriarchal God that distinguishes him from his more mundane rivals is that this God is not tied down to a fixed spot or geographical feature like the other gods, but is already of a more universal nature. "Abraham's god . . . is a wanderer like himself. He has no fixed spot, no 'house'; he wanders hither and thither" (Buber, p. 27). The seminomadic existence of the Patriarchs affected their conceptualization of their deity. Their idea of a wandering god, a god of no fixed place, was incorporated into the monotheistic notions of God developed later by Moses under the influence of literacy.

The God of Abraham, the God of Isaac, and the God of Jacob are not necessarily the same God, but possibly personal family gods. The Bible provides us with a number of examples that the Israelites worshipped idols both during the Patriarchal Age and during the time leading to the giving of the law on Mount Sinai. In Genesis Chapter 31, we find the episode in which Rachel successfully steals her father's idols. Evidence that idol worship was part of the common practice of the Israelites is found in Exodus 32, when the people, despairing of Moses' return from the mountain, ask Aaron: "Make us gods, which shall go before us; for as for this Moses, the man that brought us up out of the land of Egypt, we know not what is become of him." Aaron complied with their wishes and fashioned them a golden calf, which they worshipped.

Further evidence for the polytheistic practices of the Hebrews during the Patriarchal Age is found in the Haggadah, which is recited each year at the Jewish Passover feast: "In the beginning our fathers were worshippers of idols, but now the Ever-Present has brought us to His service, as it is said: And Joshua spoke to the whole people: Thus has the Lord, God of Israel spoken: Your fathers dwelt in olden times beyond the River Euphrates, Terah, the father of Abraham and the father of Nachor, and they served other gods."

The Hebrews were still serving other gods in the time of Moses as indicated by the following passage from Leviticus 17:7: "And they shall no more offer their sacrifices unto devils, after whom they have gone awhoring." The use of the wording "they shall no more" indicates that idol worship was once a common practice among the Israelites.

Additional evidence that Moses introduces a new form of worship can be deduced from the fact that, in the biblical accounts of the Patriarchs, the deity is always referred to in the original Hebrew as Elohim, which etymologically derives from the plural term for *god* and hence translates literally into *gods*. Beginning with Moses, the deity is referred to by the tetragram YHWH (sometimes written as Yahweh— i.e., Jehovah). It is in Exodus 6:2 that God reveals this new name to

Moses: "And God spake unto Moses, and said unto him: I am the Lord; and I appeared unto Abraham, unto Isaac, and unto Jacob, as God Almighty, but by my name YHWH was I not known to them." Not only are the Patriarchs ignorant of His name but they do not follow the pattern of the later leaders of the Israelites who prophesy and preach against idolatry.

The role of Abraham was not that of the founder of the Israelite religion; that belongs to Moses. The Patriarchs are rather a historical link of God-fearing men that joins the Hebrew nation to the first generation of men, the legendary generation of Adam, Enoch, and Noah. Abraham is portrayed as a moral and just person, but not really as a "fighter for YHWH" (Kaufman, 1960). Although legends have conferred on Abraham the honor of Patriarch of Israel, historical analysis reveals that he is not the founder of monotheism. "The absence of the essential motifs of Israelite religion in patriarchal times indicates that it was not then that the monotheistic idea came into being" (Kaufman, 1960, pp. 221-223).

THE WRITTEN LAW

Having established the absence of pure monotheism during the patriarchal age, we must also show that writing and codified law were also absent. No reference to writing is ever made in Genesis, even on a number of occasions when one would expect a written record to be made if writing were part of the culture. Abraham's purchase of a burial place for Sarah from Ephron, the Hittite, in Genesis 23 provides one such example. The deal is sealed by the exchange of 400 shekels of silver "in the hearing of the children of Heth." No receipt is drawn up. Another example is provided in Genesis 31:48, where Jacob and Laban record a covenant between them by building a heap of stones. "And Laban said, This heap is witness between me and thee this day." The absence of writing also precludes the possibility of a system codified law. No mention is ever made of any laws in Genesis. Summarizing our results, the evidence from the Bible suggests that the Israelites, whom Moses led out of slavery in the land of Egypt, were a preliterate nomadic people without a codified system of law who worshipped more than one god.

Before beginning the story of how Hebrew culture was radically transformed by the innovations of alphabetic writing, codified law, and monotheism introduced by Moses, we must first examine the context of the rich cultural milieu in which the Israelites operated. There were many influences at work that prepared the ground for the ideas Moses was to introduce. The three principal sources of cultural influence were Mesopotamia, from which Abraham departed; Canaan, where the

Patriarchs first settled; and Egypt, the land where Israel was in bondage and where Moses was born and educated.

From Mesopotamian culture, the Israelites derived "Biblical legend (especially concerning primeval times), law (especially the Covenant Code, Ex. 20:19–23:33), hymnody, and wisdom literature" (Kaufman, 1960, p. 200). From the Canaanites, they derived alphabetic writing, a linguistic transformation from the Canaanite to the Aramaic dialect, the type of poetry found in Psalms, divine names (el, baal, and adon), sacrificial practices and terminology, and a number of legends including those of David, Noah, and Job. From the Egyptians are derived many stories, hymns, names, and a concern with magic. Another possible influence, less easy to trace but often mentioned, are the religious ideas developed during the time of Akhenaton, particularly the worship of the sun disk, Aton. Although Aton worship was not exactly monotheistic, some parallels with the religious ideas of Moses are apparent.

Moses did more than bring the Hebrews out of slavery in the land of Egypt; he brought them a new concept of God, a codified system of law and alphabetic writing. As related in Exodus, the Israelites entered a covenant with their deity under the leadership of Moses and received a written form of the law: "And he gave unto Moses, when he had made an end of communing with him upon Mount Sinai, two tables of testimony, tables of stone, written with the finger of God" (Ex. 31:18).

It is our claim that the events on Mount Sinai represent the historic transition of three separate innovations in the cultural and religious life of the Israelites:

1. Their first use of an alphabetic script
2. Their first adherence to a codified system of law and morality
3. Their first acceptance of a true and complete form of monotheism

The concepts of codified law and alphabetic writing were ideas that the Hebrews borrowed from other cultures, but the introduction of monotheism at Mount Sinai represents a historic first for all of humankind.

The occurrence of monotheism, codified law, and the alphabet all at the same moment in history cannot have been coincidental. Although not suggesting a causal link, it is possible that these ideas influenced each other. The abstractness of the three innovations were mutually reinforcing: "The written letter replaced the graven image. Concentration on the abstract in writing opened the way for an advance from blood relationship to universal ethical standards, to the influence of the prophets in opposition to the absolute power of kings, and to an emphasis on monotheism" (Innis, 1971, p. 39).

Kaufman (1960), the noted historian of the early Israelite religion, saw another link between monotheism and the written law. It was not the content of the law that was the new element, because the laws of the covenant can largely be traced back to Sumerian and Babylonian codes. What is new and unique is the manner of the presentation—namely, directly from God—in fact, "written with the finger of God" (Ex. 31:18). "This law was the command of a God, his absolute will" (Kaufman, 1960, pp. 233–234). Before providing the case for our hypothesis that the stone tablets Moses brought down from Mount Sinai were inscribed with an alphabetic script, let us first make the case that literacy among the Israelites as a nation began with Moses. As mentioned earlier, there are no biblical references to writing until we come to the time of Moses, at which point there is a large number of such references, including those in which Moses is actually writing down the law: "And Moses wrote all the words of the Lord" (Ex. 24:4; see also Deut. 31:9 and 24). In addition, where God instructs Moses to write down the law: "And thou shall write upon them all the words of this law" (Deut. 27:3; see also Ex. 34:27).

There are other instances in which God is credited with having written the law:

1. I will give thee tables of stone, and a law, and commandments which I have written; that thou mayest teach them (Ex. 24:12).

2. And the tables were the work of God, and the writing was the writing of God (Ex. 32:16).

3. See also Ex. 31:18, Ex. 34:1, Deut. 4:13, Deut. 5:22, Deut. 9:10, Deut. 10:2-4, Deut. 28:58 and 61, Deut. 29:27, Deut. 30:10.

Finally, we find the following three passages that make the first references to the reading of the law:

1. And he [Moses] took the book of the covenant, and read in the audience of the people (Ex. 24:7).

2. And Moses commanded . . . thou shalt read this law before all Israel (Deut. 31:10-11).

3. And afterward he [Joshua] read all the words of the law (Josh. 8:34).

The Hebrew tradition of reading out the law before the assembled nation, which began with Moses, persists to this day in the form of Torah readings in synagogues.

In addition to its association with the law, other references to writing appear for the first time in the account of the life and times of Moses. These include:

1. The book: "And the Lord said unto Moses, Write this for a memorial in the book" (Ex. 17:14). See also Ex. 32:32.
2. Signet engravings: "And thou shall make a plate of pure gold, an engrave upon it, like the engravings of a signet" (Ex. 28:36). See also Ex. 28:9 & 21.
3. Written names: "Thou shalt write every man's name upon his rod" (Num. 17:17).
4. Records of events: "And Moses wrote their goings forth" (Num. 33:2).
5. A written bill of divorce "and writeth her a bill of divorcement" (Deut. 24: 3).
6. A written song "Now therefore writeth ye this song for you, and teach thou it the children of Israel" (Deut. 31:19). See also Ex. 31:22.

The references to writing in Exodus are more significant as evidence for Hebrew literacy at the time of Moses than those in Deuteronomy because the oldest strands of the Torah are contained in Exodus (Kaufman, 1960). The claim that the description of the events at Mount Sinai was composed 500 or 600 years later, after the Hebrews returned to Israel from exile in Babylon, is not valid. Kaufman carefully analyzed the complex set of laws on tithing and has been able to unscramble the various bodies of law in the Pentateuch. He was led to the conclusion that, although the Torah was first compiled in the beginning of the Second Temple period, the laws had already crystallized and therefore the compilers "did not alter anything of what they found written much less add to it" (Kaufman, 1960). The accounts in Exodus referring to the first appearance of writing and to the key role it plays in the revelations that take place at Mount Sinai have a valid kernel of historic truth. Next we must establish that this writing was alphabetic.

This hypothesis is consistent with epigraphic records that indicate that at the time of Moses the Proto–Canaanite (or Proto–Sinaitic) alphabet was in use in both Canaan and the Sinai peninsula (Grimme, 1923; Naveh, 1982). As mentioned, some of the earliest inscriptions were found in and near the Egyptian copper mines in the Sinai. The people who made these first alphabetic inscriptions are none other than the biblical Midianites (Sprengling, 1931). In the Bible [Num. 10.29 and Judges 4: 11] they are also called *Kenites*, a term that means "belonging to the coppersmiths"; Midian is rich in copper ore (Albright, 1957). In fact, Sprengling (1931) hypothesized it is the Midianites who actually invented the original phonetic alphabet after borrowing a number of ideas about writing from the Egyptians.

Moses lived with the Midianites for a number of years. He married the Midianite leader, Jethro's daughter, Zipporah, with whom he had two sons. Moses could have easily learned alphabetic writing from his father-in-law, who was the high priest of the Midianites. Moses, having grown up in the house of the pharaoh, was probably already familiar with Egyptian writing. Learning the simpler alphabetic system would have been an easy task. Therefore, it is not difficult to believe the biblical account of Moses delivering the law to the Hebrew people in a written form. Other references to writing appear for the first time in the scriptural account of the life and times of Moses, from which we may conclude that writing had been adopted by the Hebrews by this time.

No mention of laws or commandments is found in the Torah until we encounter Moses. According to these accounts, he is solely responsible for the transmission of God's commandments. No other lawmaker is mentioned during the period of the Exodus other than Moses. It is apparent from the consistency of all these accounts that he is in fact the historical figure who gave the Israelites the concept of law. Although not all aspects of the Mosaic law we encounter in the Torah are original, the Ten Commandments are without a doubt a unique element, which created a new level of morality not previously known to humankind.

The law of the Torah parallels in some ways the second-millennium Mesopotamian law codes, such as those of Hammurabi and others. Some connection must be assumed between the Israelite and Mesopotamian legislation. "But that Moses was the great law giver need not be questioned. Though he did not write all the laws of the Pentateuch as tradition had it, he laid down the constitutive stipulations of covenant to which all specific law must conform, and whose intent it must seek to express" (Bright, 1959, p. 59).

THE MOSAIC GOD

Next we come to the question of establishing the historical uniqueness of the Mosaic concept of monotheism. "It is not an arithmetic diminution of the number of gods, but a new religious category that is involved" (Kaufman, 1960, p. 227). Many new features incorporated in the Mosaic God never appeared until the revelation at Mount Sinai. As we show later, these new aspects of the deity and the way in which he is worshipped reflect the effects of alphabetic literacy. The God of the revelation and the covenant on Mount Sinai represents a new concept of the deity as is reflected in the name YHWH.

The God of the Patriarchs was not tied down to a physical place or shrine. He wandered with his people. The God of Moses takes on an even more abstract formulation, reflecting the abstraction of alphabetic writing. As was pointed out by Innis (1971), YHWH is invisible to his people. He cannot be looked on or the people will perish (Ex. 19:21). The people are forbidden to make any images of their God or any gods for that matter (Ex. 20:4). Yahweh sits in his tabernacle on the mercy seat situated on the wings of the two cherubim, which is placed on the ark containing the testimony of his law, but he is invisible (Ex. 25:17–22). This extremely abstract formulation of the deity produces tremendous strains in the spiritual life of the Israelites. They are constantly returning to the worship of idols, as the story of the golden calf illustrated. Throughout their history, they have to be reminded by their prophets to put aside their graven images.

A frequent representation of deities in preliterate cultures is in terms of a force of nature such as a storm or fertility god. "Yahweh, on the contrary, was a God of a wholly different type. He was identified with no natural force, nor was he localized at any point in heaven or on earth" (Bright, 1959, p. 141). Although he controls storms (Psalm 29), the elements (Judg. 5:4, 21), the heavenly bodies (Josh. 10:12ff.), and fertility (Gen. 49:25, Deut. 33:13-16), he is not a storm, sun, or fertility god.

"Yahweh was powerful over all of nature, but no one aspect of it was more characteristic of him than was another" (Bright, 1959, p. 141). The relationship between God and nature changes with the monotheism introduced by Moses. In the pagan belief systems, no matter how powerful a god became, even if he were able to dominate momentarily over all the other gods, he was still not in control of his own fate. There were always mysterious or magical forces to which he was subject and which could frustrate his will. With Moses a new concept of the deity developed, creating a new religious idea that later come to shape Christianity and Islam.

> The basic idea of Israelite religion is that God is supreme over all. . . .
> He is utterly distinct from, and other than, the world; he is subject to
> no laws, no compulsions, no powers that transcend him. He is, in
> short, nonmythological. This is the essence of Israelite religion, and
> that which sets it apart from all forms of paganism. (Kaufman, 1960,
> p. 60)

Within the context of Hebrew religious thought, nature, although still regarded as a living entity, was robbed of its personality and demythed. Once the Greeks became literate, they also demythed nature and developed a notion of causality to explain its actions. This led to their scientific approach to the description of nature. A similar development occurred with the Hebrews, but with different consequences. They also developed a notion of causation, but the prime cause they attributed to Yahweh. In fact, the name Yahweh incorporates the notion of causing to come into being.

> Linguistically the form yahweh can only be causative, and to judge from many analogies in Babylonia, Egypt and Canaan, it is an abbreviation of a longer name or litanic formula. . . . The enigmatic formula in Ex. 3:14, which in Biblical Hebrew means "I am what I am," if transposed into the form in the third person required by the causative Yahweh, can only become "Yahweh asher yihweh" (later yihyeh), [He Causes to Be What Comes into Existence]. (Albright, 1957, p. 260).

The Hebrew notion of causation did not develop along the logical scientific lines of the Greeks. Rather, they incorporated it into their unique sense of history, with its promise of the future, the Promised Land, and their role as the Chosen People.

THE ALPHABET AND HEBREW HISTORY

Israel's religion and notion of God are deeply rooted in her historical experiences, in her deliverance from slavery in Egypt, and the theopolitical covenant she reached with God under the leadership of Moses. The idea of the covenant and the promise of the future dominated the religious life of Israel and shaped her notion of nationhood.

The sense of striving for a future promise is reinforced by the prophets. The sense of history is reinforced by the forms of worship, in which there are constant reminders of the historic events of faith through the periodic reading of the law as required by Deuteronomy 31:11. There is also the biblical injunction to the Israelites to celebrate the feasts in which the covenants of the past are renewed (Deut. 16:16) and through the commandment to teach the young. "And these words, which I command thee this day, shall be in thy heart; and thou shalt teach them diligently unto thy children" (Deut. 6:6-7).

The teaching of the young took two forms: oral and literary. Each Hebrew son was to be taught to read the law. The Israelites were the first people to achieve a universal level of literacy—an accomplishment that required a relatively easy system of writing. This is exactly the role that the phonetic alphabet fulfilled. Only 22 signs had to be learned, plus the principle of phonetics. Any child could learn to read at a very early age (3–11 years).

Alphabetic literacy helped the Hebrews develop a historic sense. The other literate cultures of the ancient world—Sumerians,

Babylonians, Assyrians, Hittites, and Egyptians—also recorded historical events, but their historiography was crude. Events were recorded in
isolation. The Hebrews connected the events and imbued them with
purpose. They also had a measure of objectivity, recording both the
events of which they were proud and those of which they were
ashamed. The Egyptians, recorded only their victories, never their
defeats. (The Greeks eventually developed objective methods similar to
those of the Hebrews after they adopted the alphabetic writing system.)
The outstanding pioneer of Hebrew history was Ahimoaz, the author of
the Book of Samuel. "Ahimoaz . . . is [the father of history) in a much
truer sense than Herodotus half a millennium later. Without any previous models or guides, he wrote a masterpiece, unsurpassed in historicity, psychological insight, literary style and dramatic power" (Pfeiffer,
1948, p. 357). The influence of alphabetic writing is reflected in the codification of the law introduced by Moses and the historiography that follows this development with its new spirit of analysis and objectivity. A
similar influence is felt in the political structures that begin to emerge
with the political leadership of Moses.

THE IMPACT OF WRITING
ON HEBREW POLITICAL ORGANIZATION

During the Patriarchal Age, the Hebrews were a seminomadic tribal
people organized by clans and following a charismatic leader. Under the
leadership of Moses, a similar structure pertained; Moses served as a
leader, lawmaker, and judge. However, there was now an awareness
that these were three separate activities. One of the effects encouraged
by the phonetic alphabet discussed earlier is the fragmentation of social
roles and activities, including the separation of the executive, legislative,
and judicial aspects of government and the bureaucratization of these
functions. Moses, at the suggestion of his father-in-law, Jethro, created
the first bureaucracy in the history of the Hebrew nation. Finding that
too much of his time was occupied in settling the disputes between
neighbors that require an interpretation of law, Moses divided the case-
load by creating a hierarchy of rulers and judges to help him. "And
Moses chose able men out of all Israel, and made them heads over the
people, rulers of thousands, rulers of hundreds, rulers of fifties, and
rulers of tens. And they judged the people at all seasons: the hard cases
they brought unto Moses, but every small matter they judged themselves" (Ex. 18:25-6). In this manner, Moses ruled and judged over the
Israelites until he died, when his leadership passed to Joshua who had
served as his chief military lieutenant.

The Hebrews entered Canaan, the Promised Land, under the leadership of Joshua. Through military conquest, they acquired a modest foothold in the land. The Hebrews returning from Egypt formed an alliance with those Hebrews who had remained in the land during the time of the enslavement in Egypt. Together these tribes formed a loose decentralized confederation. The 12 tribes of the confederation would sometimes cooperate on ventures of mutual interest and at other times fought among themselves. Their structure was somewhat like that of ancient Greece during its tribal period. Disputes between tribes were settled by a judge. The judge was often chosen, as was the case with Joshua, because of his charismatic qualities, but he was not always followed. In times of war, he would lead a coalition of tribes, but there was a reluctance on the part of the fiercely independent tribes to have a centralized authority like a king. Gideon, a popular judge, was once offered the crown, but refused it because he believed it was not in the spirit of YHWH.

The threat of conquest by the Philistines, who held the coastal regions, required extreme action on the part of the Israelites. Under the prompting of Samuel, the prophet and priest, Saul, a charismatic leader, was made king over Israel. Saul defended Israel, but tribal structures remained strong during his reign because he failed to develop a rational administrative machinery or bureaucracy.

During this period, there arose another charismatic leader, David, of whom Saul was greatly jealous. David, forced into exile, became a vassal of the Philistines and created his own private army. When Saul was killed in battle against the Philistines, David was elected king by his native tribe of Judah. Saul's son, Eshbaal, became king of the remainder of the Hebrew tribes—a kingdom that took the name *Israel*. Internal strife within the house of Saul brought down Eshbaal, and David soon became king of both Judah and Israel. David then embarked on an extremely successful campaign of conquest in which he defeated the Philistines, the perennial enemies of Israel, and destroyed the remaining pockets of Canaanite power, including that housed in Jerusalem. He also conquered the surrounding states such as Ammon, Moab, Edom, and Aram. David's success was due largely to his private army, although the other tribes fought alongside him. David made Jerusalem the capital city and created machinery that divided the kingdom into taxation and administrative districts. There was a great deal of court intrigue and feuding, which David kept in check with his private army. Israel was no longer a tribal confederacy, but a centrally ruled monarchy.

During King David's time, writing was no longer used merely for ceremonial or legal purposes, but for literature. David's reign marks the beginning of the compilation of the Scriptures. The correlation between the increased use of alphabetic writing and the beginnings of an administrative bureaucracy is not accidental.

King David was succeeded by one of his younger sons, Solomon, who was able to politically outmaneuver his rivals. Solomon did not increase the size of David's empire, but consolidated his holdings and exploited them for economic gain. Making use of diplomatic channels opened by his father, King Solomon entered into an alliance with the Phoenicians under King Hiram of Tyre. He opened trade routes to southern Arabia and Africa using ships built by the Phoenicians. Other large-scale operations such as development of the copper industry and establishment of a monopoly in horse and chariot trading were established. Solomon displayed brilliant organizational skills, which no doubt were aided by the increased level of literacy that developed during his regime. Solomon's projects were examples of state capitalism in which capital was raised by heavy taxation. Labor was conscripted by the government from among conquered people. An urban proletariat was created and class structure developed. King Solomon maintained control of his political-economic empire by using repressive Machiavellian techniques. Tribal democracy was destroyed by Solomon, and people were no longer equal. Literacy seems to have created privilege.

In addition to the increased economic activity, culture flowered under King Solomon. A large-scale building program produced both the imperial residence and the Temple. Psalmody, music, wisdom literature, and historical writing flourished. The centralization of political structures and religious activities in Israel that began with the reign of David paralleled the development that occurred in other cultures as they became literate.

Literacy, particularly alphabetic writing, with its stress on linearity and uniformity, encourages centralization of social functions such as religion. This process is described in Deuteronomy, which was written during the time of King David. The other books of the Pentateuch do not stress the importance of Jerusalem because they were written (but not compiled) before the time of David and reflect the attitudes then prevalent in Israel. With David's conquest of Jerusalem and the setting up of the Ark of the Covenant on the Temple Mount in Jerusalem, the centralization of Israel's spiritual life began. This was further reinforced by the prohibition against certain practices such as making sacrifices in the former holy places scattered about in Israel and Judah, including such sites as Shechem, Bethel, Dan, Gibeon, and Beersheba. These restrictions first appear in Deuteronomy: "Take heed to thyself that thou offer not thy burnt offerings in every place that thou seest; but in the place which the Lord shall choose in one of thy tribes" (Deut. 12:13–14).

8

The Phonetic Alphabet and the Origin of Greek Science and Logic

MINOAN AND EARLY GREEK NONALPHABETIC WRITING

Long before the Greeks developed alphabetic writing, there arose in Crete in the Minoan culture that thrived there three writing systems. The earliest was a pictographic system similar to the Egyptian hieroglyphs in which the symbols were naturalistic. This system evolved with time into a linear pictographic system, which was used primarily for inventories and bookkeeping. This script evolved into Linear A containing 70 symbols, one third of which were retained from the previous linear pictographic script. Linear A, which has never been deciphered is presumed to have been a syllabary because it has too many symbols for an alphabet and too few for a pictographic or logographic system. It was used for "lists of objects, commodities and personnel as part of the palace bureaucracy" from 1650 to 1450 B.C. (Stroud, 1989). Over 1,200 examples of Linear A have been found in 20 different sites centering on Crete, but also extant on other Greek islands and also the mainland. The language of the script is non-Greek, however.

It is believed by some and disputed by others that the Minoan inventors of Linear A with their palace at Knossos were conquered by Greeks from the mainland who wanted a writing system that would accommodate their language. The result was Linear B, which borrowed many of the symbols from Linear A. Four thousand tablets were discovered at the palace Knossos in Crete, another 1,200 at the Pylos palace in southwestern Peloponnesos, and still more on other sites on the mainland of Greece. Linear B was deciphered by Michael Ventris (Ventris & Chadwick, 1973) in 1952 and found to be an archaic form of Greek. Linear B is a syllabary with 90 symbols and a sophisticated number system with a numeral as high as 10,000. Like Linear A, it was used for inventories and bookkeeping circa 1380 to 1200 B.C., when it suddenly disappeared leaving behind no literature. There is no reference in Homer to writing, for example. Greek writing does not reappear for many years and then in the form of the first phonetic alphabet complete with vowels.

ALPHABET: FOUNT OF WESTERN CIVILIZATION

The Greek alphabet is directly derived from the North Semitic alphabet as a result of commercial contacts with the Phoenicians. This fact is recorded by Herodotus in the fifth century B.C.:

> Now the Phoenicians who came with Cadmus introduced into Greece upon their arrival a great variety of arts, among the rest that of writing, whereof the Greeks till then had, as I think, been ignorant. And originally they shaped their letters exactly like all the other Phoenicians, but afterwards in course of time, they changed by degrees their language, and together with it the form likewise of the characters. Now the Greeks who dwelt about those parts at that time were chiefly the Ionians. The Phoenician letters were accordingly adopted by them, but with some variation in the shape of a few, and so they arrived at present use, still calling the letters Phoenician, as justice required, after the name of those who were the first to introduce them into Greece. (Herodotus 5.58)

The Greek alphabet, complete with vowels, represents a unique achievement in man's capacity for rendering his spoken language into a totally accurate written form; it went beyond anything that preceded it and has not been equaled since.

The 600 or 700 years that followed the transfer of the phonetic alphabet from the Phoenicians to the Greeks was one of the most creative periods in man's existence. Within this short period, there appeared many of the elements of Western civilization—abstract science, formal logic, axiomatic geometry, rational philosophy, and representational art. It is not an accident that this unparalleled intellectual development occurred immediately following the transfer of the phonetic alphabet.

Although a causal connection is not being suggested, it is apparent that the alphabet helped create the unique conditions for this development. In the next two chapters, we look at how the alphabet stimulated the abstract and rational system of thought that characterized ancient Greek culture and subsequently all of Western civilization.

THE GREEK ALPHABET:
THE PENULTIMATE IN PHONETIC LITERACY

How did the Greek phonetic alphabet differ from the Phoenician alphabet and why did it have such an enormous impact on Western thought? The Greeks modified the Phoenician system of 22 uniconsonantal signs by adding vowels and three extra consonants to duplicate sounds that occur in Greek, but not in Semitic tongues. Seven vowels signs were created by converting five unstressed Semitic consonants (which sometimes served as vowels in Semitic writing) into pure vowels and by adding two new letters. In addition to the vowels, three new consonants were added. Otherwise the Greek alphabet took on the same names, sound values, and order as the Semitic alphabet: The Semitic letter aleph became alpha, beit became beta, and gimmel became gamma.

These seemingly minor changes completely revolutionized writing and enabled the Greeks to accurately and completely transliterate every spoken word into a unique visual sign and each array of visual signs into a unique spoken word. "The original Greek invention achieved the essential task of analysis and it has not been improved upon" (Havelock, 1976, p. 61). Havelock made this claim for the Greek alphabet because it satisfies the three conditions necessary for an efficient and passive writing system of which the reader is unaware: (a) coverage of all linguistic sounds, (b) lack of ambiguity, and (c) a restricted number of elements or letters (20 to 40). Although the North Semitic alphabet comes close to this ideal, it contains a number of ambiguities due to its lack of vowels.

Havelock (1976) attributed the success of the Greek system to the fact that reading could be taught to young children before they learned other skills. This is one of the advantages of the Greek alphabet over the North Semitic alphabet. In fact, the Hebrew writing system was modified in the Middle Ages to include vowels as subscripts or superscripts of the consonants to teach children to read. These vowels signs are not used in adult literature. The Greek alphabet completely revolutionized reading and writing and its instruction by simplifying and speeding up these processes. The changes that the Greek alphabet produced, however, extended beyond the boundaries of literacy into all aspects of Greek intellectual life.

TECHNIQUES OF EDUCATION AND INFORMATION STORAGE IN A PRELITERATE SOCIETY

Before examining the effects of the alphabet on Greek culture and society, let us first see how cultural continuity was maintained and how information was transmitted from one generation to another before the advent of literacy. Essentially the learning and wisdom of a society were passed on through epics, sagas, or myths recited from memory.

The bard Homer, for example, was "at once a storyteller and also a tribal encyclopedia" (Havelock, 1963, p. 83) who provided all the information necessary for life in tribal Greek society. From Homer the listener could learn how to rig a sailing ship, dress for battle, and behave in court. Woven around the tales were the essential lore and wisdom of the culture. The customs of the society were taught by example, not by prescription. "The warp and woof of Homer is didactic, and . . . the tale is made subservient to the task of accommodating the weight of educational materials which lie within it" (Havelock, 1963, p. 61).

The reason the tribal encyclopedia took the form of poetic epics was to ensure the preservation of this vital information through memorization. The imagery, story lines, meters, rhythms, and rhymes of the epics all served as devices aiding this process. The poetic conventions and standardized imagery that were essential to the memorization of the myths and sagas had the hidden effect of severely limiting the kinds of things that the culture could transmit and hence think about. Let us consider the personification of the natural forces in the form of the Greek gods as one example. This device, which made the Greek myths so vivid and hence easily recallable, severely limited the preliterate Greek's capacity to conceptualize natural forces. Consider how far science would have developed if the natural forces had never been abstracted, but continued to be personified and represented as gods.

Nursery rhymes and nonsense verses are another example of material easily remembered because of their rhymes and meters, but limited in content by their form. Nursery rhymes serve an important role in an oral society. They prepare children for the more arduous task of memorizing more meaningful and lengthier material. Nursery rhymes are the ABCs of an oral culture (Havelock, 1971).

THE TRANSITION TO ALPHABETIC WRITING

From a comparison of the early Greek scripts with the Phoenician scripts, Carpenter (1933, 1938) claimed that the Greek alphabet first appeared in Rhodes or Cyprus somewhere around 700 B.C. In a more recent study, Naveh (1973, 1982) determined that the transfer occurred much earlier than this and pushed the date of the borrowing as far back as 1100 B.C. If Greek tradition is any guide to the dating of the transmission of the Phoenician alphabet, then the date of 1300 B.C. assigned to Cadmus by the Greeks would favor Naveh's dating rather than Carpenter's (Kenyon, 1951). Independent of the actual date of this borrowing, we know that the Greek phonetic alphabet spread from the Greek Islands and Ionia to Athens and the remainder of the Greek mainland and then to the western colonies in Italy. The Etruscans used the Greek alphabet to transcribe their language in the seventh century B.C. and eventually passed the alphabet onto the Romans. Given this early date for the Etruscan use of the alphabet, the Naveh chronology makes more sense than that of Carpenter, considering the time that would be required for the alphabet to develop and spread from Ionia to Italy and possibly through mainland Greece.

The tremendous impact of alphabetic writing on Greek thought was not uniform. Its impact on Ionia and Athens was much greater than elsewhere. Thus, although the alphabet served as a model for several intellectual breakthroughs, it was only a necessary condition for these breakthroughs, not a sufficient one. Not all communities that adopted the alphabet were affected by it as much as the Greeks. Nor was the impact of the North Semitic alphabet uniform. The Hebrews were more affected by it than the other Semitic peoples who adopted it. The impact of the alphabet was not immediate. It took about 500 years for literacy to take hold of the Greek mind, and a similar period elapsed between the introduction and widespread use of literacy among the Hebrews. "The psychic habits of centuries could not be broken quickly, especially when—and this is very important—they had exploited all the resources of sensory pleasures" (Havelock, 1963, p. 293).

THE EFFECTS OF
ALPHABETIC WRITING ON THE GREEKS

With the advent of literacy and the use of the alphabet, the transmission of ideas from one generation to another no longer required thoughts to be expressed in stylized poetry for the sake of memorization. The alphabet made possible the preservation of prose, which imposes no formulae or conventions on the ideas expressed. This fact, coupled with the model of abstraction that the alphabet provides, produced an enormous change in the nature of Greek thought.

Perhaps the most striking effect of the alphabet was the great number of new abstractions that appeared almost simultaneously. All spoken words are abstractions of the things they represent. The written word is a further abstraction of the spoken word, and phonetic letters give it an even greater abstraction than ideographs or pictographs. The use of the alphabet thus involves a double level of abstraction over a spoken word because the transcription of a spoken word takes place in two steps. A spoken word is first broken up into semantically meaningless phonemes or sounds, and the sounds are then represented by semantically meaningless signs—the letters of the alphabet.

The impact of alphabetic writing can be traced by noting the increase in abstract thought and language that occurred as Greek literature progressed from Homer to Hesiod to the pre-Socratic philosophers and then to Plato and Aristotle. There are abstract notions in Homer such as the goddess Memory or the Furies. These abstractions, however, must always be visualized, personalized, and cast within the context of the narrative of local events that limit their universality. This lack of abstraction and universality is to be expected with Homer because his poetry is composed strictly within the oral tradition. With Hesiod, however, the alphabet begins to make its mark as a new level of abstraction first takes hold of the Greek mind. "With literacy they [the Greeks] suddenly saw their universe as ordered. Their new world view, however, was in conflict with the vocabulary they inherited from their oral tradition" (Havelock, 1963, pp. 301, 304).

Under the influence of alphabetic literacy, Greek writers created the vocabulary of abstract thought still in use to this day—notions such as body, matter, essence, space, translation, time, motion, permanence, change, flux, quality, quantity, combination, and ratio. These concepts became the language of philosophy. A rational approach to analyzing problems logically and finding solutions to them developed. Ideas such as truth, beauty, justice, and reason took on new meanings and became the subject of a new type of discourse.

Havelock (1963) noted that the way in which statements of knowledge are made in the oral and literate tradition are quite different. Statements in the oral tradition must be made in the context of events in real space and time. It is only with alphabetic literacy that timeless analytic statements emerge that can express universal truths independent of the context in which they occur. The statement "Two plus two is four" is an example of an analytic statement. The same information contained with the context of a narrative would not have the same impact.

Another important difference between the oral and literate tradition is the way in which information is organized. Homer's epic served as a tribal encyclopedia, but there was no attempt to systematize the information contained in his hidden curriculum. The order in which information useful to everyday life appeared was determined by the story line of the narrative. The Greek philosophers of the classical period, in contrast, took extreme pains to systematize their material and present it in a particular order dictated by logic or reason.

SCIENCE TAKES ROOT

Hesiod, thought to be the first Greek author to write down his compositions, represents the transition point between Greek philosophy and science on the one hand and the tribal and oral tradition, on the other hand (Havelock, 1963, pp. 296–297; Webster, 1960, pp. 273–275). "Hesiod, though he knows Homer, belongs to a different intellectual and economic climate" (Hadas, 1950, p. 11). Kenyon (1951) presented a compelling argument for the thesis that Hesiod's poems were composed in a written rather than an oral form. He argued that Greek bards would have taken the trouble to memorize Homer's popular legends of the gods and heroes. They would not have done the same, however, for Hesiod's Works and Days, with its "combination of a purely personal quarrel with agricultural precepts."

Although he dealt with the same mythic material as Homer, Hesiod ordered his material into a definite pattern. Hesiod introduced the gods to the Pantheon systematically at the beginning of his theogony and then went on to explain the creation of the universe, whereas Homer introduced the gods as they arose in the course of his narrative. Hesiod's systematic treatment of nature represented the beginning of Greek scientific thought, although Hesiod still held to traditional views of creation. "He was an innovator in theology and science. His systematization and his presentation . . . of a process of reasoning rather than a statement of conclusions, made him a significant pioneer in the field of Greek science" (Kenyon, 1951, p. 35). Hesiod is best known for his stories about the gods, but he also wrote extensively about astronomy, agriculture, and even metalworking (Kenyon, 1951). His major innovation was the literary style he employed. Although he wrote poetry, he led the way toward a prose style through his careful and systematic organization of his narrative material. This innovation and achievement of Hesiod, however, was only partial because he still developed his narrative as a series of events or happenings. The creation of the world is portrayed in terms of the activities of the gods, albeit the language in which the tale is cast is abstract and elements of classification abound.

> The device exploited by the poet for organizing his panorama of living forces is the family, the genos, or genee. This concrete device is

used to arrange a hundred phenomena in congruent groups. A step
has been taken towards classification and even towards establishing
a chain of cause and effect. The genos is on the way to becoming the
"genus" or class. (Havelock, 1963, pp. 301, 304)

The contribution that Hesiod made under influence and the impact
of the alphabet was classification or systematization. The alphabet is a
natural classification scheme for words as anyone who has used a dictionary or filing system is well aware. What distinguishes *science*, a term
derived from the Latin word *scire* "to know," from *knowledge* is the organization of that knowledge. We encounter many examples of systematization and classification in early Greek science.

In addition to serving as a paradigm of abstraction and classification, the alphabet serves as a model for division and fragmentation.
With the alphabet every word is fragmented into its constituent sounds
and letters. The Greeks' idea of atomicity— that all matter can be divided up into individual distinct tiny atoms—is related to their alphabet:
"Atomism and the alphabet alike were theoretical constructs, manifesta-
tions of a capacity for abstract analysis, an ability to translate objects of
perception into mental entities" (Havelock, 1976, p. 44).

The capacity for fragmentation and separation extends far beyond
the Greek concept of the atomicity of matter. With writing, what is
recorded or remembered becomes separate from the writer. It stands
alone in a book or scroll independent of the context of the person who
originated the ideas or information. Knowledge begins to take on an
identity separate from the knower. "The phonetic alphabet was a technical means of severing the spoken word from its aspect of sound and gesture. . . . The literate man or society develops the tremendous power of
acting in any matter with considerable detachment from the feelings or
emotional involvement that a non-literate man or society could experience" (McLuhan, 1964, pp. 193, 179). Through writing, the Greeks developed a notion of objectivity—the separation of the knower from the
object of his study. This is the beginning of the scientific method and the
source of the dichotomy the Greeks created between subjective and
objective thinking. Poetry and art are examples of subjective thinking,
whereas philosophy and science are examples of objective thinking.

In addition to objectivity, the alphabet provided the Greeks with a
number of other paradigms that proved useful to their development of
science. The abstraction and systematization that the use of the alphabet
encouraged were two of the characteristics that distinguished Greek science from that of its predecessors. The Greeks borrowed a great deal
from the primitive science of their neighbors, the Egyptians and
Babylonians, but they totally transformed this material in line with their
new standards of scientific and logical thought.

LOGIC TAKES ROOT

The transformation of empirically based Egyptian geometry into an abstract and axiom-based science is a perfect example of the impact alphabetic writing had on the Greeks. Geometry arose out of the Egyptian need to measure the area of land in the possession of a landowner before the yearly inundation of the Nile. Rather than restore the boundary lines between properties that were destroyed by the flooding, each landowner was provided with a new plot of land more or less in the same location as before and with a total area exactly equal to the amount of land in his possession before the flood. Because of this need to measure the area of land accurately, an empirical science arose called *geometry*, which literally means earth (geo) measuring (metry). Egyptian geometry is not derived from a set of axioms. There are no theorems, proofs, or propositions. There are merely a set of rules that are used strictly for practical applications such as land measuring or construction calculations.

The Greeks, in contrast, almost from the instant they became involved with geometry were interested in systematizing and formalizing the Egyptian results. Greek geometry began with Thales, one of the seven wise men of antiquity, who was the first to devise formal proofs of Egyptian geometric results. Proving geometric theorems was one way that the Greeks developed deductive logic. "But whereas in Egypt mathematics like ethics and medicine had been developed empirically and stopped short of philosophy, it became to Thales a means of discarding allegory and myth and advancing universal generalization" (Innis, 1972, p. 64).

The use of the alphabet serves as a model for matching—an activity crucial for the development of logic. Each letter of the alphabet is matched with a sound and vice versa. Every time a word is read, a match between a visual sign and spoken sound is made. Matching forms the basis of rationality or logic. Rationality grew out of the concept of ratios, which in turn involves matching. A is to B as C is to D is an example of a ratio achieved by matching.

The linking together of the elements of the alphabet—the letters—to form words provided a model for the linking together of ideas to form a logical argument. Arguments are linked together to reach a conclusion. The deductive reasoning implicit in formal logic and geometry also formed the basis of early Greek science, which attempted to derive its description of nature from first principles.

THE IONIAN PHYSICISTS

The use of the alphabet also promoted the development of logic because it promoted the skills of analysis. Each rendering of a spoken word by a combination of the letters of the alphabet represents a process of analysis. To render a spoken word alphabetically, it is first necessary to analyze the sound or phonic structure of the word and hence break down the word into its basic sounds or phonemic elements. Once this is done, the matching of the letters of the alphabet with the phonemic elements can take place to render a spelling of the word. It is our claim that the constant repetition of the process of phonemic analysis of a spoken word, every time it is written in an alphabetic form, subliminally promotes the skills of analysis and matching that are critical for the development of scientific and logical thinking.

Kalgren (1926), who wrote about ancient Chinese philosophy and contrasted Chinese and Western writing systems, made a similar point:

> We look upon the alphabetical, analyzing script as something very simple and natural, the system to write a word by successively adding one sound symbol after another, analytically, as in c-a-t. This system, though it may sound simple, is one of the most ingenious ever evolved by humanity, and it is entirely foreign to the Chinese mentality. (pp. 37–38)

Thales, the first to formalize geometry, was also the first Greek physicist. The term physics comes from the Greek word for nature, phusis. Thales was the founder of the Ionian school of science on which the entire foundation of Western science rests. He derived all of nature or phusis from a single principle—namely, water.

Thales and his followers arrived at their conclusions on the basis of their observations and use of deductive reasoning. They laid the foundations of scientific methodology and thought. They believed that change and movement are caused by physical forces. They believed in the existence of atoms, the concept of a void, and the conservation of mass. They correctly held that ice, water, and steam are different phases of the same substance.

In addition to their use of logic, the Ionians also began to develop an empirical tradition. Unfortunately, this tradition did not fully flower with the Greeks, but only some 2,000 years later during the Renaissance. The story that best illustrates the new empirical spirit that emerged in Ionia concerns the philosopher and physicist Anaxagoras. On hearing of a report of the landing of a shooting star, he mounted an expedition to Anatolia to investigate the matter. On the basis of his findings,

Anaxagoras concluded that the heavenly bodies, including the moon, were made of rock. This idea offended the popular religious belief in the divinity of the heavenly bodies and almost cost Anaxagoras his life. It was not until Galileo's telescopic observations of the mountains on the moon that Anaxagoras's ideas were finally verified.

Ionian physicists even anticipated evolution some 2,500 years before Darwin. Anaximander argued that because the newborn human child is completely helpless, man must have descended from a more primitive form of life whose young are self-sufficient. Anaximander's argument for evolution might have been influenced by his observations of gills on the human embryo as well.

Each of the Ionian physicists had a unifying principle from which he derived his description of nature. This principle was different for each philosopher, but it established early in the history of science an important pattern. From the beginnings of Greek science, an explanation for the operations of nature had been sought through some universal and unifying principle or principles. For Thales the unifying principle was water, out of which the entire universe was created. Anaximander, a student of Thales, believed the unifying material of which all matter was composed and from which opposites like hot and cold emerged was a gray neutral substance he called *apieron*—"the boundless":

> The Unlimited (apieron) is the first principle of things that are. It is that from which the coming-to-be takes place and it is that into which they return when they perish, by moral necessary, giving satisfaction to one another and making restitution for their injustice, according to the order of time. (Anaximander, fragment)

Aniximenes, a student of Anaximander, believed that all matter was composed of air and the difference in materials is due to the difference in their densities. Although modern science has shown that matter is not composed of air, but of protons, neutrons, and electrons, part of Aniximenes' idea is still true. All matter is made of the same components—namely, atoms—all of which are approximately the same size. What distinguishes one type of atom from another and hence one type of material from another is the number or density of the protons, neutrons, and electrons they contain.

Heraclitus believed that fire was the unifying principle that explained nature:

> This universe, which is the same for all, has not been made by any god or man, but it always has been, is, and will be—an ever kindling fire, kindling itself by regular measures and going out by regular

measures. There is exchange of all things for fire and of fire for all things, as there is of wares for gold and gold for wares. (Heraclitus, fragment)

If one identifies fire with energy, Heraclitus' saying reads like a statement of the principle of the conservation of energy—some 2,400 years before it was first formulated and scientifically established.

UNIVERSAL LAW

Each of the early Ionian physicists based his description of nature on one universal substance. Heraclitus was no exception, but like Anaximander he also emphasized the processes of strife and justice by which the material world is ruled. Explicit in the systems of Anaximander and Heraclitus and implicit in the other Ionian systems is the notion that nature is ruled by law or Logos: "All things come to pass in accordance with this Logos" (Heraclitus, fragment).

Behind the Heraclitean notion of Logos was the idea of cause and effect, which became the basis of all Western science. The alphabet provided a positive influence for the development of the linear notion of cause and effect by providing a model for sequence and succession. "Our ideas of cause and effect in the literate West have long been in the form of things in sequence and succession" (Havelock, 1976, p. 43).

The concept of universal law developed by the Ionian physicists forms one of the fundamentals of modern science. Universal law also appears as a product of Hebrew monotheism and Babylonian codified law. Before Hebrew monotheism, the law or rule of a god was limited to the geographical zone over which he held sway. With the advent of an omnipresent god whose law applied everywhere, the idea of a universal law developed.

One can only speculate as to whether the early Greek physicists borrowed the idea of universal law directly from the Hebrews. They were certainly in a position to develop the concept on their own, because each of the pre-Socratic philosophers was a lawmaker in his own community and was monotheistically inclined. Each believed that the universe was ruled by a single principle, which for Anaximander was apieron, for Heraclitus, Logos, and for Anaxagoras, Mind. "Mind set in order all that was to be, all that ever was but no longer is, and all that is now or ever will be" (Anaxagoras, fragment). The Greeks were in contact with Hebrew literature, however, and some degree of borrowing no doubt took place.

WHY SCIENCE BEGAN IN THE WEST

Having examined the influence that the alphabet, codified law, monotheism, and logic had on the formulation of science, we are in a better position to see why science began in the West and not the East despite the technological superiority of the Chinese. The alphabet, codified law, monotheism, and logic are all unique to the West where they were first formulated. They prepared the ground for the development of abstract science.

The alphabet provided a model for abstraction, classification, and analysis. The linking together of the repeatable elements of the alphabet also provided a model for analytic deductive logic, which also played an important role in the invention of abstract science. With the alphabet, a new style of writing developed—namely, prose—with which it is possible to create analytic statements. Abstract science without prose and analytic statements would be impossible. The Chinese never developed prose style. It is only recently that they have begun to imitate the Western novel. Their lack of alphabetic writing and a prose style, I believe, handicapped their development of abstract science despite their impressive technological achievements.

Without an alphabetic writing system to encourage analysis, logic, and classification; without a system of codified law to encourage a belief in natural law; and without monotheism to encourage abstraction and universality, the Chinese were never able to achieve Western-style science. Chinese ideas and inventions carried to the West by traders were incorporated in Western science, but the Chinese were unable to create their own scientific revolution simply because they lacked these tools to do so (Needham, 1979).

HOW LOGICAL DOUBLE-TALK DAMPENED THE EMPIRICAL SPIRIT OF GREEK PHYSICS

Although Greek science contained many of the elements of modern abstract science, it took 2,000 years for a fully mathematical description of nature á la Newton to develop. Because two major factors were missing from Greek science, full flowering was held back until the European Renaissance. One factor was the lack of an experimental orientation, and the other was the absence of the concept of zero. Paradoxically, the same rational, logical way of thinking that contributed to the early development of abstract science also inhibited both of these factors.

The importance of zero to science is twofold. First, it led directly to a place number system (Arabic numerals) and, as a consequence, to simpler arithmetical calculations. Second, zero also encouraged the development of algebra. The Greeks precluded the possibility of inventing zero when they accepted Parmenides' arguments for the impossibility of nonbeing as described later. (The story of how the Hindus were able to make this discovery is discussed in chap. 10, this volume.)

The early Greek physicists were all strong supporters of the empirical approach of observation. Anaxagoras' arduous expedition to observe the remains of a shooting star was a testament to that spirit. So are the following fragments from Heraclitus: "The things of which there can be sight, hearing and learning—these are what I especially prize." "Eyes are more accurate witnesses than ears." Despite these early encouraging signs, an attack on empiricism was mounted by Parmenides, who forced Greek thinkers to choose between trusting their senses and trusting logic. They chose logic. Parmenides was historically the first philosopher to construct a logically self-consistent argument. Reacting strongly to the Heraclitean notion of change and flux, which held that one cannot step twice into the same river, Parmenides set out to show, using logic, that change was impossible.

Parmenides started with the premise that the concept of nonbeing is logically self-contradictory, and therefore nonbeing cannot be. If *nonbeing* cannot be, then nothing can change, because if something changes from State A to State B, then A would not be. But according to Parmenides' original premise, A cannot not be; therefore, nothing can change.

Parmenides' proof demonstrating the impossibility of change was extended by his disciple, Zeno, to show that motion was also not possible: Either a thing is in its place or it is not in its place. If it is in its place, then it cannot move, and it is impossible for a thing not to be in its place; therefore nothing moves.

RESOLUING THE PARADOX

The arguments of Zeno and Parmenides would be dismissed today as logical double-talk or sophistry. Unfortunately for the progress of science, they were taken seriously by the Greek thinkers of that day, who were unprepared to deal with the new system of rational thought that logic made possible. As with any new technology, there are always abuses at the beginning when, through a lack of experience and understanding, the new techniques are used in an inappropriate manner. Such was the case with the first scientists and philosophers who, when confronted with the either–or choice between logic and observation, chose logic. Even the empirically minded Anaxagoras wrote: "Because of the weakness of our senses we are not able to judge the truth."

Parmenides presented a paradox to Greek philosophy and physics— namely, the contradiction between the commonsense observations of change in the everyday world of experience and his logically consistent arguments against change. Each of the Greek thinkers responded to this challenge by finding a way to resolve this paradox, in each case by carefully inserting into his worldview some element that did not change.

The empiricist Empedocles constructed a universe composed of four basic and immutable substances that no change could invade: earth, air, fire, and water, of which every material substance in the universe is composed in some unique ratio. Change consists simply of the rearrangement of these four basic elements into new combinations. The combinations change, but not the four basic elements of which these combinations are composed. Change is also motivated by the desire of these four basic elements to form pure states. This explains why heavy things fall back to earth and air and fire rise up. The universe, in this picture, strives to return to an equilibrium position composed of four pure layers of matter consisting of earth, water, air, and fire, which approximates the physical world as we observe it. The bottom layer is the earth on which sits the ocean or water, above which floats the atmosphere or air. Fire in this picture is represented by the heavens with their luminous bodies, the sun, the moon, and the stars.

Empedocles' division of the material universe into four basic, immutable, and repeatable elements parallels the division of the phonetic universe into the 26 basic, immutable, and repeatable letters of the alphabet from which all words are composed. Empedocles' system eventually evolved into the classification scheme of modern chemistry, in which all material substances are described in terms of the approximately 100 immutable atoms or elements of which they are composed. An intermediary step in this evolution was that of the alchemists, who added mercury, salt, and sulfur to Empedocles' four elements to describe the material world. The alchemists were on the right track in the way they described nature in terms of elements and compounds. They made the simple error of assuming that gold was an amalgam rather than a pure element. Alchemist's dreams of transmuting elements was realized in the 20th century with the use of nuclear reactions.

The desire to resolve the paradox posed by Parmenides and accommodate change within a static world also led to the formulation of the concept of atoms by the two Greek physicists Leucippus and Democritus. According to these philosophers, the process of dividing and subdividing matter could not be carried out ad infinitum, but would eventually lead to particles called atoms, which could no longer be subdivided. They were right. The universe is composed of tiny indivisible immutable atoms or particles invisible to the human eye. The Greek word atom literally means "uncut." According to the atomists, there are a finite number of different types of atom that differ from one another, like the letters of the alphabet, by their size and shape. Each object of the universe is composed of a different combination of atoms just as each word is composed of a different combination of letters. "They saw the analogy with what the alphabet had done to language and likened their atoms to letters" (McLuhan, 1964, p. 86). The atomists explained change as the formation of new combinations of atoms. The individual atoms, however, did not change—consistent with Parmenides' idea of immutability. The prediction of atoms some 2,500 years before their actual discovery is a tribute to the imagination of the early Greek physicists. The first modern proponents of the atom, Boyle and Dalton, borrowed the idea directly from them.

Although the effects of the Parmenidean paradoxes on Empedocles and the atomists was a creative spur to their imagination, the influence on other thinkers was not always so positive. The impact in the long run proved to be destructive to the empirical spirit of Greek philosophy and science. Plato, for example, resolved the Parmenidean paradox by creating the concept of two worlds. There is the World of Perceptions, where things appear to change, and there is the World of Ideas, where all is static and unchanging as Parmenides had proved. The artificial separation of these two domains—the empirical and the theoretical—reinforced by alphabetic writing, discouraged the empiricism of the pre-Socratic philosophers and reinforced the theoretical bias of Greek thinking.

Aristotle, also responding to the Parmenean challenge, created an artificial separation between the imperfect changing sublunar world and the ethereal unchanging heavens—the domain that lies beyond the moon. Aristotle's a priori assertion that the heavens are unchanging and a physical domain distinct from the earth provided an obstacle to the development of empirical astronomy against which Copernicus and Galileo had to struggle some 2,000 years later. Plato and Aristotle diverted the Greek spirit away from learning through empirical observation to speculation and philosophizing by means of logic and rationality. Logic and rationality later proved to be critical ingredients in the development of modern science, but only when integrated with empiricism and experimentation.

9

The Impact of Alphabet Writing on the Greek Spirit

THE GREEK READING PUBLIC

We have traced the influence of alphabetic literacy on the Greek intellectual achievements of science, logic, and philosophy. Now we focus on its effect on social, cultural, economic, and political affairs in ancient Greece.

At first the impact of the alphabet was confined to a few elite in the society who were able to read and write. A reading public did not emerge in Greece until over 500 years after the first introduction of the alphabet. There are few references to the reading of books or libraries during the "golden age of Greek literature. Those rare libraries that did exist were small private collections consisting of less than 100 scrolls each" (Kenyon, 1951, pp. 35-36).

In the transition from Plato to Aristotle's generation, an increased use of books became evident. It is obvious from the study of Aristotle's writings that he had access to a library of philosophical works. Many of his own works represented compilations of the ideas of other philosophers or collections of empirical evidence published in earlier works. Reference to Aristotle's library is found in the writings of Strabo (XIII, 1.54). By the time of Aristotle, the habit of reading was being established.

This development completely changed the nature of Greek society, particularly Athenian society. The Greek spirit before the golden age was deeply rooted in the oral tribal traditions as epitomized by Homer. The new literature as represented by Plato and Aristotle actively opposed this particular mind-set and attempted to create a new mentality and a new mode of education based on rationality and the preeminence of the individual.

Their position eventually prevailed, due more to the activities of the book manuscript copyists and booksellers than to the actual arguments Plato and Aristotle presented in their books. As McLuhan (1964, chap. 1) pointed out, "the medium is the message," and the mere use of books promoted rationality and a new style of education independent of the content of what was written. Even the written forms of Homer's oral poetry contributed to the downfall of the oral tradition. Homer in book form had a much different impact on Greek culture than when presented in its original oral form. Plato had a sense that the impacts of writing were complex as the following passage from his dialogue Phaedrus indicates:

> [Letters,] said Theuth, will make the Egyptians wiser and give them better memories; it is a specific both for the memory and for the wit. Thamus replied: O most ingenious Theuth . . . this discovery of yours will create forgetfulness in the learners' souls, because they will not use their memories; they will trust to the external written characters and not remember of themselves. The specific which you have discovered is an aid not to memory, but to reminiscence, and you give your disciples not truth, but only the semblance of truth; they will be hearers of many things and will have learned nothing; they will appear to be omniscient and will generally know nothing; they will be tiresome company, having the show of wisdom without the reality.

THE VISUAL BIAS OF THE ALPHABET

Media not only have an impact on social patterns, but also directly affect the psyche and ways in which people think and learn. "The effects of technology do not occur at the level of opinions or concepts, but alter sense ratios or patterns of perception steadily and without any resistance" (McLuhan, 1964, p. 18). A medium of communication creates a sensory bias and, hence, a new cognitive style. Preliterate cutures existed in an acoustical world where all information was processed simultaneously in real time. Literate societies, in contrast, developed a visual bias in their perceptions because literacy involves the use of the visual faculty in which information is processed in a linear sequential manner letter by letter or word by word.

The alphabet—by separating the sound, meaning, and appearance of a word—separated the eye from the rest of the senses, especially the ear. Preliterate man is multisensual, whereas alphabetic man is highly visual. "Between Homer and Plato, the method of storage began to alter, as the information became alphabetized, and correspondingly the eye supplanted the ear as the chief organ for this purpose" (Havelock, 1963).

The Greeks created visual space, the geometric space treated in Euclid's elements. With alphabetic literacy, visual metaphors for knowledge crept into usage in the Greek language. We use similar metaphors in English as the following examples illustrate. Our word idea derives from the Greek word *eidos*, "the appearance of a thing." Theory derives from the Greek word *theorein*, "to view" (the word *theater* has the same root). The term *speculate* derives from the Latin specere, "to look."

The English word *see* refers to either knowledge or sight by eye. The terms *vision* or *sight* (insight, foresight) connote knowing. Other visual metaphors abound; *light* refers to knowledge and *darkness* to ignorance, whereas to reflect is to think. The term *contemplate* comes from the Latin contemplate, "to observe." Terms such as *bright, brilliant, illuminate, clear,* and *lucid* also link knowing and seeing. The Greek words *idea* and *theory* cannot be found in Homeric Greek. Both these words are products of the alphabet and the new visual stress it fostered.

Plato acknowledged the new role of the eye in the postliterate revolution of rationality and learning:

> The sight in my opinion is the source of the greatest benefit to us . . . given us a conception of time, and the power of enquiring about the nature of the universe; and from this source we have derived philosophy, that which no greater good ever was or will be given by the gods to mortal man. This is the greatest boon of sight. (Plato, Timaeus, 47a).

The visual bias of the Greeks reflected itself in the special emphasis placed on geometry. It is reported that above the doorway into Plato's Academy hung the sign LET HIM NOT ENTER WHO KNOWS NOT GEOMETRY. "Geometry was used to develop a conception of the earth and of the universe . . . Science found its ideal in geometry" (Innis, 1972, pp. 64–65).

THE INVENTION OF NATURE

With the alphabet the Greeks began to see things differently, in a more fragmented manner. They invented the idea of nature, which they called phusis (or physics). The Greeks separated man and his artifacts from nature. Nature for the Greeks was simply the totality of the universe minus man and his culture. Once the Greeks had objectified nature, they treated it as something to be studied scientifically. "The discovery of nature has been described as one of the greatest achievements of the human mind since it was the basis of the idea of universal law."

The objectification of nature by the Greeks has had implications in the West far beyond the development of natural science. It soon became an object to be exploited, subdued, and conquered for man's economic benefit. This parallels the similar attitude of the Hebrews whose deity is quite separate from his creation. Man is also considered separate from the rest of creation over which he was given dominion: "And God created Man in His own image . . . And God said unto them, Be fruitful, and multiply, and replenish the earth, and subdue it: and have dominion over the fish of the sea, and over the fowl of the air and over every living thing that moveth upon the earth" (Genesis 1:27-28).

The Hebrews considered themselves created in the image of the Creator with license to subdue the earth for their own needs. A nonliterate people would never conceive of this role for themselves. Tribal people are unable to separate themselves from nature; they are nature, an integral part of the environment. Wilfred Pelletier, a Canadian Indian, claims that Western-trained environmentalists, no matter how sophisticated their training and how earnest their concern, can never have the same feeling, understanding, or concern for the environment as a native person. "We are the trees, we are the rivers," he exclaims. "You can never know them the way we do."

The separation of man and his artifacts from nature explains why the Greeks never studied the effects of their own tools or artifacts despite their avid interest in nature. Unfortunately, this tradition has become part of our Western heritage—to ignore the impacts of our technology. Hall and Hall (1975) observed the inability of science to grasp environmental forms: "Quite simply the Western view is that human processes, particularly behaviour, are independent of environmental controls and influence." The specialization that the alphabet encourages discourages one from thinking holistically or environmentally.

Another reflection of the fragmentation and specialization that alphabetic literacy encourages is the way the Greeks subdivided knowledge. They separated their studies by subject and created the fields of geometry, logic, physics, cosmology, astronomy, metaphysics, ontology, epistemology, aesthetics, ethics, politics, rhetoric, and dialectics. This spirit also influenced the way in which social, political, and economic activities were organized in Greek society and the new role played by the individual.

THE EMERGENCE OF THE INDIVIDUAL WITH ALPHABETIC LITERACY

With the emergence of a reading public through the increased access to books, a new attitude developed in Greek society regarding the way in which an individual related to his society and family. The fragmentation that alphabetic literacy encouraged led to the separation of man from nature and also the individual from his society and family. "They [the Greeks] created the Individual Man. Individualism was born, where alone perhaps it could have been born, in the narrow cradle of the diminutive republic founded by a people endowed with unique social and intellectual gifts" (Robinson, 1948, p. 195). One of the unique intellectual gifts Robinson referred to was alphabetic literacy. Greek individualism was spread first by Alexander's conquests and then by those of Rome until it became the norm in the Western world.

Before literacy the Greeks had little notion of the individual, as the epics of Homer indicate. The Iliad celebrates glory even at the price of death. The Homeric heroes put the well-being of Hellas or their tribe before their own personal well-being. Homeric man is judged solely on the basis of his success, independent of his volition or intentions. Homeric man has no conception or experience of knowledge. Knowledge is never separated from action nor is it separated from the emotions into the subjective and objective. There are few boundaries in the Homeric world that separate the individual from his society.

It is only with Hesiod that we first encounter an individual who speaks for himself. Homer never referred to himself in all of his works. Hesiod, in contrast, provided autobiographic details, admonished his reader in the first person, and developed his own unique literary style. The individuality that arises is not based on selfishness, but shares the acceptance of individual moral responsibility that parallels the developments in Hebrew Scriptures. "Hesiod too has a Fall, and if man himself escapes divine retribution for wrongdoings, yet his house will pay the penalty. Men have a moral responsibility which animals do not" (Hadas, 1952, p. 36).

Hesiod was followed by a number of lyric poets—Archilochus, Alcman, and Sappho—who gave expression to their individual experiences and personal feelings. Seventh-century Greece was characterized by two developments: the gradual rise of "free non-nobles" and the individual (Ehrenberg, 1968, p. 21). The cause of the non-nobles was championed by the tyrants who exploited the discontent of this class to usurp power. Codified law was introduced to meet the demands of individuals for greater justice. It also introduced a separation between *nomas*, or public law, and *ethos*, or private practice and personal habit. In the oral tribal world of Homer, no such separation existed. With the emergence of individualism, the uniformity of a shared ethos is replaced with the enforced uniformity of nomas through codified law.

Individualism also influenced religious practices and created a new religious movement among the Greeks of the sixth century B.C. Orphism provided a "new consciousness of the self and a new feeling for human life" (Innis, 1972, p. 57). The Orphic religion gave impetus to the concept of the soul, which was later elaborated by Heraclitus, Socrates, and Plato and formed the basis of their humanism and individualism (McLean & Aspell, 1971, p. 11). The Ionian philosophers contributed greatly to the development of the idea of the individual. The empirical and rational approach of these early philosophical physicists increased the individual sense of self-sufficiency. Heraclitus, who believed that man shared in the Logos that ruled the cosmos, strongly supported the aspirations of the individual over the masses. "To me one man is ten thousand if he be the best."

Heraclitus looked to himself as the source of his strength: "Man's character is his 'daemon,' his destiny. I searched for myself." With Heraclitus the meaning of the Delphic saying "Know thyself" changed. The Homeric interpretation was that the Greek should realize his limitations as a mortal by pursuing the golden mean of moderation and following the gods. With Heraclitus, "Know thyself" became an indispensable part of a program of individual self-enhancement. This goal overlapped with part of the program pursued by the Sophists. The Sophists were private tutors who taught young men the art of self-improvement and self-sufficiency. Their credo was expressed most succinctly by Protagoras: "Man is the measure of all things, of those being, that they are, of those not being, that they are not."

The Sophists carried their individualism to extremes. They believed that truth and morality were relative and depended on the individual. It was for this reason that they were opposed by Socrates and Plato. Aside from his opposition to their relativism, Socrates actually shared many of the concerns of the Sophists. For Socrates, man was also the measure of all things, but his concerns were more spiritual than those of the practical-minded Sophists. He is credited with shifting the emphasis of Greek philosophy from natural science and materialism to humanism and ethics. At the core of Socrates' teaching was the idea of improving the individual by improving his soul.

The concern for the individual expressed by Socrates and the Sophists also manifested itself in the arts. Painters, sculptors, poets, and playwrights continuously chose man as the subject of their artistic works. "Wonders are many in the world, and wonder of all is man" (from Sophocles' *Antigone*). The tragedies of the fifth century concerned themselves with the problem of the individual vis-à-vis religion, the state, and society.

With the conquests of Alexander the Great and the creation of an empire consisting of culturally mixed groups, a new era in Greek politics was born in which the individual played an even more prominent role. "Man as a political animal, a fraction of the polis or self-governing city had ended with Aristotle; with Alexander begins man as individual" (A. J. Carlyle). Within the confines of the Greek city-state in which all the citizens shared a common racial origin, language, religion, and cultural background, elements of tribal traditions survived despite the rise of the rationalistic, individualistic, alphabetic man. With the Alexandrian conquests, a new mosaic of races, religions, and creeds was created in which cultural uniformity could not be taken as the norm. To facilitate the administration of such a contingency, a new form of uniformity was required. Alexandrian officials created the notion of an empire of subjects who, although culturally and linguistically diverse, were nevertheless distinct individuals and hence were equal before the law.

The Hellenistic solution for administrating a diverse empire based on the rights of the individual within the context of a codified law became a pattern to be imitated by other administrations. The Roman, Byzantine, Islamic, and modern European empires provide a number of examples of this pattern.

THE SEARCH FOR TRUTH AND BEAUTY

One of the most dramatic impacts of alphabetic literacy was an increase in the level of abstraction of Greek thought as reflected in religious and legal practices and in the development of abstract science, deductive logic, axiomatic geometry, and rational philosophy. This abstraction is also seen in a new vocabulary not found in Homer, which spontaneously emerges with alphabetic literacy and includes the notions of truth, beauty, and art.

In Homeric society, as in all other preliterate societies, no distinction was made between art and technique. The Balinese, for example, have this expression: "We have no art; we do all things well." The Greeks, however, under the impact of alphabetic literacy, which encourages analysis and other forms of fragmentation, abstracted the notion of art and objectified it. They invented art just as they invented nature.

The Greek concept of art incorporated the abstract notion of beauty, which was distinguished from skills or crafts. The word *art* still retains both of its original meanings: the original preliterate idea of technique and the newer notion of a beautiful object or performance, as reflected in *Webster's New World Dictionary* definitions: (a) skill, (b) any craft or its principles, and (c) a making of things that have form as beauty.

Another abstraction pursued by the Greeks was truth. The Hebrews were also concerned with truth, but from a moral point of view, as in the admonition in the Ten Commandments: "Thou shall not bear false witness against thy neighbor" (Ex. 20:16). The Greeks developed a much more abstract and objectified notion of truth. The truth for the Hebrews was more intuitive and self-evident. It stemmed directly from their faith in God and the maintenance of their covenant with him.

For the Greek, a new form of truth emerged based on rationality and differing from traditional values of tribal solidarity. Plato attacked poets like Homer because they epitomized the old style of education based on imitation or mimesis rather than his new style, which entailed training young people to reason through each problem on its own terms. "Once Plato's Republic is viewed as an attack on the existing education apparatus of Greece, the logic of its total organization becomes clear" (Havelock, 1963, p. 13).

Plato encouraged his students to use logic, science, and rationality (Havelock, 1963, p. 25) to find fresh solutions to problems instead of relying on the traditional remedies of the past. Together with a training in mathematics and logic, Plato encouraged his students to formulate the problems of human existence in scientific terms (Havelock, 1963, p. 31).

The impact of the alphabet was to introduce both a new style of education and a new approach to problem solving. The new rational philosophers such as Plato could feel only disdain for the poets whose roots extended back to the oral tradition. "The oral state is still for Plato the main enemy" (Havelock, 1963, p. 41). "The imitative poet who aims at being popular is not by nature made, nor is his art intended, to please or to affect the rational principle in the soul; but he will prefer the passionate and fitful temper, which is easily imitated" (Plato, Republic, 605). "Plato attacked the pedagogical value of poetry and of Homer by pointing to the contrast between philosophy and poetry, truth and sham, and expelled poets from the state" (Havelock, 1963). He believed that there existed "an ancient quarrel between philosophy and poetry," and that the only salvation for society was the triumph of philosophy and rationalization over the poets—in other words, the triumph of alphabetic literacy over the oral tradition. "Until philosophers are kings, or the kings and princes of this world have the spirit and power of philosophy . . . cities will never have rest from their evils; no, nor the human race as I believe" (Plato).

10

The Hellenistic and Roman World Empires

THE HELLENISTIC WORLD

One of the alphabet's influences was to establish a uniformity of the written word and hence of administrative procedures. It was in this climate that the Greeks began to implement their policy of cultural uniformity. They attempted to Hellenize the rest of the world through colonization and military conquest. Alexander the Great, a student of Aristotle, conquered the entire civilized world, from the eastern end of the Mediterranean to India, establishing outposts of Greek culture wherever he went. The dispersal of Greek ideas and administrative forms was facilitated by the easy transport of books and documents made possible by the use of papyrus and the alphabet. His world empire was short lived and did not survive beyond his own untimely demise after which it split into four dynasties: the Antigonids in Macedonia; the Attalids in Pergamum; the Ptolemies in Alexandria, Egypt; and the Seleucids in Persia.

Alexandria was a particularly active center and became the focus of Hellenistic learning through the growth of the famous library there. The library also functioned as a university, a center of research, and a museum housing the greatest number of scientific specimens that had ever been assembled up to that point in history. It was here that Euclid developed his famous Elements of Geometry in 300 B.C. Alexandria was also famous for its systematic study of astronomy. Aristarchus showed that the distance from the earth to the sun was much greater than that to the moon and proposed a heliocentric theory of the universe 1,800 years before Copernicus. The quality of astronomical data collected at Alexandria was so accurate that it was not equaled or surpassed until the observations of Tycho Brahe. Other notable scientific accomplishments included the biological classification schemes and the geographical studies of Strabo.

At its height, the library at Alexandria contained 700,000 volumes. Books were collected from all over the world. The Hebrew Scriptures were translated into Greek. Educated slaves serving as scribes were organized to produce large numbers of books. In fact, book publishing became such a lucrative enterprise that the Ptolemies banned the export of papyrus to Pergamum where another library had been organized to rival the one in Alexandria. This led to the large-scale production and use of parchment as a medium for writing in Pergamum.

As a result of the publishing activities at Alexandria and Pergamum, a mass reading public emerged for the first time in history, which created an even greater demand for books. The existence of a widely distributed reading public in both Hellenistic and Roman Egypt has been deduced from the examination of papyrus fragments representing a broad range of literary works found in archaeological ruins of a large number of provincial towns of ancient Egypt (Kenyon, 1951, pp. 21–25).

GREEK ORIGINS OF LATIN CULTURE

The spread of Greek culture through conquest took place to the east, whereas its spread to the west was through colonization. Cumae, the first historical Greek colony in Italy, was founded by the Chalcidians about 740 B.C. and soon thereafter became a center of civilization. The Etruscans and Romans both received their alphabets from this Greek colony. The achievements of the Greek settlements in Italy in turn influenced the mother country and contributed to the Hellenization of the southern Italians and the spread of Greek influence to the Romans, Etruscans, and other peoples of northern Italy.

Greek influences not only entered Rome directly from the Greek settlements to the south but also from the Etruscans, a partially Hellenized culture that exerted the greatest influence on the development of early Rome of all the non-Latin cultures in Italy (Hadas, 1952, pp. 3-11). They taught the Romans many of the practical skills of organization and engineering that later proved to be Rome's greatest strength.

The Romans freed themselves from the Etruscans through conquest in 510 B.C. after which they gained military control of Italy. They then turned their attention to the remainder of the Mediterranean world, successfully invading and conquering all of these states, including Carthage and Greece, and establishing a world empire.

Like the Akkadians who had conquered the Sumerians and then adopted their culture, the Romans absorbed Greek culture. "Captive Greece took her fierce conqueror captive and introduced her arts into rude Latium" (Horace, Epistles 2.1.156). The Romans connected their history with that of the Greeks by relating their origins to Greek mythology. They claimed they were descendants of the Trojans through Aeneas. "No observer ancient or modern, could fail to be impressed by the extent of Roman indebtedness to Greece" (ibid.).

ROMAN LETTERS AND LITERATURE

The Romans borrowed their alphabet directly from the Etruscans who in turn had borrowed it from the Greeks and just as the Greeks had borrowed it from the Phoenicians. The first Latin alphabet bears an almost exact resemblance to the alphabet used in the southern Etruscan cities of Veii and Caere where Latin-Etruscan contact was strongest. The Etruscan had the practice of inscribing their gifts such as vases filled with wine with an inscription. As they traded with the Romans they presented them with inscribed tributes and the Romans borrowed this practice. The first Latin inscriptions of this nature date back to the period between 620 and 600 B.C. Within approximately 50 years, Latin inscriptions were being used to inscribe law codes and other public functions.

As with the Greeks, the Romans transformed the alphabet to serve their own needs. The Etruscan alphabet did not have the Greek letter omicron, so the Romans borrowed it directly from the Greeks and transformed it into o. They retained the same order of the Etruscan/Greek letters as well as their sound value, but changed their names, shortening them for convenience; Alpha became A; beta; B: gamma, C; delta, D. They also inserted a newly divised letter G to replace Z, for which they had no use. During the first century B.C., they reintroduced Y and Z, which they placed at the end of the alphabet. Our English alphabet is based almost exactly on the Roman alphabet. The letters J, U, and W, however, were added during the Middle Ages. The J is a variant of I and hence was placed just after it. U and W are variants of the letter V, which explains their position just before and after this letter.

The early Latin alphabets had a diversity of letter forms, and the direction of the writing was left to right, right to left, and in some cases, boustrophedon. With the emergence of Rome as the dominant political power in Latium in the beginning of the third century B.C., the writing system became normative and settled into a left-to-right direction. The first grammar school appeared in Rome circa 250 B.C. Over the next 250 years, Rome imposed its writing system over the entire Italian peninsula, "replacing the writing systems of Etruscans, Umbrians, Samnites, Picentes, Messapians, and Greeks" (Wallace, 1989). From the Italian peninsula, the Romans spread their alphabet through conquest and civil administration to the far corners of Europe.

Roman literature, which did not appear until the end of the third century, began as little more than translations of Greek literature. Latin literature, even according to the standards of the Romans, never equaled that of the Greeks. Literature served a different function for the Romans. It was not a central concern, but rather an adornment of cultivated life. Because in later times Rome stood as the transmitter of Greek culture to the rest of Europe, Roman literature was destined to have an important impact on the development of Western or European culture despite that it was not central to its own culture.

The Romans made their mark on Western civilization not on the basis of their writings, but on the basis of their accomplishments in the practical arts, including architecture, civil engineering (roads, aqueducts, bridges, and water mills), town planning, civil administration, law, and military technology and organization. Their bias to the practical is reflected in the words Virgil used in describing Rome's destiny through the speech of Aeneas' father, Anchises:

> Others, I doubt not, shall beat of the breathing bronze with softer lines, shall from marble draw forth the features of life; shall plead their causes better; with the rod shall trace the paths of heaven and tell the rising of the stars: remember thou, O Roman, to rule the nations with thy sway—these shall be thine arts—to crown Peace with Law, to spare the humbled, and to tame in war the proud. (Aeneid, 6.847)

The Romans clearly looked on the practical arts as the fulfillment of their destiny and the fine arts as only an afterthought. In some cases, they actually expressed disdain for literature, as in a saying of Cato the Elder: "The art of poetry was not respectable; if a man engaged in it or applied himself to junketings he was called a wanton." The Latin term for poet, poeta, is not native, and the same term, scriba, was used for both *poets* and *scribes*.

Despite the Romans' disdain for the arts and the paucity of their literary output compared with the Greeks, the technology of the alphabet ,nevertheless, had an important impact on the development of their culture vis-à-vis the practical arts to which they applied their energies. The alphabet provided a model for the organized and systematic way in which they pursued their practical arts.

Although the Romans did not excel at literary creativity, they did make considerable use of writing. As in Alexandria, there was an active trade in books (Hadas, 1954; Kenyon, 1951), and publishers made use of slaves as readers and copyists to mass produce (by the standards of those days) books for commercial sale to supply the private libraries that, according to Seneca, "had become as common as baths in the houses of the rich" (Hadas, 1954, p. 68).

There is also evidence from a number of literary sources that Roman schoolboys were taught the art of reading and writing. "Boys learn in accordance with a written model (praescriptum); their fingers are held, and they are guided by the hand of another through the forms (simulacra) of the letters, then they are told to copy what is put in front of them and improve their handwriting by comparison with it" (Seneca, Epistulae Morales, 94.51).

A more elaborate passage of Quintilian suggests an improvement on the technique described by Seneca as well as the importance of penmanship :

> As soon as the child has begun to know the shapes of the various letters, it will be no bad thing to have them cut as accurately as possible on a board, so that the pen may be guided along the grooves. Thus mistakes such as occur with wax tablets will be rendered impossible; for the pen will be confined between the edges of the letters and will be prevented from going astray. Further by increasing the frequency and speed with which they follow these fixed outlines we shall give steadiness to the fingers, and there will be no need to guide the child's hand with our own. The art of writing well and quickly is not unimportant for our purpose, though it is generally disregarded by persons of quality. Writing is of the utmost importance in the study which we have under consideration and by its means alone can true and deeply rooted proficiency be obtained. But a sluggish pen delays our thoughts, while an unformed and illiterate hand cannot be deciphered, a circumstance which necessitates another wearisome task, namely the dictation of what we have written to a copyist. (Hadas, 1954, p. 25)

Another technique apparently employed by the Romans, according to Quintilian, was the fashioning of ivory letters to be used as toys by young children to acquaint them with the alphabet (Hadas, 1954, p. 25).

One measure of the importance of writing to the Romans was that they developed a technique of shorthand stenography, which they used to provide written minutes and proceedings of the Senate, the acta diurnal, and the acta senatus (Harvey, 1978). The practice of using shorthand was introduced by Cicero and taught to his secretary, a freedman named Tiro (Hadas, 1954).

The widespread use of writing in Rome is attested to by the frequent references to this form of personal communication and the description of a number of schemes for writing in codes or ciphers. Suetonius, describing Augustus' private communications, wrote, "Whenever he wrote in cipher he wrote B for A, C for B and the rest of the letters on the same principle, using AA for X" (Hadas, 1954, p. 17). (Note that X was the last letter of the Roman alphabet in those days.)

ROMAN ORGANIZATION

The impact of the alphabetic writing with which all educated men in Rome were acquainted can be seen more in the nonliterary practical affairs in which the Romans prided themselves than in their actual literary output. The influence of the uniformity, regularity, and linearity that the alphabet subliminally promotes is reflected in all Roman forms of organization—from their military and civil administration to their architecture and town planning. As with the Greeks, literacy greatly influenced all aspects of Roman life, transforming an oral tribal society into a civilized one. "They extended lineality into an Empire and homogenization into the mass processing of citizens, statuary, and books" (McLuhan, 1962, p. 76).

This highly visual bias of the Roman spirit is reflected in town planning and road building. "Roman roads and Roman streets were uniform and repeatable whenever they occurred. There was no adaptation to the contours of local hills or custom" (McLuhan, 1964, p. 99). The roads that carried the messages, the papyrus on which the messages were written, and the alphabetic code in which they were written all contributed to the vast administrative apparatus that constituted the Roman Empire. "The spread of writing contributed to the downfall of the Republic and the emergence of the Empire. With the growth of administration the power of the emperor was enhanced" (Innis, 1972, p. 100).

Uniformity and fragmentation also influenced the organization of the military. "The phonetic alphabet was the greatest processor of men for homogenized military life that was known to antiquity" (McLuhan, 1964, pp. 104–105). The Roman legions not only defended Rome, but became a public-works machine re-creating the pattern of Roman organization all over the world.

Rome further exploited the principle of fragmentation by using its military to divide and conquer and, once that was accomplished, to divide and rule. The Romans perfected the military techniques of division through the creation of the legions, which today go by the names of *battalions* and *divisions*.

One of the paradoxical aspects of this fragmentation is that, looked at another way, it becomes centralization, in which all of the fragments are controlled by one authority. "All roads lead to Rome" expressed the extreme form of centralization that constituted Roman administration of its empire.

ROMAN LAW

The organization of a bureaucracy based on writing influenced other aspects of Roman life, such as the codification of the law and the rise of individualism; these have survived to become an integral part of Western civilization. Roman law did not begin as a written code, but rather arose out of an oral law whose roots can be traced back to the time before writing had been introduced to the Italian peninsula. Law was at first in the hands of the priests who had absolute control over its enactment and administration.

As democratic institutions developed, deliberative assemblies demanded that the law be made accessible by reducing it to a written form. The codification of Roman law followed the patterns established by the Greeks. The Romans, however, placed a greater importance on law than did the Greeks and soon developed legal forms far more sophisticated than their predecessors. The importance of law to the Romans was alluded to in the earlier quotation of Virgil, in which he stated that Rome should "crown Peace with Law." Cicero also stressed the importance of law to Romans: "We are servants of the law in order that we may be free."

One of the innovations and achievements of the Romans was the development of contract law, which dealt with both the conveyance of property rights and the entering into of mutual obligations on the part of the contractors. Roman law tended to be more practical and less abstract than Greek law. "The reasons underlying the legal system should not be inquired into, otherwise much that is certain would collapse" (Neratius). As a result of this spirit, a great deal of emphasis was placed on precedents. As a consequence, compendia and digests of the law and legal decisions were needed—a factor that led to the organization of law libraries.

A natural consequence of the emphasis on law was the rise of the individual. "The development of the Empire and Roman law reflected the need for institutions to meet the rise of individualism and cosmopolitanism which followed the breakdown of the polis and the city state" (McLuhan, 1964, p. 99). The new emphasis the law placed on the individual as distinct from his society or family also had consequences in Rome in terms of religion.

The law carefully distinguished between the civil and religious responsibilities of the Roman citizen. Jesus, who lived under Roman law in the province of Judea, invoked this principle when he was forced by his interrogators to choose between his religious beliefs and civic duty. "Render therefore unto Caesar the things which be Caesar's and unto God the things which be God's" (Luke 20:25).

11

The Arabs
and Islamic Culture

THE PROPHET AND LITERACY

In each of the cultures studied, the acquisition of alphabetic literacy has had a major impact on the social interactions and intellectual development of the society. This pattern is dramatically repeated in the case of the Arabs. The roots of Islam and the rise of Arab culture can be traced back to the introduction of alphabetic literacy to this people. The Arabian peninsula, before the arrival of the Prophet Muhammad, was the home of a preliterate polytheistic society ruled by tribal mores and traditions, particularly in the northern and central regions. In the fertile areas of the south in what is presently Yemen, there thrived a prosperous culture, the Sabeans, with a literary tradition. The Sabeans utilized an alphabetic script, but it was not destined to become the predecessor of classical Arabic. This honor fell to the Nabatean script developed from the Aramaic writing system by the Nabateans who occupied that part of the Fertile Crescent bordering on the northern edge of the Arabian peninsula. Through trading activities, the nomads of northern and central Arabia came in contact with the Nabateans and borrowed their script, which they used primarily for economic activities in their trading cities. This script, however, eventually evolved into the classical Arabic into which the Koran was eventually transcribed.

According to tradition, this script was also used in pre-Islamic times to transcribe special poems that were the prize winners of the famous poetry contests held yearly at the sacred stone in the Ka'bah at Mecca. Seven odes, the al-Mu'allaquat, were honored by being inscribed in golden letters and hung on the walls of the Ka'bah, originally the Arabian center for polytheistic worship (Safadi, 1978, p. 7).

Aside from the few instances of writing just referred to, communications in pre-Islamic Arabia were totally oral. The people were basically nomadic and mistrustful of the written word (Hitti, 1964). The Prophet Muhammad changed all of this through the Koran, a collection of the transcriptions of his prophecies and revelations. The Koran became the centerpiece of Islamic culture and transformed the Arabs from an oral people to a literate one.

Some scholars such as Hitti believe that Muhammad specifically wanted to create a literary tradition. "Evidently what was primarily weighing on Muhammad's heart was the observation that the Jews had a book, a revelation, and the Christians had a book and were all progressive and prosperous, whereas the Arabians had no book and were comparatively backward" (Hitti, 1964, p. 31).

Hitti's assertion is partially true, but his statement must be qualified. The Koran was not composed in the same way that the other books were written. It contains revelations and teachings of the Prophet that had originally been transmitted orally directly to the people (Nicholson, 1969). The elements that now constitute the Koran were collected over the period of the Prophet's lifetime and were only canonized after his death. All unauthorized versions were burned, leaving one single authorized version, which has remained unchanged to this day.

The following passage describes the Prophet's first vision, which took place in a cave on Mount Hira when Mohammed was 40 years old. It reveals the subtle tension that exists between the literate and oral traditions in Islam.

> One night in the month of Ramadan the Angel appeared to him and said, "Read." He answered "I am no reader." Then the Angel seized him with a strong grasp, saying, "Read," and as Muhammad still refused to obey, gripped him once more and spoke as follows: "The Sura of Coagulated Blood (XCVI) Read in the name of the Lord who created man of blood coagulated. Read! Thy Lord is the most beneficent who taught by the Pen. Taught that which they knew not unto me." The prophet was frightened and thought it a dream at first. "I awoke," said the Prophet, "and me thought it was written in my heart." (Nicholson, 1969, pp. 150–152)

The two episodes indicate that perhaps the Prophet was not literate or at least wished not to appear so, as has been suggested by some scholars. "He himself is said to have been illiterate, and merely to have 'recited' the words he heard out of heaven" (Arberry, 1964, p. ix). The epithet ummi, which is applied to Muhammad in the Koran and is translated as "illiterate," does not necessarily indicate that he was unable to read and write, but only that he was not acquainted with Hebrew Scriptures. The Koran suggests that he may have had other reasons to appear illiterate (Nicholson, 1969). "Thou [Muhammad] didst not use to read any book before this [the Koran] nor to write it with thy right hand; else the liars would have doubted" (Koran XXIX, 47).

Despite the possibility that the Prophet may have been illiterate, it is still evident that writing was an important part of the new tradition, as the use of the many metaphors referring to reading and writing indicate. The reference in Sura XCVI to the Lord "who taught by the Pen" is rendered by some translators as "who taught the use of the Pen" (Nicholson, 1969; Safadi, 1978).

ISLAM AND THE
INTRODUCTION OF WRITING INTO ARABIA

Further evidence for the integral part played by writing in Islam is the historical correlation between those who introduced writing into Arabia and those who played a role in the development of Islam in its earliest days. Many of these figures were the students of Harb, the man who popularized writing among the aristocracy of Quraysh, the tribe of the Prophet Muhammad. One such figure was Muawiyah, the founder of the Umayyad dynasty, which ruled the first great Muslin empire.

Shortly after its establishment in Mecca, writing spread to the nearby town of Medina. It was the Medina scribe, Zayd ibn Thabit, who became the Prophet's most famous secretary and was entrusted with the task of collating and writing the first codex of the Koran. There is a clear association between the earliest scribes of Islam and those who introduced writing into Arabia. It is obvious that writing played a vital role in the spread of Islam and that in turn Islam played a vital role in the spread of literary in Arabia and many of the lands that the Arabs conquered in the name of Islam.

The following story of the Umm al Kitab illustrates the important role that writing and the notion of the book play in Islamic tradition. "According to tradition God sent the Book to the Jews but they distorted its true meaning. He then sent it to the Christians who also distorted its meaning. Finally he sent it to the Arabs and they got it right." This story also reflects the Islamic belief that Moses and Jesus were also prophets of God, but Muhammad was the final Prophet who completed the divine revelation to man.

ISLAM AND THE PRESERVATION OF THE ORAL TRADITION

Despite the importance of written communication to the advent of Islam, the oral tradition remained vital. The Koran was not first transmitted through the written word, but by the oral tradition. In addition to the Koran, the comments on the Koran, known as the Hadith, were also transmitted orally at first, but later were transcribed and transmitted in a written form. A mixture of both the written and oral traditions has always coexisted in Islamic culture. The name of the Koran is derived from *kara'a*, "to read, recite, or discourse," which indicates the oral manner in which these writings are interpreted. "In Sura XVII 92 it [kara'a] certainly stands for 'to read,' but the most frequent meaning is rather to recite, to discourse" (Gibb & Kramer). Even the written transmission of the Koran and Hadith was achieved through a combination of oral and written activity. The professor or teacher would read aloud his written copy, which the students would copy down. They would then tidy up their versions through further study and present them to their professor for his signature to testify that the copy was an authorized version.

The Koran, as the sole source of authority in the Islamic world, was subject to careful reading and study. Despite the intimate connection with the oral tradition, the Koran became the vehicle whereby the Arabs acquired alphabetic literacy. "The Koran is the most widely read book ever written" (Hitti, 1964, p. 42). In addition to its use for religious purposes, it also became the textbook from which almost all young Moslems learned to read Arabic.

THE ISLAMIC WORLD EMPIRE

Inspired by the Prophet and fired by the zeal of Islam, the Arabs soon conquered and controlled a world empire stretching from Spain and North Africa in the West to Indonesia and the Chinese border in the East. Within a couple of centuries, the nomadic polytheistic, preliterate tribal people of Arabia were world rulers, making use of a well-organized administrative bureaucracy that governed with the aid of a legal code based on the abstract ethical principles of monotheism. Part of this transformation was due to the alphabetic literacy encouraged by the Koran, and part was due to borrowings from the sophisticated cultures of Egypt, Syria, Iraq, and Persia, all of which had employed one or another of the alphabetic scripts in pre-Islamic times.

In the earliest days of Islam, a distinction was made between Arabs and foreigners. Most of the administrators were actually members of these conquered cultures and hence foreigners. As time passed, the distinction between Arab and foreigner began to diminish under the egalitarian principle fomented by Islamic law, in much the same way that the distinction between Greek and barbarian disappeared in Hellenistic culture. Cultural uniformity was reinforced by the uniformity of a common language and script. A universal culture emerged whose capital moved from Mecca to Damascus under the Umayyad caliphs and then to Baghdad under the Abbasid caliphs. In our ensuing discussion, we use the term *Arabic* to refer to the world culture based on the Arabic language, rather than restricting the term to the culture of the Arabian peninsula.

We turn now to an examination of the influence of alphabetic writing on the development of Islamic or Arabic culture. It is not possible to establish any causal relations or direct impacts. As with the other cultures we have studied, we find, however, that the alphabet provided a climate in which abstract notions such as monotheism, codified law, science, and logic could flourish.

ISLAMIC LAW

One of the areas where the alphabet had a particularly dramatic impact on Arab culture was in the administration of justice and formulation of law. Although the form of the law was influenced by alphabetic writing, its authority was derived directly from the Prophet and the divine origin of his revelations. "In the eyes of a Muslim, the law is an integral part of his religion; in Islam, law is more important even than theology" (Savory, 1976, p. 54).

This attitude toward law represented a major change in Arabic culture when contrasted with pre-Islamic values. In pre-Islamic Arabia, the tribe was preeminent, and the rights of the individual were secondary. Any legal rights an individual had were vested in his family and tribe, the tribe being an extension of the family. The family and tribe looked after "his rights, avenged his wrongs, inherited his property, and answered for his crimes" (Savoy, 1976, p. 55).

Another element in this legal transformation was the increase in the abstract and universal character of an individual's ties to his community.

The blood tie of family and tribe was abandoned and replaced by loyalty to the Muslim community. All Muslims were equal in the sight of God and the law. The aristocratic structure of pre-Islamic society disappeared. "The personal life of the individual emerged—even though, in certain respects, the community assumed legal and social rights which were formerly vested in the tribe" (Savoy, 1976, p. 57).

What is important about this development, from the point of view of our study, is the parallel transformation that occurred in Mesopotamia, ancient Israel, Greece, and Rome, in which the alphabet (or phonetic writing) was accompanied by three developments: (a) the demise of tribal society, (b) the rise of law based on the rights and the responsibilities of the individual, and (c) the creation of a universality of humankind that transcends family and tribal links. The transformation of the system of justice was not immediate. Although religion became the sole authority for law in the Muslim world, only 80 verses of the Koran deal with legal matters. At first Islamic society did not possess a formal legal code or system of justice. Yet as with the Mesopotamians, Hebrews, Greeks, and Romans, phonetic writing soon suggested a codified pattern of legislation that, in the latter part of the eighth and ninth centuries manifested itself in a body of religious law, the Shari'ah, which regulated all aspects of Muslim life (Savoy, 1976).

Law schools at Medina and Kufah in Iraq were established to study, expand, interpret, and administer this body of law. At first the different schools caused a fragmentation of interpretation of the law as each school developed its own unique point of view. This situation was soon rectified, and a unification of the law and its interpretation were realized by Al-Shafi'i, "the father of Islamic jurisprudence." He enunciated four principles as the basis of his legal system: (a) the Koran, (b) the accepted doctrine of the Prophet, (c) the consensus of the Islamic community, and (d) analogical reasoning (Savoy, 1976). The first two principles were key. However, it is interesting to note that, as with the Greeks and Romans, logic entered into the consideration of jurisprudence.

In addition to the religious law and courts covered by Shari'ah, there also developed a secular system of jurisprudence administered by the Mazalim courts, which dealt with civil and criminal matters not covered by the Koran.

ARABIC LITERATURE AND SCIENCE

The influence of alphabetic literacy on the development of Arabic literature followed a pattern similar to that of other cultures. Poetry appeared before prose in pre-Islamic Arabia in a form highly developed linguistically, metrically, and artistically (Maramura, 1976, p. 61). Arabic prose did not emerge until the eighth or ninth century.

Before this time, prose was confined to the Koran, the Hadith, and oratory, which is largely an oral form. The links to prose are through the Koran, that is, religious thought based on monotheism, as was the case initially for Hebrew prose and to some extent for Greek prose. At first the alphabet, monotheism, and codified law developed together in Islamic culture following a pattern similar to that of the Hebrews. There then followed the introduction of science, logic, and philosophy, which were borrowed from ancient Greek sources through Jewish, Syriac, Christian, and Persian mediators.

Baghdad, the capital of the Abbasid dynasty from 750 to 1258, became a center of learning. The philosophical and scientific works of the Hellenistic world were translated and introduced to the Muslims. This stimulated new and original research and study in which the Arabs made significant and lasting contributions (Maramura, 1976, p. 65). Baghdad became, as an Arab historian described it, "the market to which the wares of the sciences and arts were brought, where wisdom was sought as a man seeks after his stray camel, and whose judgment of values was accepted by the whole world" (Gibb, 1963, p. 46). Baghdad soon possessed a library and an academy that in many ways rivaled the original library at Alexandria (Hitti, 1964).

One of the factors that contributed to the intense literary activity in the Arab world was the sudden availability of paper in the mid-eighth century, replacing the more expensive media of parchment, papyrus, and leather (Gibb 1963). The Arabs borrowed this know-how from the Chinese and eventually passed it onto the West.

The contribution of the Arabs to the overall development of modern science was twofold. First, there are the advances and discoveries they made totally on their own. Second, there is the role they played in the preservation of and transmission to Europe of the scientific accomplishments of ancient Greece, India, Persia, and China. The Arabs built upon the base of Greek learning contained in the Syriac and Persian literature both in translation and in the original Greek (Wickens, 1976).

One area of Arab success was the field of *chemistry*—a term that derives from the Arabic *alkimiya*, "alchemy" (the prefix al means "the"). Although alchemy eventually came into disrepute in Europe, historians of science recognize that alchemy as practiced by the Arabs laid the foundations for modern chemistry.

Another area where Arabic science was extremely successful and went far beyond the Greeks was medicine and pharmacology, particularly in observation, diagnosis, and treatment with drugs (Savory, 1976). "It was they who established the first apothecary shops, founded the earliest school of pharmacy and produced the pharmacopoeia" (Hitti, 1964, p. 141). Important contributions were also made in agriculture, magnetism, geography, optics, ophthalmology, astronomy, and mathematics.

Arab mathematicians transmitted the Hindu place number system to Europe and made significant advances in algebra (Savory, 1976). Arabic astronomical observations were more accurate than those previously made because of improvements in the instruments of astronomical observation. They increased the size of the armillary sphere and astrolabe and thus reduced the errors of observation. They were able to calculate the radius of the earth and the meridian degree with only 1% error, by A.D. 820 (Savoy, 1976). In the meantime, Europe still slumbered under the illusion that the earth was flat.

Although the Arabs made vital contributions, they fell short on the development of modern science. "They introduced the objective experiment, a decided improvement over the hazy speculations of the Greeks. Accurate in the observation of phenomena and diligent in the accumulation of facts, the Arabs nevertheless found it difficult to project proper hypotheses and draw truly scientific conclusions" (Hitti, 1964, p. 147). However, they did lay the foundations for modern science, which they transmitted to Europe.

12

Numerical Notations
and the
Mystery of Zero

Thirty spokes share the wheel's hub, but it is the hole in the
center that provides its usefulness.

—*Lao Tsu from the Tao Te Ching*

THE MYSTERY OF THE DISCOVERY OF ZERO

In our review of Mesopotamian, Hebrew, Greek, Roman, and Arab cultures, we have seen how the abstract nature of alphabetic writing has
provided an environment in which abstract intellectual ideas and social
institutions could flourish. The only other notation or system of visual
signs that has played as important a role in promoting abstract thought
has been the place number system, whereby all numbers can be represented by 10 numerical signs, the Hindu–Arabic numerals: 0, 1, 2, 3, 4, 5,
6, 7, 8, and 9. The key to the whole place number system is the zero element or sign, 0, whose invention was an achievement of Hindu mathematics and thought.

Numerical notation and writing systems have always been closely
linked. In fact, the first forms of notation were numerical and took the
form of tallies etched on bones. This might explain the fact that in the

Semitic languages the words for *scribe* and *count* are the same (i.e., SPR). Writing and the notation for abstract numbers emerged in Sumer at precisely the same moment in history, from a common progenitor, clay accounting tokens.

In the earliest alphabetic scripts (e.g., Semitic and Greek), the letters of the alphabet were also used to represent numbers. The first 10 letters represented 1 through 10, respectively. The next nine letters represented 20, 30, and so on to 100. This system of numerical notation required virtually all of the letters of the alphabet.

The Romans also developed a number system using the letters of the alphabet, but in a more abstract manner. A much smaller number of letters was needed—namely, I, V, X, L, C, D, and M. The system was also more abstract because the numerical values depended to some extent on the placement of the signs. For example, IV = 4, whereas VI = 6. There is no zero element in this system, and numerical calculations are extremely clumsy. Consider the product 56 X 6 = 336 using Hindu–Arabic and Roman numerals:

$$
\begin{array}{r}
56 \\
\underline{\times\, 6} \\
336
\end{array}
$$

versus

$$
\begin{aligned}
\text{LVI} \times \text{VI} &= \text{L} \times \text{V} + \text{V} \times \text{V} + \text{I} \times \text{V} + \text{L} \times \text{I} + \text{V} \times \text{I} + \times \text{I} \\
&= \text{L} + \text{L} + \text{L} + \text{L} + \text{L} + \text{V} + \text{V} + \text{V} + \text{V} + \text{V} + \text{V} + \text{L} + \text{V} + \text{I} \\
&= \text{CC C X X X V I}
\end{aligned}
$$

The calculations involving long division or fractions become even more complicated with Roman numerals. The advantages with Hindu–Arabic numbers are obvious.

Arabic numerals are obviously the most abstract numerical notation possible, just as the alphabet is the most abstract form of writing. It is ironic that the alphabet achieves its abstraction through phonetization, whereas the Arabic numerals are logograms or ideograms that represent 10 numerical values including zero. The letters of the alphabet and the Arabic numerals, however, share four important features that enable them to act abstractly:

1. Each system contains a small number of elements: 26 letters (for the English alphabet) and 10 numerals.

2. Both systems form a complete set. The total set of possible spoken words can be represented alphabetically, and any number, no matter how large it may be, can be represented in terms of some combination of the 10 numerals 0 through 9.

3. The individual elements of the two systems, the letters and the numerals, are atomic. That is, they are identical and repeatable.

4. The values (sound or numerical) of the aggregate elements (the words or numbers) of the system depend not only on the atomistic components (the letters and numerals) of which they are made up, but also on their order. In other words, both the letters and their order determine a word, and both the numerals and their order determine a number. For example, ON is not the same as NO nor is 18 the same as 81.

The development of the place number system depended on the invention of the concept of zero—an idea that seems extremely simple and yet is quite sophisticated. For this reason, the discovery of the concept of zero is often taken for granted. Many assume that the Greeks, the originators of formal geometry and logic, made use of it. We are taught about zero in elementary school, geometry in high school, and logic in college. Therefore, many people believe logic and geometry are mathematically more sophisticated than the concept of zero. This is not true and is an example of the distortion of the history of science effected by textbooks and school curricula, as pointed out by Kuhn (1972). The Greeks never developed the operational notion of zero, yet their achievements in geometry and logic were unparalleled. As a result of not having a concept of zero, their arithmetic calculations were laborious and their development of algebra was stunted.

Hindu mathematicians invented zero more than 2,000 years ago. Their discovery led them to positional numbers, simpler arithmetic calculations, negative numbers, algebra with a symbolic notation, as well as the notions of infinitesimals, infinity, fractions, and irrational numbers. The historians of mathematics have always been puzzled that the germinal idea of zero was a discovery of the Hindus and not the Greeks. Laplace, the great mathematician of the 18th century, wrote:

It is India that gave us the ingenious method of expressing all numbers by means of ten symbols, each symbol receiving a value of position as well as an absolute value, a profound and important idea which appears so simple to us now that we ignore its true merit. But its very simplicity and the great ease which it has lent to all computations put our arithmetic into the first rank of useful inventions, and we shall appreciate the grandeur of this achievement the more when we remember that it escaped the genius of Archimedes and Apollonius, two of the great men produced by antiquity. (Dantzig, 1954, pp. 19–20)

More recent historians of mathematics have been equally surprised. Particularly puzzling to Tobias Dantzig was the fact "that the great mathematicians of Classical Greece did not stumble on it" (Dantzig, 1954, p. 30). For Constance Reid, the great mystery of zero is that "it escaped even the Greeks" (Reid, 1964, p. 4).

Why did the ideas of zero and algebra develop in India and not ancient Greece? The explanation of this phenomenon does not lie in an examination of Greek mathematics, but rather in a comparison of Greek and Hindu philosophy. Paradoxically, it was the rational and logical thought patterns of the Greeks that hindered their development of algebra and the invention of zero.

THE INHIBITION OF GREEK IMAGINATION DUE TO LOGICAL RIGOR

As discovered earlier, it was the ancient Greeks who invented and developed formal logic. Their achievement has only been surpassed within the past 300 or 400 years by logicians and mathematicians, who based their work on the foundations laid by the Greeks. Logical arguments permeated all areas of Greek scientific and philosophical thinking. A high value was placed on analytic thought, which the Greeks applied to almost all fields of human knowledge. The Greek thinkers, however, became captives of their own methods. They rejected the validity of empirically observed phenomena such as motion and change because of the logical arguments of Parmenides. Certain other theoretical ideas such as infinity, infinitesimals, atoms, and the vacuum were similarly rejected because of logical considerations. In a sense, the Greeks became slaves to the linear either–or orientation of their logic. As a result, their imagination was limited, making it difficult for them to conceive of the concept of zero.

The Hindus, in contrast, had no such intellectual tradition of formal logic. They were less constrained in their thinking and more imaginative, which proved to be an invaluable asset and led to the development of zero. The history of zero actually begins with the Babylonians long before Greek or Hindu mathematics. The Babylonians used a primitive notion of zero for special applications. They were never able to develop this concept any further, however. The Babylonian scribes used a symbol as a place holder to denote a blank space (Van der Waerden, 1954). Zero in their system never became a number to be added or subtracted or to be used to simplify their calculations as was the case with the Hindus.

The only other independent development of zero was that of the Mayans. They used zero for place numeration, but zero never entered into mathematical calculations such as multiplication or division. Like the Babylonian zero, the Mayan zero represented a dead end—a mere historical curiosity.

The Mayan zero was a completely independent discovery, but there is a possible connection between the Hindu zero and that of the Babylonians. Because commerce existed between Mesopotamia and India, there could be a link, but finding historical evidence to support this hypothesis is not easy. However, even if it is true that the Hindus borrowed the idea, the question remains of why the Greeks were unable to borrow the Babylonian idea and develop it in the same way. In fact, the ancient Greeks were nearer in time and closer geographically to the Babylonians, and hence would have been in a better position to borrow the idea than the Hindus. The transmission of other mathematical ideas from the Babylonians to the Greeks during the Seleucid period of the third century B.C. took place a full century before the first appearance of zero in the Hindu literature. Neugebauer (1952) indicated that Babylonian material was available to both Greeks and Hindus.

Whether borrowed or invented, we are still left with the mystery: Why were the Hindus able to deal with zero and not the Greeks? To gain insight into the great mystery of why zero escaped the mathematically sophisticated Greeks, let us recall the impact that the alphabet had on the development of Greek thought. Soon after the introduction of alphabetic writing into Greece, a unique transformation of its intellectual life began (Havelock, 1963; McLuhan, 1962). Thales marks the beginning of the Greeks' use of the deductive logic and rationality that, within a short time, invaded all areas of Greek thinking, unleashing new powers of analysis. Rationality became the be all and end all of Greek thought, but it eventually hamstrung its development by restricting its creativity to the narrow confines of logical rigor.

Parmenides' logical arguments against change and the notion of nonbeing poisoned the intellectual climate for nurturing the ideas of zero. Remember how he argued that State A could not change into State B because then State A would no longer be, but nonbeing was not possible? Nonbeing could not be (see chap. 7 for more details). In contrast to the Greeks, Hindu thinkers accepted nonbeing.

In Buddhism, negativity and non-being are positive and good because the Buddhist takes his point of departure in the negative side of life and the world. For him the being of existence is a "nothing"; likewise non-being is the negation of something negative and is, therefore, something positive. The Greeks and the Hebrews were united in the idea that nonbeing is something dreadful; being, however, is a genuine reality and the true good. (Boman, 1960, pp. 57–58)

Nonbeing was a state that Hindus and Buddhists actively sought in their attempt to achieve Nirvana or oneness with the whole cosmos. Nonbeing was something concrete—a state that could be discussed. Therefore, the concept of zero was totally consistent with Hindu philosophy, and hence presented no problems to Hindu mathematicians. The Hindus did not have any logical cultural stumbling blocks to overcome as the Greeks did. Nothing stood in the way. In fact, their religious ideas reinforced their notion of nonbeing and, hence, zero. In conclusion, my hypothesis is that Greek thought, particularly that of Parmenides, discouraged the conceptualization of zero, whereas Hindu thought encouraged this notion.

Our explanation of why the Hindus, and not the Greeks, invented zero solves only one mystery. There remains the question of why the Hindus also developed the notions of negative numbers, simple arithmetic computational methods (algorithms), algebra with a symbolic notation, infinitesimals, and infinity. Although the Greeks made progress in these areas, they never developed them as fully as did the Hindus. They had no notation for an unknown quantity in their algebra. Dantzig (1954) suggested that the Greeks were at a disadvantage in developing a symbolic notation because they used their letters to denote numbers and hence had no symbols available for representing unknown variables. This excuse is lame. The reason that the Hindus developed algebra, negative numbers, and infinity is simply that they pioneered the concept of zero and the Greeks did not. Each of these mathematical concepts, as we show, is related to the concept of zero.

FIRST APPEARANCE OF ZERO

One of the first uses of the zero symbol was made by the Hindu mathematician Pingal sometime before 200 B.C. (Datta & Singh, 1962). The use of zero in calculations appeared for the first time in the Bakhshali manuscript (A.D. 200), where use of place value was also found. The treatment of zero as a number, with equal status to other numbers such as 1 or 2, was found in the Pancasiddhantika: "In Aries the minutes are seven, in Gemini they are three, two, one, zero (sunya) each repeated twice" (Datta & Singh, 1962, p. 75–81). The name for zero used in this and later texts is sunya (pronounced *shunya*), which literally means "empty space" or "blank." Zero was first symbolized as dots in the

Bakhshali manuscript and later as small circles or Os. The use of dots to represent zero is used as a metaphor in the Vasavadatta: "The stars shone forth . . . like sunya-bindu (zero-dots)" (Datta & Singh, 1962, pp. 75–81).

The Hindus developed all the arithmetic and algebraic properties of zero. The operations of addition and subtraction with zero first appeared in A.D. 505 and a century later the definition of zero as a - a = 0 (Datta & Singh, 1962, p. 239). By A.D. 750, zero had all the algebraic properties it now possesses as can be found in the Trisatika by Srîdhara:

> In addition cipher makes the sum equal to the additive, when cipher is subtracted (from a number) there is no change in the number. On multiplication and other operations (division by another number, squaring, square rooting, cubing, cube rooting) on zero the result is zero. Multiplication of a number by cipher also gives zero. (Datta & Singh, 1962, p. 240)

PLACE NUMERATION

The development of place numeration, whereby all numbers can be represented by the 10 symbols, 1, 2, 3, 4, 5, 6, 7, 8, 9, and 0, is probably the most important application that was made of the zero or sunya symbol. Our present number system was invented by the Hindus and transmitted to Europe by Arab and Persian scholars. The mathematicians of Baghdad adopted the Hindu system around A.D. 1000. They translated the Hindu term *sunya* into the Arabic *sifr*, which also means "empty space."

Originally, the term *cipher* was intended to denote only the zero element, the unique element of the number system, but eventually the entire number system became known as the *cipher system*. As with other innovations, the new number system was forbidden in some European cities because the Church objected to their Islamic origin. As a consequence, Arabic numbers had to be used secretly. The word *cipher* soon came to mean "a secret code," as indicated by the word *decipher*. To distinguish between the entire number system and its unique element, 0, the term *zero*, short for *zepharino* (the Latinized form of cipher), came into use to denote 0.

Place numeration not only simplified the expression of numbers; it made possible a tremendous simplification of arithmetic calculations. All present-day procedures of multiplying, dividing, and square and cube rooting were developed using the place number system invented by the Hindus. Many of the Hindu techniques were transmitted to

Europe by the Arab mathematician, al-Khwarizmi, from whose name is derived the term *algorithm*, meaning a procedure for performing a mathematical calculation. The scientific revolution of the Renaissance could never have taken place if these simpler modes of calculation had not been made possible by the Hindu place number system.

The scientific revolution also benefited from the Hindu development of algebra. The Hindus' successes in developing algebra stemmed, like their success with zero, from their ability to work intuitively without being unnecessarily held back by the need for logical rigor. The essential element in their development of algebra was their invention of zero, which proved to be a powerful mathematical concept.

ALGEBRA OR *AVYAKAT-GANITA*

Algebra or aryakat-ganita (literally, the science of calculation with the unknown) first appears in Hindu literature in the Bakhshali manuscript, one of the first works in which the concept of zero appears. It is here that we also first find the concept of negative numbers (Srinivasiengar, 1967). The number -7 is denoted by 7+. It is believed that the + sign represents the letter kha, the first letter of the Hindu word ksaya, which means "to diminish." In later works, -7 is denoted by $\dot{7}$ or $\overset{o}{7}$ where the ˙ sign or ° sign stands for zero. The numeral 7 lies below the zero sign to explicitly denote that -7 is seven less than zero.

The first representation for the unknown is also found in the Bakhshali manuscript. The expression used was *yadrccha venyase sunya*, which literally means "put a zero [sunya] in the place of the unknown or desired quanticy" (Srinivasiengar, 1967, p. 32). The symbol **o** was also used to represent the unknown, sometimes in an elongated version, 0, to distinguish it from zero.

The use of the sunya (zero) to denote the unknown incorporated the idea of leaving a space blank for the unknown. The idea started the Hindu mathematicians off along the road, which led to the development of algebra. The use of the symbol for zero to denote the unknown suffers, however, limitations. For one thing, there is the possibility of confusing the unknown with zero. It is sometimes useful to incorporate zero into an algebraic equation, which would be difficult if the unknown were also represented by the 0 symbol. Another limitation is that sometimes more than one unknown appears in an equation. Once the Hindus had developed the notion of dealing with equations by incorporating an unknown through the use of the sunya symbol, they expanded their notation to include more than one unknown. One of their tricks was to use the abbreviations of the colors to represent multiple unknowns.

An example of this is found in the representation of the equation
197x + 1644y + z = 6302:

ya 197	ka 1644	ni 1	ru 0
ya o	ka 0	ni 0	ru 6302

The two lines are equated to each other. The symbols ya, ka, and ni are abbreviations for *yakava* (red), *kalaka* (blue), and *nilaka* (yellow)—the unknowns. The symbol ru means "to this add. The term *ka 1644* means 1644 times ka, and *ka 0* means no ka (Datta & Singh, 1962). This latter device was particularly useful for problems with multiple unknowns. The idea of representing the unknown with a symbol, however, first derived from the use of *sunya*.

INFINITY, INFINITESIMALS, FRACTIONS, AND IRRATIONAL NUMBERS

The mathematics of infinitesimals and infinities was first pioneered by the Hindus and then later refined by the mathematicians of the Renaissance. The concept of infinity arose through the consideration of the division of a finite number by zero:

> In this quantity consisting of that which has cipher for its division, there is no alteration, though many may be inserted or extracted as no change takes place in the infinite and immutable God, at the period of the destruction or creation of worlds, though numerous orders of being are absorbed or put forth. (Datta & Singh, 1962, p. 243)

The Hindu mathematical concept of infinity was related to and reinforced Hindu theological notions:

> At the time of the world's creation, the Infinite and Indestructible Lord Almighty created crores [1 crore = 10 million] of beings. At the time of the great Deluge, all these beings go back to His form and are immersed in Him. Neither process makes any change in Him. (Srinivasiengar, 1967, p. 82)

This passage illustrates the notion that the sum of a finite quantity and infinity is still infinity: x + □ = □.

The Greeks, in contrast, were uncomfortable with the notion of infinity, which they rejected out of hand as meaningless, irrational, and

logically impossible (Dantzig, 1954). The concept of infinity leads naturally to the idea of an infinitesimal through the division of a finite quantity an infinite number of times. The Greeks came close to the idea of the
infinitesimal as expressed by: (a) Zeno's paradoxes, (b) Eudox's method
of exhaustion, and (c) Archimedes' method of determining pi by succes-
sively inscribing and circumscribing polygons to a circle. In the end, the
Greeks horror of infiniti led to their rejection of the notion. The Hindus,
however, felt no such revulsion, and evidence for a primitive form of the
infinitesimal is found in the Bhaskara II manuscript of A.D. 1150: "The
product of [a number and] zero is zero, but the number must be
returned as a multiple of zero if any further operations impend" (Datta
& Singh, 1962, p. 242). One also finds the example a/0 x 0 = a, which is
correct only if the 0 symbol is taken to represent the infinitesimal (Datta
& Singh, 1962, p. 243).

The Greeks rejected fractions, arguing that the "unit was indivisible," although they did make use of ratios:

> Official Greek mathematics before Archimedes does not have any
> fractions at all. This was not, however, because they were not
> known, but rather because one did not wish to know them. For
> according to Plato, the unit was indivisible and, in Plato's words,
> "the experts in this study were absolutely opposed to dividing the
> unit. (Republic 525E) Fractions were scorned at, left to merchants;
> for, so it was said, visible things are divisible, but not mathematics
> units." Instead of operating with fractions, they operated with ratios
> of integers. (Van der Waerden, 1954, p. 49)

The Hindus, in contrast, had no ideological aversion to dealing with
fractions: "The rational operations with integers and fractions, as they
are taught in our schools, are formed in exactly the same forms in the
Hindu arithmetic books. With the number themselves, they reached us
by way of the Arabs" (Van der Waerden, 1954, p. 57). The Greeks also
had an aversion to irrational numbers. There is a legend that a member
of a Pythagorean society was thrown overboard on a voyage for reveal-
ing to a member of the crew the darkly held secret that the length of the
hypotenuse of a right triangle whose sides were each of unit length
could not be expressed as the ratio of two integers. This fact, which was
so disturbing to the Greek mathematical mind, posed no problem to the
Hindus. "The Hindus, unlike the Greeks, regarded irrational roots of
numbers as numbers. This was of enormous help in algebra, and Indian
mathematicians have been much praised for taking this step" (Bayer,
1968, p. 242).

CONCLUSION

We have considered a number of examples of how the logical rigor of Greek thought hampered mathematical development and led to the rejection of (or failure to develop) a number of ideas, such as zero, place numbers, fractions, negative numbers, irrational numbers, infinity, infinitesimals, and a symbolic notation for algebra. These concepts were embraced and developed by the Hindus, who were logically less rigorous than the Greeks, but were perhaps, as a consequence, more intuitive. These Hindu discoveries have played a key role in the subsequent development of Western science and mathematics.

It is ironic that the evolution of Western theoretical thought required a detour into the East to develop the essential mathematical tools of place numbers and algebra so essential for the development of modern science. We have explained the necessity of this detour in terms of the logical rigidity that took hold of the minds of the Greeks as they developed their tools of rationality and logical analysis under the influence of the phonetic alphabet. If our hypothesis is correct, we must explain why the alphabet had such a negative effect on the Greeks and not on the Hindus.

The Hindus also made use of an alphabetic script, but did not seem to be overwhelmed by logic although they made use of it. There are several factors that might explain the difference in the impact of logic. First of all, the Greeks were the first to develop a totally phonetic alphabet complete with vowels, which exactly and precisely rendered their spoken language into a written form. The Hindu alphabet was derived from the Aramaic alphabet, an offshoot of the original 22 consonant Semitic alphabet. As a consequence, it did not incorporate the vowels in the same explicit way as the Greek alphabet did. Second, Hindu society retained its oral traditions much more strongly than the Greeks did. As a consequence, the alphabet effect was not as powerful as it was in Greek society. In fact, it can safely be said that no other culture was as strongly affected by the alphabet as was ancient Greece. Perhaps this because it was the first society to develop three radically new techniques for organizing information: (a) the totally phonetic alphabet complete with vowels, (b) deductive logic, and (c) abstract science. The Greeks were simply unprepared for some of the negative side effects of being logically too rigorous.

Another interesting lesson emerges from this story of the discovery of zero in India. This chapter, which was originally written in 1978 and published in *ETC: A Review of General Semantics* (Logan, 1979), was written in reaction to the following passage in Tobias Dantzig's (1954) book *The Language of Science*:

One who reflects upon the history of reckoning up to the invention of the principle of position is struck by the poverty of achievement. This long period of nearly five thousand years saw the fall and rise of many a civilization, each leaving behind it a heritage of literature, art, philosophy, and religion. But what was the next achievement in the field of reckoning, the earliest art practiced by man? An inflexible numeration so crude as to make progress well nigh impossible, and a calculating device so limited in scope that even elementary calculations called for the services of an expert. . . .

When viewed in this light, the achievement of the unknown Hindu who some time in the first century of our era discovered the principle of position assumes the proportions of a world event. Not only did this principle constitute a radical departure in method, but we know now that without it no progress in arithmetic was possible. . . .

Particularly puzzling to us is the fact that the great mathematicians of Classical Greece did not stumble upon it. Is it that the Greeks had such a marked contempt for applied science, leaving even the instruction of their children to slaves? But if so, how is it that the nation that gave us geometry and carried this science so far did not create even a rudimentary algebra? Is it not equally strange that algebra, that cornerstone of modern mathematics, also originated in India and at about the same time when positional numeration did?

When I read this account of the invention of zero and others, which I did not bother to quote because their Eurocentric bias was so distasteful to me, I was outraged that historians of mathematics were surprised the Greeks "did not stumble upon it (zero)." Although Dantzig is at least respectful of the achievement of the Hindu and Buddhist mathematicians, he, like other historian of mathematics who were much more scurrilous in expressing what they considered to be a paradox, angered me because of their assumption that all that was good in the Western scientific tradition should somehow follow directly from ancient Greek culture. As I have shown, there is no real mystery in the invention of zero in India; as a matter of fact, if it were not for the cultural diversity of the world's civilizations, there would have been little or no progress in our intellectual development. We in the West owe thanks to both the Indian and Islamic cultures for their contribution of the scientific revolution, which took place in Europe in the Renaissance and quickly spread to the entire globe. A similar debt is owed to the Chinese and other oriental cultures for their many inventions that traveled westward and were another essential ingredient in the development of abstract science.

I have made a particular point of explicitly acknowledging the contribution of non-European cultures in this edition of *The Alphabet Effect* because of the misreading of some critics who accuse me of a Eurocentric bias. Nothing could be further from the truth. What motivated this study was the recognition that the Science Revolution that took place during the Renaissance would have been impossible without the contribution of so many non-European cultural sources. I thank the reader for indulging me in this mission of setting the record straight. What is clear to me from my study is that it is cultural diversity that gives rise to new ideas and human progress.

There is one other addition I would like to make to this edition, and that concerns the possible role of the abacus in the development of zero or *sunya* (leave a space). If one wanted to record a result of an abacus calculation in which therewere 5 hundreds, no tens, and 8ones, and one were to write this as 58, it would not represent 508 but fifty-eight. The Hindu mathematicians did not use the characters 5 and 8 but rather the 5th and 8th letters of their alphabet, but let us for the sake of discussion use the Arabic numerals 5 and 8. I believe that the concept of zero might have arisen as a desire of the Hindu mathematicians wanting to distinguish 508 from 58 or 580. So they wrote 5 'sunya' 8 or 5 'leave a space for no tens' 8. Sunya or *leave a sapce* indicated that there were no tens and evolved into what we know as zero.

13

The Middle Ages and the Return of Alphabetic Literacy

THE FALL OF ROME AND THE RISE OF CHRISTIANITY

After the fall of Rome, alphabetic literacy underwent a sudden eclipse popularly known as the Dark Ages. This was followed by a slow, but steady recovery that culminated in the High Middle Ages and finally the Renaissance. To understand the role of literacy during this vast historic period stretching from A.D. 400 to 1400, we must study the collapse of the Roman Empire in the West and the rise of Christianity in Europe. These two major historic events are linked and can be traced back to the actions of Constantine, who became the emperor of Rome in A.D. 312.

Up to the time of Constantine, the practice of Christianity was regarded as a subversive activity that undermined the authority of Rome. As a result of the influence of his mother, Helena, a devout follower of Christ, Constantine put an end to the persecutions of the Christians. He also lent his support to the religion to which he finally converted at the end of his life. His actions led directly to the eventual adoption of Christianity as the official religion of the Roman Empire in A.D. 380.

Equally significant was Constantine's founding of Constantinople (city of Constantine) as the capital of the eastern half of the Roman Empire in A.D. 330. Constantinople became a great center of political power and has remained, to this day, one of the great cities of the world. Constantine's action, however, led directly to the split of the Roman Empire. When Constantine's successor, Theodosius, died 65 years after the founding of Constantinople, he left one half of his empire to each of his two sons. The division of the Roman Empire into two halves eventually led to the foundation of the Byzantine Empire and the fall of Rome. The Roman Empire at this time was economically exhausted from overtaxation to support its military adventures, decadent lifestyle, and other excesses. The resources of the western part of the Empire were particularly depleted, whereas Constantinople still thrived through its trade with the East. Rome survived less than 100 years after being severed from its richer eastern provinces. It was sacked by the Visigoths in 410 and again by the Vandals in 455. Its last emperor was deposed in 476 by the barbarian general, Odoacer, who declared himself King of Italy. Italy was then conquered in quick succession first by the Ostrogoths and then by the Lombards.

THE BYZANTINE EMPIRE
AND THE GREEK ORTHODOX CHURCH

Before returning to our discussion of the plight of Europe after the fall of Rome, let us first examine the developments in the eastern part of the Empire, which continued to prosper after its separation from Rome as the Byzantine Empire. The capital city, Constantinople, was in an extremely favorable geographic position to profit from trade between Europe and Asia. At first Byzantium competed with Persia for the control of Asia. It was then challenged by the Islamic empires that arose. Although the Arabs totally conquered the Persians and completely dominated the Middle East, Byzantium was able to withstand their repeated attacks until it was eventually defeated by the Turks after a reign of over 1,000 years.

At first Latin was the official language of Byzantium, but gradually Greek assumed this role, becoming the official language during the reign of Heraclitus (A.D. 610–641). Christianity was the official religion from the first, with Constantinople serving as the seat of the Chief Patriarch of the Greek Orthodox Church. Christianity spread to Russia and the rest of Eastern Europe through the office of the Patriarch.

The relationship between Constantinople and Rome was complicated. The Roman emperor, Honorius moved his capital to Ravenna in 400.

The Germanic tribes that took over Italy also set up their capital in this city. They were Christians, but adhered to the heretical Arian sect, which did not accept the concept of the Trinity. The Bishop of Rome, who wished to maintain political independence from these Arian regimes, accepted the overlordship of the Byzantine Empire. This resulted in a somewhat paradoxical relationship between these two cities, in which Rome claimed religious authority over Constantinople while at the same time accepting its political or temporal authority. Rome played a double role of supreme religious authority of the Christian world and that of a small geopolitical state in Italy. Its political fealty to Constantinople continued until the eighth century, after which Rome looked to France for its political protection.

THE ROMAN CATHOLIC CHURCH

With the passing of Imperial Rome, followed by many years of chaos and military conquests, the only source of moral authority that remained in Italy was the Roman Catholic Church. The Pope, or the Bishop of Rome, as the head of the Church in the capital city of the Empire had historically been in a special position as far back as the second century. Tradition held that Christ had entrusted the care of the Church to Peter, the first Bishop of Rome, and hence to his successors. In the early years of the Church, the Pope's authority was challenged by other bishops who claimed to be his equal. In the fourth century, Ambrose, Bishop of Milan, was in fact the most influential bishop of his time. Eventually the Pope came to be regarded as the leader of the Church, and there soon developed in Rome a bureaucratic apparatus to administer the Church.

With the fall of Rome, there was a total discontinuity in the form of political organization and a natural displacement of the Roman autocracy or ruling class, which no longer held temporal power (Innis, 1971). In an attempt to preserve their way of life this political elite became members of the hierarchy of the Roman Catholic Church. They borrowed many of the organizational forms of Imperial Rome, which they incorporated into the Church structure. These legacies included the Curia and the office of Pontifex Maximus (the Pope). The canon law by which the affairs of the Church were administered and by which many civil matters were governed were all based on the principles of Roman law.

Although the content had been changed, the literary medium was the same, and its message was that of strict adherence to the letter of the law. As had been the case in Imperial Rome, the fathers of the Church organized and regulated human affairs through written legal codes. The medieval Christian Church, which became the dominant social institution of its time, inherited this tradition and synthesized Oriental mysticism, "Hebrew justice, Christian love, Greek belief in intellect, Roman organization and Hellenic asceticism" (Hitti, 1961, p. 162).

THE MIDDLE AGES AND THE ORAL TRADITION

The Roman Catholic Church in Europe maintained the tradition of alphabetic literacy prevalent during the classical period. Christianity, like Judaism and Islam, was a religion of the Book—in this case of both the Hebrew Scriptures (or Old Testament) and the Gospels (or New Testament). The preservation of literary skills was absolutely necessary to maintain this tradition. Literary forms were also used in canon law and in the administration of the Church.

The use of literary media in the secular world of medieval Europe, however, did not survive the fall of the Roman Empire. Political power was constantly changing hands as the various Germanic tribes vied with one another to establish their kingdoms throughout what is now modern Europe, including the Italian peninsula. This was such a chaotic and volatile period that the forms of civil administration the Romans had established over most of Europe could no longer be maintained. They gave way to a new form of government based on the older oral traditions of the Germanic tribes, which had incorporated a personal relationship between a ruler and those he governed. Loyalty to a liege was symbolized by a verbal oath of allegiance and fealty by the *vassal*—a term derived from the medieval Latin word *vassus*, "servant" (Easton, 1970, p. 293).

The personal nature of government is illustrated by the fact that the highest offices in the land were held by the personal household servants of the king, such as the chamberlain, master of the castle, marshal, or master of the stables and hence the military leader of the state. The household offices would have been relegated to servants in Roman times and the duties of the chamberlain and the marshal carried out by consuls and generals.

The system of personal loyalties extended throughout all civil interactions in medieval society. The landlord–tenant relationship of the Roman period was transformed through the infusion of the Germanic sense of personal fealty and resulted in the feudal system, with its intricate web of personal relations connecting everyone in the society from the lowliest serf to the king.

The economic unit of feudal life was the manor, which was a fundamentally self-sufficient household. Without the imperial order to maintain the road system and trade routes, the regions of Europe became more isolated from each other and came to depend only on their own resources to satisfy their needs. This decentralized economic order was closer to that of the tribal society of Europe before Roman rule than to the highly centralized mode of organization that characterized imperial times.

Another index of importance of the oral tradition in medieval life is the role played by the poets and minstrels who gave expression to the secular and religious values of the culture. It was the trouvéres of northern France, the troubadours of southern France and Spain, and the minnesingers of Germany who created and then promulgated medieval notions of nobility and chivalry.

THE DARK AGES: MYTH OR FACT?

The collapse of the Roman Empire marked the end of an era and resulted in a dramatic discontinuity in the political and social structure of Europe. As the literate forms or organization gave way to those of a more oral nature, the civil servants who processed the paperwork in the Roman bureaucracy were suddenly unnecessary. One of the major incentives to learn reading and writing suddenly disappeared. There was a dramatic drop in the level of literacy in the general population, and scholarly activities came to a virtual standstill.

Historians have branded this period the Dark Ages and have tried to characterize it as a time of ignorance and little learning. More careful scholarship has revealed that only book learning atrophied. The mechanical arts and agriculture actually thrived, with steady but modest advances being made throughout the Middle Ages.

The entire notion of the Dark Ages becomes even more absurd when one considers the steady level of accomplishments in that time (Easton, 1970). These include such outstanding achievements as the evolution of the vernacular languages of Europe and the first fruits of their respective literatures. During this period, significant steps toward the establishment of Western democracy included the proclamation of the Magna Carta and the formation of the Swiss cantons. The Middle Ages also saw numerous breakthroughs in the invention and / or application of mechanical devices, especially in the harnessing of power, and tremendous improvements in agricultural techniques, such as the development of the heavy plow and crop rotation suited to northern European farming. Finally, there were innovations even in the field of learning and scholarship, including the founding of universities, which are still operating to this day.

It was the practical arts that flourished in the Middle Ages and eventually set the stage for the Renaissance. In fact, it is difficult to distinguish the boundary between the Middle Ages and the Renaissance

(Easton, 1970, p. 545). To characterize the period as the Dark Ages simply because of the decline of book learning reflects a literary bias of historians (White, 1962).

THE TRANSITION FROM ANCIENT LEARNING TO MODERN SCIENCE

A popular misconception exists that modern science arose directly from Greek science due to the revival of learning in the Renaissance after a 1,000 years of inactivity. Not only does this analysis ignore the accomplishments of the Middle Ages alluded to earlier, but it also fails to take into account some of the negative effects of the alphabet on classical learning. The abstractness of the phonetic alphabet promoted a divorce of brain and hand, a disdain of empiricism, and excessive adherence to logical rigor among Greek thinkers, each of which inhibited the development of modern science. Greek and Latin learning, rather than being 2,000 years ahead of its time, had in fact run its course and exhausted its possibilities for further development. The decline of book learning and channeling of intellectual activity into the practical arts during the Middle Ages had a positive effect on Western learning. It permitted an infusion of new ideas from the so-called *barbarian cultures*. As a result, classical learning was revitalized when it resurfaced during the Renaissance.

With the political chaos and economic depression that followed the collapse of Rome, the luxury of abstract scholarship could no longer be indulged. Men turned their minds to the practical questions of survival and, as a consequence, made significant breakthroughs in technology. They built on the foundations of Greco–Roman technology to which they added their native innovations or those borrowed from the Islamic world or from China. When Western Europeans finally returned to the tradition of Greek learning, they no longer divorced the practical arts from scholarly activity. A new amalgam had been created that combined the logical rigors of classical Greek learning and the mathematical achievements of the Arabs with the empirical spirit of medieval mechanics. This led to the systematic experimentation and astronomical observations of Galileo, Torricelli, Brahe, and others.

MEDIEVAL TECHNOLOGY

The historical scholarship of Lynn White has shown that the Middle Ages was a period of great technological progress (White, 1962, 1968), which resulted in a steady increase in the standard of living of the ordinary peasant. "In technology, at least, the Dark Ages mark a steady and uninterrupted advance over the Roman empire" (White, 1940, p. 141). A steady increase in the level of prosperity was realized through a string of improvements in metallurgy and mechanical devices applied to agriculture and the harnessing of animal, water, and wind power (White, 1962). Health standards also improved as a result of the increasing level of technological sophistication (Giedion, 1969).

Oddly enough, the motivation for improvements in metalworking likely grew out of the increased violence of warfare made possible by another medieval invention, the stirrup (White, 1962). The metal stirrup developed from the Asian toe stirrup permitted a mounted warrior to hold a lance in his arms and use the full momentum of the horse to deliver a mortal blow instead of relying on the strength of his arms. This innocent invention had many implications. To protect the mounted warrior, metal armor became sophisticated, and techniques for metalworking improved. The high cost of equipping a mounted warrior or knight was one of the key motivations for the inauguration of the feudal system, in which an estate was granted to a landlord so that he could supply a number of knights to the king's army (White, 1962).

Another medieval invention, the heavy plow, permitted large tracts of land to be plowed at once and gave rise to the manor as a cooperative agricultural community (White, 1962). The heavy plow changed the face of Europe both literally and figuratively. First, it altered the shape of fields from small square plots to long narrow tracts; and second, it increased the prosperity of those fields through the improvement of field drainage. The opening up of the most fertile soils by the heavy plow increased production and made possible the accumulation of surplus food. Other technological improvements also increased the prosperity of farming in the Middle Ages, including use of open fields, rotation of crops on the basis of a 3-year cycle, the modern harness, and nailed horseshoes.

The net effect of the increased agricultural yields was "population growth, specialization of function, urbanization and the growth of leisure" (White, 1962, pp. 43–44). It also provided a base for the beginnings of an industrial way of life. The improved standard of living allowed peasants to buy manufactured goods. "In the new cities there arose a class of skilled artisans and merchants, the burghers who speedily obtained control of their communities and created a novel and characteristic way of life, democratic capitalism" (White, 1962, pp. 78–79).

With its emphasis on profit and efficiency, capitalism proved an ideal climate for the harnessing of power for human purposes, which in the later Middle Ages took many forms:

Animal Power: The collar harness permitted the use of horses for plowing and hauling—a task relegated to the slower moving oxen before this development. The importance of horsepower is reflected in our use of the term, to this day, as a measure of power.

Water Power: The harnessing of waterpower dates back to the Roman period, but it is not clear where the idea originated because water mills seem to have simultaneously appeared in the Mediterranean region, northern Denmark, and China (White, 1962, p. 81). The Middle Ages saw the widespread diffusion of waterpower and its application to a number of different activities, including grinding grain, cutting marble, cutting wood, fulling, tanning, beer making, laundering, metal polishing, forging, and knife sharpening. The Domesday Book of 1086 indicates the existence of 5,624 mills in approximately 3,000 English communities (Hodgen, 1939). The water mills became the laboratory in which the mechanical skills of the Middle Ages developed a proficiency in the use of gears (star, crown, and worm types), cams, axles, wheels, screw mechanisms, cranks, trip hammers, and the like.

Wind Power: The principles of harnessing waterpower were applied to the wind in Europe and resulted in the windmill (White, 1962).

The harnessing of power in the Middle Ages, with its by-product of mechanical inventions, led directly to a number of subsequent innovations that affected the use of the alphabet and enhanced alphabetic literacy and the learning associated with it. Among these were the invention of the printing press and the advent of the Industrial Revolution, which is the subject of our next chapter. It also affected the nature of scientific thinking and the revitalization of classical learning to which we now turn our attention.

One influence of alphabetic literacy on the harnessing of energy was the way in which the components of a system were linked together to form a whole so that energy could be transmitted from its source to where it was needed. This achievement set the stage for the industrialization of Europe.

CLASSICAL SCHOLARSHIP

Although the level of abstract scholarship declined during the Roman period as compared with Greek learning, there was a general increase in the number of people who acquired alphabetic literacy. With the collapse of the Roman Empire, its bureaucratic structures, and the level of literacy, classical learning almost totally disappeared.

The only organized group to carry on the literary tradition of classical scholarship was the Church, which had a narrow set of interests and was not an innovative institution. Not many new scholarly works arose out of this milieu except those of a theological nature, such as the philosophical writings of Saint Augustine. His Confessions and The City of God expressed the spirit of his time. Other purely scholarly works were those of Isidore of Seville, Boethius, and the English Benedictine monk Bede, but their quality was not high.

The one valuable service that the Church provided to scholarship was preservation. Cassiodorus in the fifth century directed his monks to collect and copy Greek and Latin manuscripts, which started the Benedictine tradition of preserving classical learning. The efforts of the Church, together with the preservation of texts by the Islamic and Byzantine cultures, permitted the eventual transmission of Greek and Latin learning to Renaissance scholars.

The Church also preserved the Latin language, albeit in a medieval form. It served as the vernacular and *lingua franca* among both churchmen and scholars. As time passed, the vernacular forms of medieval Latin evolved into the early versions of the Romance languages French, Italian, Spanish, Portuguese, and Romanian. The use of Latin as a *lingua franca* of scholarship became even more valuable as a result.

CAROLINGIAN RENAISSANCE

Certain secular authorities also kept alive the Roman tradition of learning and literacy. After a period of extreme anarchy and chaos, some order began to return to Europe during the reign of Charlemagne (Charles the Great), whose empire included most of France, Belgium, the Netherlands, Germany, Switzerland, Austria, and northern Italy. Although he was illiterate, he created cathedral schools and encouraged the monasteries to spend more time on teaching and studying.

One of the immediate impacts of this short-lived Carolingian Renaissance was the development of an extremely legible and neat hieratic script known as the *Caroline minuscule alphabet*, from which we derive our modern-day lowercase Roman letters. Another fallout of this revival of learning was the medieval school curriculum of the seven standardized liberal arts consisting of the trivium of grammar (literature), rhetoric, and logic and the quadrivium of arithmetic, geometry, astronomy, and music. The trivium taught the students to read and write using the alphabet. They also learned to express themselves orally.

The quadrivium focused on mathematics, including music, which consisted of the study of the ratio of the frequencies of notes. Taken together, the trivium and quadrivium basically amount to what today we might call the 3Rs—reading, writing, and arithmetic. After a student had mastered the trivium and quadrivium, he was allowed to go on to study theology.

Unfortunately, the Carolingian Renaissance was short lived and did not survive much beyond Charlemagne's reign of peace, prosperity, and good order. One reason for this was the absence of printing to sustain the revival. Charlemagne's cathedral schools, however, eventually evolved into the medieval universities, and learning was initiated in other places.

Alfred the Great began a similar revival of English literature. Johannes Scotus Erigena created a system of Neoplatonic metaphysical thought. Benjamin of Tours, studying at the cathedral school in Chartres, applied the lessons of logic from the quadrivium to his theological speculations. He argued that reason should be used by man to reinforce his faith in certain theological issues. He used logic to attack the doctrine of transubstantiation. Saint Anselm carried the use of logic further in his attempts to develop proofs for the existence of God. He also entered into a debate regarding the nature of abstractions such as universals. Although he was an advocate of the use of logic in theology, Saint Anselm always put faith before reason. This was not the case with Abelard, a logician, who attracted a strong following of students in Paris. Although Abelard's activities were thwarted by reactionary churchmen such as Saint Bernard, who accused him of heresy, in the end, Abelard triumphed through his students who later rose to positions of influence. They included the theologian Peter Lombard and Pope Alexander III.

It was at this point in history, when alphabetic literacy was reinforcing an interest in logic, that Europe rediscovered classical learning. Scholars became particularly interested in Aristotle through contacts with the Arabs. Greek works were retranslated from Arabic into Latin, although some Greek manuscripts survived and were translated directly into Latin (White, 1940).

The works of Aristotle were at first ignored by the Church. As they came to have an increasingly greater influence in the universities, the Church tried unsuccessfully to suppress their use. When the works of Averroes, the Islamic theologian, challenging Christian dogma, were translated into Latin, the Church defensively embraced Aristotle. His ideas were incorporated into its theology, first through the works of Albertus Magnus and then through those of Thomas Aquinas. At first the acceptance of Aquinas' Aristotelian-based theology was opposed by mystics, but it eventually triumphed to become part of the official doctrine of the Roman Catholic Church. Aquinas was made a saint.

The victory and acceptance of Aquinas had an impact on science and scholarship that was as great as that on religion and theology. Aristotle's ideas moved into the mainstream of European thought. The slavish adherence to his ideas that had characterized much of classical learning, however, was challenged, paradoxically enough, by the Church. Catholic clerics challenged a number of Aristotle's positions in physics on the grounds that they seemed to limit the powers of the Creator. Aristotle's contention that a vacuum cannot exist or that the universe is finite were ruled by the Bishop of Paris in 1277 to be null and void.

This challenge to Aristotle's authority led to secular arguments repudiating elements of Aristotle's physics, such as his theory of motion that held that a body must have a force continually acting on it to remain in motion, contrary to our modern ideas of inertia. Shortly after the ruling of the Paris bishop, Jean Buridan, a philosopher at the University of Paris, proposed a theory of impetus that was a direct forerunner to Galileo's and Newton's ideas of inertia.

Buridan's work was important because it converted a scientific question based on empirical observations into a valid topic of philosophic discourse. Buridan's investigations were carried out in a new empirical philosophical climate, where the idea of putting theoretical questions to an experimental test was first taking root.

This new attitude was inspired by the work of the medieval scientist and philosopher, Robert Grosseteste and his pupil, the friar Roger Bacon, who were active at the University of Paris. Bacon actively lobbied the Pope to support the testing of scientific theories through the science of experience. Bacon's actual experiments were rather small in number and limited to optics, and his science of experience was based more on observation than controlled repeatable experiments. Nevertheless he helped create a new attitude toward science that eventually led to the experimental work of Galileo and others.

In addition to encouraging empiricism, Bacon also promoted the notion that science and technology would increase humankind's material well-being:

> Machines may be made by which the largest ships, with only one man steering them, will move faster than if they were filled with rowers; wagons may be built which will move with unbelievable speed and without the aid of beasts; flying machines can be constructed in which a man may beat the air with mechanical wings like a bird . . . machines will make it possible for men to go to the bottom of seas and rivers.

Bacon's faith in science and experimentation was motivated by the desire to solve practical problems and drew little support or inspiration from theoretical science. He correctly foresaw that empiricism would transform science. His vision was realized with the rise of modern science during the Renaissance. The new spirit of science was a marriage of the empirical, technology-based mechanics of the Middle Ages, with abstract science based on mathematics and deductive logic as originated by the Greeks operating under the influence of the alphabet effect.

14

The Printing Press: Enhancing The Alphabet

In our study of the alphabet effect, for the most part we have taken the media for the transmission of the alphabet for granted. These media included papyrus, parchment, paper, pens, brushes, and ink. These adjunct technologies naturally have had an important impact on the way in which the technology of the alphabet has been deployed. It is perhaps no accident that the greatest library in the Greek world was built in Alexandria near the Nile River. The Nile was a source of an abundant supply of papyrus, a much cheaper writing material than parchment. The invention of paper in China and its transmission to Europe in the late Middle Ages had a greater impact on the spread and use of alphabetic literacy than any other development up to that time. A good supply of paper, as we soon see, was also instrumental in the development of the art of printing.

With the printing press, we finally encounter a technology whose impact on the use of the alphabet is so great that it must be ranked in importance with the alphabet. Not only did the printing press greatly multiply access to alphabetic texts, it also, through the regularity it introduced, transformed the way in which the alphabetic text was placed on the page and was perceived by its readers. The differences between the handwritten manuscript and the machine-manufactured, printed artifact are so great that these two forms of alphabetic text must be considered as completely different media. This fact is reflected in the dramatic change in European civilization and society that the printing press effected. The impact of the printing press was of the same order of magnitude as the impact of the alphabet approximately 3,000 years earlier. The impact of the printing press, however, was more sudden and hence more dramatic.

"The discovery of printing was one of the great turning-points in the history of mankind . . . It changed the very warp and woof of history, for it replaced precarious forms of tradition (oral and manuscript) by one that was stable, secure, and lasting" (Sarton, 1957).

THE INVENTION OF THE PRINTING PRESS

Before examining the dimensions of this turning point in the history of humankind, let us first review the history of printing from its earliest origins before the invention of the alphabet. The first form of printing can be traced back to the cylinder seals used by the Sumerians to make impressions on wet clay. The first large-scale use of the technique was made by Buddhists in sixth-century China to print religious texts. They would carve a page of text in reverse on a wooden block that was then used to create multiple copies of a printed page on paper. This system did not prove to be economically viable in either China or Europe. By the 11th century, a system of movable type had been created in which there was one Chinese character per font.

The use of movable type in China never reached the stage development it eventually did in the West because of the large number of characters or type fonts required. The idea of printing with block prints and movable type spread to Europe, however, where it met the more receptive environment of alphabetic literacy. At first block prints were carved in wood as the Chinese had done. Within a short period of time, there arose a technique for printing with movable type in which each font carried one letter of the alphabet. The success of the printing press and movable type was due to the unique character of the alphabet, which permitted the mechanical production of large numbers of the same type fonts at relatively low cost, which encouraged their mass production. Relatively small-scale entrepreneurs were able to set up printing shops in every major urban center in Europe. In China, however, it was only in government-sponsored enterprises that printing could be managed (Innis, 1972).

The timing of the introduction of print (Innis, 1971) was fortuitous because it coincided with the arrival in Europe of another Chinese invention—namely, paper manufacturing. Without a cheap supply of writing materials, the printing press might not have been invented nor become the commercial success that it was.

The impetus for the invention of printing was commercial. With an increased supply of paper in Europe, there was a marked increase in the manufacture of books in *scriptoria* and *stationarii*, where copyists were employed and organized to mass-produce books. As the market for books increased, especially for the Bible and other religious texts, the early printers were economically motivated to expand their operations. Economic factors also contributed to the success of the printing press and the book trade to which it gave rise. The phonetic alphabet, with its limited number of elements, was capable of an infinite number of combinations and allowed the printing press to serve a variety of markets (Innis, 1972, p. 234).

The market for manuscripts or books existed before the invention of the printing press and was in fact one of the factors leading to this innovation. The widespread literary interest and popular demand for books increased even more once printing prices were reduced (Putnam, 1962).

The demand for books began in the Middle Ages, and we can trace three distinct periods for the production of manuscripts. The first—stretching roughly from A.D. 550 to 1200—involves exclusively the activities of the monasteries in the preservation of classical texts and the organization of scriptoria to carry out the copying tasks.

The second stage, roughly from 1200 to 1400, corresponds to the period when production of books was dominated by academics and the university booksellers or stationarii. The stationarii were licensed by the universities and charged with stocking those books required for particular courses of study at the university ((Putnam, 1962). Students obtained their books either by renting manuscripts through the offices of the stationarii or making their own manuscripts from dictations read out loud to them by lecturers at the university.

The third period, starting in 1400 and running until print took over manuscript production, began when publishing activities were commercialized outside the university (Putnam, 1962). Three major markets for manuscripts can be identified in this period: (a) the market for Bibles and other religious books, (b) the market for the newly emerging vernacular literatures, and (c) the university market. The vernacular movement in literature began with Dante's *Divine Comedy* in 1300 and Boccaccio's *Decameron* later in the century. This movement spread from Italy north to France, Germany, and England. One measure of the popularity of vernacular literature is the fact that 80 handwritten manuscripts of Wolfram von Eschenbach's *Parzival* and 60 of Chaucer's *Canterbrry Tales* have survived to this day (Steinberg, 1955). Another index of the extent of the book market in Europe is the fact that approximately 10,000 scribes or copyists made their living through the production of manuscripts (Chassant, 1864).

What contributed to the economic success of printing with the alphabet was the use of type fonts that could be mass-produced because there was such a small number needed, approximately 100, which included the upper and lowercases of the alphabet, the 10 numerals, and punctuation marks (: ! , ? ;.). The other factor is the constant repeatability of these elements so that, once a page was composed with type and printed, the type fonts could be disassembled and used again for another page. The reassembling of already manufactured typecast fonts was naturally much faster than having to carve a page in reverse from scratch.

The true innovation of the European printing press, the invention of which is usually ascribed to Johann Gutenberg, was not the press so much as the idea of using movable type. A certain amount of controversy surrounds the question of who should be honored as the first inventor of the printing press, if indeed such a person exists. It would seem that the printing press arose as a consequence of a number of experiments and innovations carried out in different places by different individuals (Putnam, 1962).

Laurens Janszoon, surnamed Coster (or Koster sacristan), of Haarlem in the Netherlands, who originally worked with block prints, was certainly one of the pioneers of movable type, as documented by Hadrian Junius, who wrote a history of Holland a century later (Putnam, 1962; Usher, 1954). Koster used wooden type fonts together with wooden block prints for the production in 1428 of *Speculum Humanae Salvationis* (*The Mirror of Human Salvation*)—a religious prayer book popular among the Benedictines. Junius also reported that Koster's workshop closed its activities after his death, but that one of his workmen conveyed his ideas to Germany where they presumably reached Gutenberg.

The development of the printing press depended on a number of other innovations in addition to the two supposedly introduced by Gutenberg. These were the use of movable, mass-produced, cast-metal type fonts and an improved mechanism for the handpress, which permitted large sheets of paper to be printed. The original handpress was derived directly from wine and cloth presses. Among the most important supporting innovations for print were paper manufacturing and an oil-based ink derived from the work of oil painters.

Perhaps Gutenberg's true contribution was to organize all of these innovations and create a commercial enterprise that made printing possible. Prior to his work on the press, Gutenberg was not concerned with manuscripts, but with the manufacturing of mirrors, according to local records. These historic records reveal that while Gutenberg was engaged in activities involving mirrors, he was also working on a printing press. He was engaged for a number of years in research and development. Gutenberg required investment capital for this activity and entered into a joint venture with Johann Fust. A misunderstanding ensued between the two, followed by a lawsuit in which Fust gained control of one of Gutenberg's presses.

Fust not only became a printer like Gutenberg, but, being a more astute entrepreneur, also became Europe's first publisher and set about systematically marketing the products of this new invention. He traveled to Paris to sell his printed edition of the Bible at one-fifth its normal price, causing a total panic among the copyists who claimed he was in league with the Devil because he was able to produce as many copies of a manuscript as he wanted.

Gutenberg received credit as the inventor of the first printing press as early as 1499 in the *Chronicle of Cologne* (Mori, 1921): "The first inventor of printing was a burgher at Mainz, and he was born at Strasbourg, and named Johann Gutenberg." Gutenberg deserved the credit he received given the lack of reward or commercial success he enjoyed during his lifetime. He gave up successful business interests and devoted all his energies and resources to perfecting his invention. We are indebted to him for his contribution, which totally transformed Western civilization.

THE PRINTING PRESS AND THE RENAISSANCE

The main market to which the printers addressed themselves was not the nobility (who prior to the press were the only class who could afford books), but rather the newly emerging middle class (Burckhardt, 1883). They were able to afford the new books and also had time to learn how to read.

The early critics of print were unable to gauge the truly revolutionary impact this medium was to have on their society and culture. To understand the magnitude of the impact of the printing press, we must carefully analyze the vast differences between the handwritten manuscript and the mechanically mass-produced printed book despite that the content of these two media was virtually identical. The first books printed were those available in manuscript form. The printers basically provided a duplicating service that reproduced existing manuscripts in larger numbers and at lower prices (Eisenstein, 1979).

McLuhan (1962) pointed out that, although the handwritten manuscript and printed book are quite different media of communication, the first producers and consumers of the printed pages considered print a continuation of the manuscript. This was the only perception the first users of print could reach because the contents of the first printed books and handwritten manuscripts were the same. They could not fathom the effects the printing press, through increased accessibility, reduced cost, and multiple copies, would have on the spread of culture and education. They could not imagine the ways in which information was to be organized or how it would be influenced by the regularity and uniformity of the printed page, or that it would introduce a visual bias into their thinking. They did not foresee how the permanency of the multiple copies of printed texts would affect the preservation of both scientific data and literary texts.

Each of these features of the printing press—uniformity and regularity, visual bias it encourages, permanency of its record, increased literacy it permits—are all features the alphabet promoted before the advent of print, albeit to a lesser degree. The printing press, however, enhanced and amplified each of these features of the alphabet, unleashing a powerful new force that completely transformed Western civilization, leaving in its wake the Renaissance, rise of science, Reformation, individualism, democracy, nationalism, systematic exploitation of technology, and the Industrial Revolution—in short, the modern world. "It brought about the most radical transformation in the conditions of intellectual life in the history of western civilization" (McLuhan, 1962, p. 159).

One of the printing press' major impacts was to reinforce or enhance a transition that was already in progress when it was first invented— namely, the transition from the Middle Ages to the Renaissance. The exact point when this transition took place is impossible to determine. However, there is no doubt that the revival in learning that took place in Italy in the 14th century, the "quattrocento revival," occurred well before the advent of the printing press in the middle of the 15th century. Therefore, the printing press cannot be said to have been a causative agent of the Renaissance. Nonetheless, many historians regard the printing press as the dividing line between the Middle Ages and Renaissance. "Four men, Gutenberg, Columbus, Luther and Copernicus, stand at the dividing line of the Middle Ages" (Kapp, 1886). The printing press marked the end of the literacy style associated with the Middle Ages and the beginning of a new one (Chaytor, 1945). It also represented a new beginning for science and technology. "The development of printing, more than any other single achievement, marks the line of division between medieval and modern technology" (Usher, 1954).

Scholars regard the advent of the printing press as a significant transition point, despite that it arrived on the scene after the quattrocento revival, because of the way in which it reinforced this revival of learning. The printing press allowed the Italian Renaissance to sustain itself, unlike the two previous renascences: the 9th-century Carolingian revival and the so-called 12th-century renaissance (McLuhan, 1962). These two earlier revivals were dependent on the spoken word and handwritten manuscripts for the transmission of their spirit. With the advent of print, the quattrocento revival could continue to gain momentum because the printing press provided a reliable medium for preserving the fruits of alphabetic literacy, freeing the energy of scholars for production of new ideas rather than merely preserving those of the past.

The printing press also encouraged a greater retrieval of manuscripts from the past as publishers looked for new grist for their mills. The new means for disseminating texts ensured that documents retrieved from the past would remain in circulation (Debus, 1978). The printing press not only increased the number of titles available, but also increased access to them. Scholars were no longer limited to the few libraries that existed during the Middle Ages; they were now in a position to create private libraries, which permitted a greater amount of scholarship to take place. Scholarship was no longer restricted to the monasteries and universities. In fact the most innovative and successful scientific and scholarly work took place outside these two medieval institutions (Putnam, 1962).

Printing allowed the impetus of the quattrocento revival to be preserved so that the Renaissance could come to full bloom, rather than dying in the bud as had happened with the revivals in the 9th and 12th centuries. Printing allowed a critical mass to develop, which led to a lift-off of the spirit of learning and created what Eisenstein and Panofsky referred to as the "permanent Renaissance" (Debus, 1978, p. 6). "To put it briefly, the two medieval renascences were limited and transitory; the Renaissance was total and permanent" (Panofsky, 1972, p. 106).

In attempting to describe the interaction of the printing press and the Renaissance, there are those who claim that the Renaissance inspired the printing press while others take the opposite view. Eisenstein claimed that, "the Renaissance probably did less to spread printing than printing did to spread the Renaissance" (Debus, 1978, p. 6). In contrast, Putnam (1962), argued that the Renaissance must have had an enormous influence in furthering the speedy development and diffusion of the printing press.

In fact both positions are correct. The message of the printing press was the Renaissance, and the medium of the Renaissance was the printing press. In other words, a bootstrap operation was in effect in which the printing press and Renaissance created the conditions for their mutual development.

UISUAL BIAS

The influence of the printing press was not limited to the dissemination of ideas. Rather, it shaped the character of the Renaissance. As a multiplier of alphabetic literacy, the printing press tended to reinforce many of the patterns that emerged with the alphabet. One of the effects of the alphabet was to transform the oral bias of spoken communications to the visual bias of the written word. "When words are written, they become, of course, a part of the visual world. Like most of the elements of the visual world, they become static things and lose, as such, the dynamism which is so characteristic of the auditory world in general and of the spoken word in particular" (Carothers, 1959, p. 311). Of all writing schemes, the alphabet enhances the visual bias the most because of the abstract nature of alphabetic coding and the repetition of the same 26 elements. Print reinforces the visual bias of the alphabet. It makes literary material more available and hence creates a greater dominance over the spoken word than manuscript writing does.

Print also reinforces the visual element through standardization of the written text—something totally lacking in handwritten texts.

> The lack of assistance to readers, or of aids to facilitate reference, in ancient books is very remarkable. The separation of words is practically unknown, except very rarely when an inverted comma or dot is used to mark a separation where some ambiguity might exist. Punctuation is often wholly absent, and is never full and systematic. (Kenyon, 1957, p. 65)

With the printing press, words are uniformly separated, punctuation is used systematically, texts are regularized, and spelling and grammar are standardized. As a result, the printed page is a much more regular arrangement of alphabetic script than the manuscript form. The letters appear in neat rows straight as an arrow. Each line begins at the same place on the left-hand side of the page and ends at the same place at the right-hand side of the page—two neat, absolutely straight margins sandwiching the text. The words in the text are evenly spaced. Paragraphs are indented so that the reader is aware each time a new set of ideas is begun. Each page is numbered, making reference back to the text easy. All of these devices enhance the visual appeal of the text and reinforce the visual bias of alphabetic writing.

Also greater care was given to the creation of a printed text compared with a handwritten one.

Manuscript culture is producer-oriented, since every individual copy of a work represents the great expenditure of an individual copyist's time. Medieval manuscripts are turgid with abbreviations, which favor the copyist although they inconvenience the reader. Print is consumer-oriented, since the individual copies of a work represent a much smaller investment of time: a few hours spent in producing a more readable text will immediately improve thousand on thousands of copies. (Ong, 1982, pp. 122–123)

The regularity of the printed page also allows silent reading, which increases the speed by which the text may be read as well as its visual character. Handwritten manuscripts are irregular and more difficult to read. To increase the comprehensibility of the text, the handwritten manuscripts were read aloud, as is done by youngsters just learning to read. This practice stressed the oral rather than visual character of the text.

Another factor contributing to an increased rate of silent reading was the use of serifs on the letters of the type fonts. The serifs are the little horizontal marks at the bottom and/or top of the letters as is the case with the typefont used in this book. Before print, these served as decoration; after print, they facilitated the reading of the text. The serifs at the top and bottom of the letters serve as guides to move the eye along the printed line of text more rapidly, much the way railroad tracks guide a train. The tunnel vision and linear thinking characteristic of the highly literate are, in part, due to the railroading that the serifs create, which enhances the linearity of the page. They keep the eyes from wandering off. The readers of the first printed pages with serifed type fonts were history's first speed readers. The alphabet, and in particular the printed alphabet, according to Innis and McLuhan, creates a visual bias on the part of the reader:

A decline of the oral tradition meant an emphasis on writing (and hence on the eye rather than the ear) and on visual arts, architecture, sculpture and painting and hence on space rather than time. . . . The discovery of printing in the middle of the fifteenth century implied the beginning of a return to a type of civilization dominated by the eye rather than the ear. (Innis, 1971, pp. 130-131, 138)

Printing brought back the visual bias of the Greeks with their strong emphasis on geometry in mathematics and realism in the arts (McLuhan, 1962, 1964). During the period following the introduction of the printing press, the first significant new progress was made in geometry since the time of Alexandria. The algebraic advances made by the Hindus and Arabs were integrated with geometry, leading to the analytic geometry of Descartes.

The Renaissance also gave rise to realism and the classical Greek sense of aesthetics. Not only did the Renaissance artists recapture the tradition of sculpture, they also mastered perspective, which enabled them to portray three dimensions on a two-dimensional canvas. The new fascination with portraying accurate three-dimensional visual images led to the invention of the camera obscura or pinhole camera.

Another reflection of visual bias was the division by scientists and philosophers of the perceptions into primary and secondary qualities. The primary qualities are those that can be apprehended with the visual sense. The secondary qualities, with the exception of color, are appre-hended with the nonvisual senses. "As with Galileo, extension and movement were the only physical realities that he [Descartes] recog-nized as 'primary'; other aspects of existence such as colours, tastes and smells were referred to as secondary qualities" (Bernal, 1954, p. 304).

The visual bias of the printed page and the linear succession of the letters of the alphabet created a new sense of order that contributed to the systematic way in which science and other forms of scholarship came to be practiced during the Renaissance. This spirit manifested itself in Newtonian mechanics and the metaphor of God as the clockmaker who set his ordered universe into a predictable form of motion.

ALPHABETIZATION

Another factor contributing to this sense of orderliness was that the alphabet and the printing press, working together, unleashed new ways to organize information to cope with the information overload they had created. One of the techniques employed for catalogs, indexes, and ency-clopedias or compendia of information was alphabetization—that is, the arrangement of topics, book titles, or authors in alphabetic order. The term *index* is actually an abbreviation of *index locorum* or index of places; it did not become a common practice until after the invention of the printing press. Although indexing was possible in the manuscript era, it was not a practical feature because the pagination of each copy of a manuscript would be different, and hence a new index would have to be created for each copy of a handwritten manuscript. With printing the pagination was the same for each copy of the book, and therefore the alphabetic indexing only needed to be done once (Ong, 1982).

Alphabetization occurred before the introduction of printing and dated back to the Alexandrian library. However, it was not commonly used during the Middle Ages or in ancient Greece or Rome (Daly, 1967). At first, alphabetizing was a matter of arranging words according to their initial letters and ordering them according to the alphabet. It was only later, around A.D. 200, that absolute or near absolute alphabetization was practiced, and it was only after the introduction of printing that the practice became widespread. It would seem that alphabetization was first used by the librarians at Alexandria for cataloging purposes (Daly, 1967, pp. 79, 94).

Alphabetization, however, can be traced back to the period before Greek literacy to the Semitic peoples. One of the prime pieces of evidence for the borrowing of the phonetic alphabet by the Greeks from the Phoenicians is the fact that the names, sound values, and order of the letters of the alphabet were preserved. Although the names of the Phoenician letters were meaningless and the order of their presentation arbitrary, the Greeks nevertheless preserved these two features of the alphabet. This would indicate that the order of the letters was important to the Semites. In fact, it is known that the order of the letters dates back to the earliest abecedarian. If the order were preserved by the Semites, then it is altogether possible that they too might have resorted to alphabetic ordering. In fact, there are a number of places in the Hebrew Scriptures in Psalms, Proverbs, and Lamentations where the letters of the alphabet are used to order the verses of a chapter.

The order of the letters of the alphabet was retained by the Greeks and exploited to create their number system. The first nine letters of the alphabet stood for the numbers 1 to 9 and so on as described earlier. The Hebrews also used this number system, but it is believed that they borrowed the idea from the Greeks. The ordering of the letters of the alphabet was also retained by the Romans despite that they changed the names of the letters.

Alphabetization in Semitic, Greek, or Roman culture did not become important until the period of the Alexandrian library in the third century B.C., when the techniques of organization used by the librarians spread to other sectors of the information industry, such as authors and public administrators. One of the earliest uses of alphabetic order is found in a late third-century B.C. inscription from the island of Cos, in which the participants in the cult of Apollo and Heracles are listed alphabetically (Paton & Hicks, 1891).

Alphabetization, once introduced in Alexandria, was used primarily by scholars for glossaries and lexica. Although there was a transfer of the technique of alphabetization to Roman scholars, in actuality it was not widespread. Pliny made use of it in his *Natural History*, but this is thought to be a direct translation from the Greek reference material he copied. Only certain lists are alphabetical—namely, those of botanical specimens, gems, sea fish, and artists. Plautus and Virgil also made use of alphabetization as did a limited number of Roman administrators, who tended to file information topographically or chronologically. The use of alphabetization during the Middle Ages and Byzantine period was also sporadic. In the Latin West, Isidore of Seville prepared an etymology in alphabetic order and Phorius a lexicon in the ninth century. A number of Latin glossaries, a bilingual Greek–Latin lexicon attributed to the circle of Robert Grossereste, and a biblical concordance by Hugh of St. Cher, all alphabetized, appeared in scattered European libraries. In 1053, Papias explained the organization of his dictionary in the earliest known description of alphabetization: "Anyone who wishes to find anything quickly must also notice that this whole book is composed according to the alphabet, not only in the first letters of the parts but also in the second, third and sometimes even in the further determinative arrangements of the letters" (Daly, 1967, pp. 25–26).

Giovanni of Genoa, the author of the popular 13th-century encyclopedia, the *Catholicon*, also made the effort to describe his organizational principle to his readers hoping that they would appreciate the efforts he had made.

> You may proceed everywhere according to the alphabet. So, according to this order you will easily be able to find the spelling of any word included here. For example I intend to discuss amo and bibo. I will discuss amo before bibo because a is the first letter of amo and b is the first letter of bibo and a is before b in the alphabet. [He then explains why abeo appears before adeo, amatus before amor, etc.] Now I have devised this order at the cost of great effort and strenuous application. Yet it was I, by the grace of God working with me. I beg of you, therefore, good reader, do not scorn this great labour of mine and this order as something worthless. (Daly, 1967, pp. 71, 73, 91)

Alphabetization did not become a standard procedure for organizing textual material until after the advent of the printing press. One of the reasons was that creating an alphabetic list was not easy because of the high cost of paper or parchment. The standard way to create an alphabetic listing is to list each item on a card and then order the cards. There seems to be no evidence of this technique before printing. Another method was to write the items to be ordered on a sheet of paper one line at a time. The paper was then cut up into individual slips each containing one item. They were ordered alphabetically and then pasted back onto a piece of paper. Another technique for ordering items was to write them out in a long list and then number each item according to their order, starting with the first letter of the first word and proceeding to the second, third, and so on. A third technique was to set aside so many pages for each letter of the alphabet and then place items according to the first letter in the title. This resulted in cases where there were blank spaces between pages because too much space had been allocated or where the text was crowded and cramped because not enough space had been allocated.

Once printing was introduced and multiple copies were to be made, the expense of creating an alphabetic ordering could be absorbed. Also as the amount of information rapidly exploded, alphabetization became a necessity once again as it had at Alexandria. Still, the technique of alphabetization remained a novelty as late as 1604, when Robert Cowdray tendered the following advice in his dictionary, *Table Alphabetical*: "If thou be desirous . . . rightly and readily to understand, and to profit by this Table, and such like, then thou must learne the alphabet, to wit the letters as they stand, perfectly without booke, and where every letter standeth" (cited in Daly, 1967).

The learning of the order of the letters of the alphabet—the ABCs— is to this day the child's first step in becoming literate. It is ironic that this first step to literacy, the memorization of the alphabet, takes place totally in the oral mode. Children reciting the alphabet employ a rhythmic cadence just as they do with a nursery rhyme.

The commercial considerations of the printers further enhanced the natural orderliness that the printing press promoted. To compete with each other, they prepared carefully organized catalogs. "The competitive commercial character of the printed book-trade when coupled with typographic standardization made more systematic cataloguing and indexing seem not only feasible but highly desirable as well" (Daly, 1967, p. 94). The publishers were also careful to prepare their texts in a systematic way to make their products more desirable in the marketplace. They used title pages, tables of contents, and, in some cases, an index. Consequently, the reading environment in which scientists and scholars operated was a well-organized one, and this affected their thinking and scholarship. The medium is the message and the message of print was organization, alphabetization, systemization, and standardization.

Accuracy also became an important factor in the preparation of texts; when publisher–printers discovered their errors, they printed errata so that their errors would not be propagated. They also put much more effort into editing and correcting texts before they were typeset because any error would be multiplied many times over on the press. "Clarity and logic, the disposition of matter on the printed page became . . . a preoccupation of editors" (Strauss, 1965). The scholars and printers influenced each other, each reinforcing the tendency in the other to become more organized, accurate, standardized, and systematic until these values became the norm of modern science, scholarship, and publishing.

15

Print, the Alphabet, and the Science

THE PRINTING PRESS AS A MEDIUM FOR SCIENTIFIC THOUGHT

The phonetic alphabet played a major role in ancient Greece in the development of deductive logic and abstract science. The new system of writing induced in its users the powers of abstraction, uniformity, classification, and analysis. The printing press, as we have noted, enhanced the effects of the alphabet. Written material became even more abstract because of the ease and speed with which it could be read. The reader no longer needed to sound out each word, but could read phrases and sentences in a single glance. The printed medium became transparent and hence its effects more abstract. Because of the neat and uniform way in which information could be organized on the printed page, typography also increased the trend toward uniformity, classification, and analysis.

It is for these reasons that the printing press exercised such a stimulating effect on the whole field of science and mathematics. "If science helped give birth to the printed book, it was clearly the printed book that sent science from its medieval habits straight into the boiling scientific revolution" (de Solla Price, 1967).

The rapid dissemination of information and knowledge to a mass audience was one of the essential elements in the use of modern science. One indication of the importance of the printed book in this respect was the close association of the scientists with printer publishers. In some instances, scientific pioneers were printers (Drake, 1970). Scientists were anxious to publish their results, and they were also avid readers of scientific materials. Newton was a prime example of this spirit, as revealed in the notebooks that catalog his readings of Boyle, Hooke, Galileo's *Dialogues,* and Descartes' *Principles of Philosophy.* These summaries show how he arrived at many of his own new principles and results (Whiteside). Galileo, another author of the scientific revolution, paid the following tribute to the power of alphabetic literacy: "but of all the stupendous inventions, what sublimity of mind must have been his who conceived how to communicate his most secret thoughts to any other person, though very far distant either in time or place? And with no greater difficulty that the various arrangements of two dozen little signs upon paper? Let this be the seal of all the admirable inventions of man" (Shlain, 1998, p. 1).

The printed book was important not only because it served as a medium for the diffusion of ideas, but also because it provided a way to preserve scientific data through the rapid creation of multiple copies. This is probably what motivated Tycho Brahe to assemble a printing press on the remote island of Hveen, where he established his astronomical observatory. He also built a paper mill on the island to accommodate his steady stream of publications (Christianson, 1972; Dryer, 1890; Gade, 1947).

The printing press had a role to play in the overall revival of ancient learning, and the resurrection of an ancient scientific text would often provide the medical student or practitioner with new information and insights. In fact, reading through ancient texts was a valid form of medical research, and in the early days of modern science it often yielded more knowledge than practical laboratory experiments.

The medical field was not the only one to benefit from the literary research that the new humanist's literary tradition promoted. The spin-off into the science of classical Greek and Latin scholarship was formidable. The humanists simplified and clarified language. They made available the great wealth of Greek mathematics and science. The study of biology was stimulated by the desire to identify the plants, animals, and minerals that classical authors mentioned in their texts (Crombie, 1963).

Print promoted self-learning and hence provided would-be scientists with an independent point of view for evaluating hypotheses and the validity of empirical data. Jacobo Foresti in the *Supplementum Chronicarum* published in Venice in 1483 expressed this spirit with the question, "Why should old men be preferred to their juniors now that it is possible for the young by diligent study to acquire the same knowledge?"

This spirit led to a great deal of research and scholarship outside the university where a slavish conformity to the ideas of the ancients created an environment hostile to innovation. For example, the university community first attacked Galileo long before the Church did. The spirit of true science was carried out by "self-educated men and talented amateurs of liberal education." The academic monopoly on science during the Middle Ages was broken by the printed book (Drake, 1970).

The university, with its small body of students and teachers, had been the only medium for the exchange of scientific ideas. Because of its insularity, the conservative academic community was able to "police any unorthodox ideas it wished to squelch." The printing press broke this monopoly of knowledge and allowed the reading public to participate in the exchange of ideas. The Velikovsky affair, in which academics in the 1960s tried to suppress publication of his books, shows that the academic monopoly of knowledge is still a force with which to be reckoned (Innis, 1971).

The search for larger markets resulted in publications in the vernacular tongues, including work of a scientific and mathematical nature. This dramatically increased the number of people who had access to technical ideas. Prior to the printing press, a knowledge of Latin acquired through the Church or university was the only key to learning. The printing press allowed works that were translated by university-trained scholars to be disseminated to the general public.

The story of Tartaglia, who published the first vernacular translation of Euclid in 1543, captures the spirit of the new kind of scientists that the printing press made possible. Tartaglia, a gifted mathematician, despite his publications and the notoriety he won in his famous dispute with Cardano, failed to win a place in the university system. He had a tremendous impact on science, however, training Benedetti, one of Galileo's most important Italian predecessors, and Ostilio Ricci, Galileo's teacher of mathematics!

Another positive effect of the printing press was the dramatic way in which it changed the patterns of scholarship, increasing the time available for developing new ideas. Instead of being forced to wander from one center of learning to another to view the limited number of manuscripts available, a scholar could remain in one place and collect printed editions of the books he wanted to study. Once the ancient texts appeared in printed editions, scholars were released from the tasks of recovering, preserving, and copying them. They were free to work or develop new ideas.

The same applied to the recovery and preservation of astronomical data. Once these tasks were taken over by printers, astronomers had more time for observations. Tycho Brahe made more observations than any other astronomer before his time. Printed mathematical tables of logarithms and trigonometric functions also saved astronomers and other scientists vast amounts of labor, freeing them for more creative work. They could collect and organize much larger amounts of data in a systematic and orderly fashion. Naturally, new patterns emerged with the new visualization of information that print made possible.

Copernicus, for example, developed his ideas after print had been introduced, but before the vast amount of new data collected by Brahe was available. He analyzed basically the same data as Ptolemean astronomers 1,300 years earlier. However, Copernicus saw the data differently. This was due in part to the new print format, which made handling the data so much easier. Copernicus was able to analyze the vast amount of data virtually on his own, whereas the Ptolemean astronomers needed all of the vast resources of the great library at Alexandria to do their work.

The printing press provided an easily accessible format not only for data, but also for scientific ideas. Print, by making it possible to reproduce thousands of copies of a text cheaply and quickly, made the diffusion of ideas over space and time simple. Kepler, one of those most affected by print, was well aware of its impact:

> Do we not today by the art of printing bring to light all the ancient writers? . . . Through them a new theology has been created today, and a new jurisprudence; the followers of Paracelsus have created a new medicine, and the followers of Copernicus a new astronomy. For my part, I believe that now at last the world is alive, and indeed is in a state of intense excitement. (Kepler, 1606)

Not only were the scientific works of the ancients available, but also those of the more practical medieval scientists. The ancient writers excited and inflamed the imaginations of Renaissance thinkers, but it was the more down-to-earth thinkers of the Middle Ages who steered science in the direction of empiricism and practicality. The early printing presses made medieval scientific ideas available to Renaissance scientists (Crombie, 1963).

Printing also provided a mechanism whereby new ideas spread even when attempts were made to suppress them by the Church or State. Copernicus did not publish his famous *De Revolutonibus* until the end of his life, receiving the first printed copy, according to tradition, on his deathbed. He wrote the book using a highly technical language so that only the community of astronomers could read it. It was for this reason that at first it was ignored outside of scientific circles. This permitted its superior mathematical techniques to become indispensable to all astronomers before the formidable lay and clerical opposition to its central thesis developed. By then it was too late to suppress it because Copernicus' ideas had penetrated or perhaps more accurately infiltrated the spirit and imagination of European thought. A revolution in scientific thought had been launched through a printed book that had experienced a rapid and wide dissemination throughout Europe (Kuhn, 1957).

In addition to the book, the printing press created another medium for the dissemination of scientific ideas—namely, journals in which scientists were able to report on the results of their research periodically, rather than after a line of research was completed after many years of work. This enabled a much more rapid turnover of new ideas through the feedback of readers and authors. It also promoted cooperation among scientists who could feel they were contributing to a joint venture. Because of the preservative power of print and the cooperative spirit it fostered, a critical mass of scientific activity soon emerged. The scientific community that the printing press created at first rivaled and then surpassed the size of the community at the great library in Alexandria.

PRINT SETS THE STANDARD FOR SCIENCE

Typography made possible a new level of standardization of textual material, which in turn promoted greater accuracy. Contradictions or errors stood out like sore thumbs in the visually uniform format of the printed page. The repeatability of print and its powers of preservation also promoted greater accuracy and precision in the data captured in textual material, and this had a positive impact on mathematics and science.

A new confidence in the accuracy of mathematical constructions, figures and numbers was predicated on a method of duplication that transcended older limits imposed by time and space and that presented identical data in identical form to men who were otherwise divided by cultural and geographic frontiers. (Eisenstein, 1979, p. 669)

By creating a standardized format for the presentation of textual material, the printing press encouraged a similar standardization in the way all information was handled and presented. Each sheet printed from the same plate was identical to all the others, and the information on it was arranged in exactly the same way. This permitted an author to refer to the exact line and page of another's work without ambiguity. The cross-referencing from one text to another allowed comparisons between ideas or similar sets of empirical data (Eisenstein, 1979, p. 72).

The printing press not only permitted and promoted greater accuracy with alphabetic texts and numerical figures, but also with pictorial representations. This was of prime importance for the transmission of scientific drawings and diagrams. "Hand drawn illustrations were replaced by woodcuts and engravings which could be more easily reproduced. Repeatable pictorial statements revolutionized technical literature reinforcing the uniformity and standardization that the printed word had created" (Eisenstein, 1979, pp. 52–53). The fact that identical images, maps, and diagrams could be viewed simultaneously by scattered readers constituted a kind of communications revolution in itself, which impacted most on medicine, botany, zoology, geography, and astronomy.

The repeatability of visual images and diagrams is not explicitly part of the alphabet effect. However, alphabetic literacy helped make the printing press a success and, hence, contributed to the development of a medium for the lithograph and engraving. The visual bias that the alphabet and print encouraged also created an environment in which printed pictorial images could thrive. Ong (1982) pointed out that block printing was practiced in Europe long before the invention of the movable type printing press, and hence could have been used to create accurate drawings. Yet this was not done because manuscript books were created one at a time. The effort to make an accurate drawing that would be used in only one copy of a book was not deemed to be worth the effort. However, when multiple copies of the book were being made and the same press could be used to make both illustrations and pages of text, more printed books were illustrated with engraved prints.

The importance of the role of the printed book in the development of science is reflected in Galileo's use of the metaphor of the book to describe the physical universe:

> Philosophy is written in that vast book which stands forever open before our eyes, I mean the universe; but it can not be read until we have learnt the language and become familiar with the characters in which it is written. It is written in mathematical language, and the letters are triangles, circles, and other geometric figures, without which means is it humanly possible to comprehend a single word. (*Saggiatore*)

THE RISE OF EMPIRICISM AND THE DIVORCE OF SCIENCE FROM ITS LITERARY PAST

The initial interest in science, its diffusion to a large audience, and its development into a systematic study were all due in part to the printed book. Literary activities, however, came to dominate scientific thought as they had during the classical Greek period. To create the experimental spirit that characterizes modern science today, Renaissance scientists had to rebel against the literary tradition that permeated their study of nature and develop a more empirical approach to physics, chemistry, biology, and medicine.

The alchemists, despite their use of certain magical practices, laid down many of the foundations for empirical research that evolved directly into modern chemistry. Alchemists today are more remembered for their allegorizing and mysticism than for the new emphasis they placed on observational evidence. Paracelsus called on alchemists to learn from nature rather than from books (Debus, 1978). The empirical tradition of alchemy can be traced back to its roots, which was the practical goal of the transmutation of base metals into gold.

> If you wish to know that pepper is hot . . . that the magnet attracts steel, that arsenic whitens brass, you have to verify the assertion by experience. It is the same in Geometry, Astronomy, Music and Perspective, and other sciences with a practical aim and scope. A like rule applies with double force in alchemy. (Debus, 1978, pp. 17–18)

The spirit of turning from books to the empirical observation of nature was also encouraged by Severinus, a Danish physician and follower of Paracelsus. In his book *Idea Medicinae Philosophicae*, published in Basel in 1571, Severinus wrote:

> Search the valleys of the deserts, the shores of the sea, and the deepest recesses of the earth; mark well the distinctions between animals, the differences of plants, the various kinds of minerals, the properties and mode of origin of everything that exists. Be not ashamed to learn by heart the astronomy and terrestrial philosophy of the peasantry. Lastly, purchase coal, build furnaces, watch and experiment without wearying. In this way and no other, you will arrive at a knowledge of things and of their properties.

The empirical spirit that developed in the Renaissance was due in part to the increased interest in mechanical devices in the late Middle

Ages. The invention of the printing press, which marked a dramatic transition to modern technology, also promoted an interest in empiricism, especially among the educated who were associated with the book trade. The operation of publishing books and using a printing press involved a wide range of technical matters in addition to the mechanical aspects of the press, such as the use of screws and levers. Knowledge concerning the production of paper and inks, the chemistry associated with them, and a number of issues in metallurgy and metal casting associated with the production of the type fonts were also required.

The groundwork for the Industrial Revolution was also laid at this time. The printing press represented the first large-scale, mass-production manufacturing operation and the first reduction of any handcraft to mechanical terms (McLuhan, 1962). The printing press with movable type provided the first uniformly repeatable commodity, the first assembly line, and the first mass production. "Printing marked the first stage in the spread of the industrial revolution" (Innis, 1971, p. 30).

THE PRINTING PRESS REINFORCES
THE ABSTRACTION OF ALPHABETIC LITERACY

The alphabet naturally played an important role in the birth of modern science. Its effects were even more pronounced in the print form than in the manuscript form. Many of the features of the alphabet that contributed to creating a positive environment for the birth of abstract science in ancient Greece, such as abstraction, regularity, uniformity, and linearity, were enhanced by the print format. The powers of the alphabet as a tool for analysis and classification were strengthened with print because of: (a) the greater amount of data that could be accommodated on a single page of print, (b) the increased uniformity of print, (c) the stronger visual bias of the printed page, and (d) the increased capability for cross-referencing.

One of the primary characteristics of the modern physics that followed on the heels of the printed word was a new level of abstraction. The Copernican revolution did more than replace the earth with the sun as the center of the universe. It was a triumph of abstract thinking in which the dictates of logic triumphed over common sense. In the Copernican system, the earth was required to move through the heavens—a notion that totally violated all the sensibilities of contemporary thought. The motivation for this bizarre system was Copernicus' abstract reasoning that a world system that required fewer epicycles to describe the movement of the planets was more logical. He also argued on equally abstract grounds that the Ptolemaic system must be wrong because the earth was not really in the center of the universe, but ever so slightly displaced from the center.

Galileo was extremely impressed by the abstractness of Copernicus' thinking. This undoubtedly influenced his own thinking and gave him the courage to develop his ideas along abstract lines of his own. He wrote in his *Dialogue on the Two Principal Systems of the Universe*: "I cannot find any bounds for my admiration how reason was able, in Aristarchus and Copernicus, to commit such a rape upon their senses and in spite of them, to make herself mistress of their belief."

Descartes captured the new spirit of abstraction in philosophy with his dictum "Cogito, ergo sum" ("I think, therefore I am") and in mathematics with his analytic geometry. The latter led directly to Newton's breakthroughs in which classical mechanics was described in terms of three mathematical laws of motion. This achievement represented perhaps the greatest leap in abstract thought in our intellectual history. The following passage from Query 31 in Newton's Opticks captures the spirit of this new attitude, in which he rejected all occult explanations for motion and sought "to derive two or three general Principles of Motion from Phaenomena, and afterward to tell us how the Properties and Actions of all corporeal things follow from those manifest Principles."

PRINT: THE MEDIUM OF CLASSIFICATION AND SPECIALIZATION

It was the new level of abstraction of Newton's Laws that provided a measure of the depth of the new science. It was the work of the catalogers and classifiers of scientific information, however, that provided an indication of the scope and breadth of the new thirst for knowledge. Scholars collected and compiled information in the fields of botany, zoology, philology, linguistics, library science, geology, and astronomy. Catalogs, dictionaries, encyclopedias, data collections, and compendia of all sorts appeared in increasingly larger numbers during the Renaissance, stimulated by the organizational possibilities that the printing press made possible.

The large compilations or catalogs of data were more systematic and orderly in the printed format than they had been when they were compiled by scribes. The accuracy of printed compendia of data and information increased because of the increased ability of scholars to visibly spot errors and inaccuracies. Readers were often invited to correct any errors they found or to supplement the information provided. Print permitted a rather rapid feedback from many readers because of the speed at which multiple copies of a text would be distributed to interested scholars and also because the reader was readily able to identify the author and printer, and hence transmit his views to the author. David Hume recognized this advantage of print in a letter to his publisher: "The Power which Printing gives us of continually improving and correcting our works in successive Editions appears to me the chief Advantage of that art" (Cochrane, 1964).

The manner in which the printing press promoted the classification of scientific data is illustrated by the work of the 16th-century Swiss scholar Konrad von Gesner. He produced the first comprehensive bibliography, the *Bibtiotheca Universatis*, in 1545, which listed approximately 10,000 titles by some 3,000 authors writing in Greek, Latin, and Hebrew. Three years later, he released the *Pandectarum*, which cataloged 30,000 titles cross-referenced and classified by topic. Gesner's passion for cataloging and systematizing went well beyond library science. He worked in the fields of botany and zoology, and with the help of 50 correspondents, compiled vast amounts of information including illustrations, which earned him the title "father of zoology." Other botanists were collecting information from India, the New World, and a variety of countries and climates (Sarton, 1957).

The printing press unleashed and stimulated the gathering of scientific information in a number of fields in the natural, social, and linguistic sciences. Scholars and printers developed organizational tools to deal with the sudden surge in information. The alphabet served as a model for the various orderings of data, which included alphabetization, chronological ordering, geographic ordering, typologies, indexes, and registers.

In response to the flood of information, an old institution from the classical period was resurrected and revitalized—namely, the encyclopedia. A typical 16th-century example of such a compendium of knowledge and information was Sebastian Münster's *Cosmography*, which went through 35 editions—20 in German, 5 in Latin, 6 in French, 3 in Italian, and 1 in Czech. In his preface, Münster explained the nature of his encyclopedia:

> The art of cosmography concerns itself not only with the countries, habitations, and lives of various peoples of the earth, but also with many other things, such as strange animals, trees, metals, and so on, things both useful and useless, to be found on land and in the sea; [also] the habits, customs, laws, governments of men, the origins of countries, regions, cities and towns, how nature has endowed them and what human inventiveness has produced in them, [also] what notable things have happened everywhere. (Strauss, 1965)

During the course of its 35 editions over a period of 84 years (from 1544–1628), the volume of the *Cosmography* exploded. It began with 650 folio pages, but 1575 the French edition contained over 4,000 pages (McLuhan, 1962). Not only did this new encyclopedia enjoy public acclaim, but Pliny the Elder's *Natural History* in a printed edition enjoyed a greater popularity than the original edition had in Rome 1,500 years earlier. Over 40 editions appeared during the 15th and 16th centuries.

The printing press encouraged an explosion of new information, which in turn led to the specialization and fragmentation of knowledge. The alphabet had encouraged a specialization and division of subjects or topics in classical Greece, in sharp contrast to the holistic approach of the oral tradition of Homer.

This encyclopedic division of knowledge into special topics was a continuation of the tradition of specialization that began in classical Greece, where Aristotle had divided philosophy into specific topics. The print format reinforced these divisions, which were elaborated by Renaissance scholars such as Ramus. As the cost of books fell, specialized monographs were published, which could support a small community of experts interested in a fairly narrow range of study. The disciplines of science, including mathematics, astronomy, geology, physics, chemistry, and zoology, evolved because they were more sharply differentiated as a result of print.

The use of the alphabet through the medium of print served as a paradigm for classification and organization within each of these individual fields. For example, in physics the principle of linear superposition, by which the components of motion in the x, y, and z directions can be separated and treated as individual problems, is a direct fallout of the type of analysis that alphabetic literacy inspired. It is probably no accident that the letters of the alphabet are used to designate the three dimensions of space into which all motion can be subdivided and analyzed.

The Cartesian coordinates x, y, and z that Newton employed enabled him to abstract and simplify the description of the dynamic interactions of mechanical systems. It also set the tone for the age of mechanization that the printing press had ushered in. The division of all systems into their basic components parallels the way in which words can be broken down into their basic sounds and then represented by the letters of the alphabet. This form of organization encourages or invites a linear cause-and-effect analysis of the relationships between the components of a system. Newton's formulation of mechanics in terms of forces (causes) and accelerations (effects) can therefore be traced back to the linear form of analysis inspired by the alphabet.

The modern scientific revolution, which began in the Renaissance and culminated in the breakthroughs of Newtonian mechanics, led directly to the Industrial Revolution, mass production, and the assembly line, all of which are based on segmentation and specialization of task. "The restructuring of work and association was shaped by the techniques of fragmentation, that is the essence of machine technology" (McLuhan, 1964, p. 8). This spirit infused the engineers and mechanics who built the machinery of the Industrial Revolution, basing it on the same principles of piecing together the repeatable uniform elements of gears, screws, and levers in linear configurations to achieve specific mechanical tasks. The waterwheels, windmills, and other devices from the Middle Ages provided the early impetus for the mechanical revolution. It was the printing press, however, where the repeatable uniform type fonts were used and reused in an infinite number of permutations, that inspired the transformation to the semi-automated machinery of the Industrial Revolution.

In the field of chemistry, the analog between the 92 elements out of which all chemical substances are composed and the letters of the alphabet out of which all words are built is immediately apparent. The parallel is further strengthened by the fact that the elements in chemical equations are referred to by the letters of the alphabet, such as H for hydrogen or C for carbon. For each element, there corresponds an atom, which is the smallest building block or unit of chemistry, just as the phoneme and letter of the alphabet are the smallest building blocks or units of speech and writing, respectively. Molecules, which are composed of various combinations of atoms, are like words composed of different combinations of letters. The atoms that form these combinations are guided by the syntax of the chemical forces. The symbols used to describe the molecules also involve the letters of the alphabet in that an individual molecule is represented by the atoms of which it is composed. For example, water is written as H_2O (two hydrogen and one oxygen) and hydrogen peroxide as H_2O_2.

The atoms are made up of *still* smaller *bits* of matter called *elementary particles*, which include electrons, protons, neutrons, and mesons (the nuclear glue that keeps the nucleus together). These building blocks of the atoms—the elementary particles—also operate like the letters of the alphabet, combining according *to* the syntax of nuclear and electric forces to form individual atoms. The symbols used *to* represent them are also the letters of the Roman or Greek alphabet (e.g., *e* for the electron, *p* for the proton, and *pi, omega,* and *rho* for the mesons). Recent experimental studies in particle physics seem to indicate that the proton, neutron, and mesons are composed of still smaller bits of matter referred to as *quarks,* of which there are at least six different types. The up, down, strange, charm, beauty, and truth quarks are also represented by the letters of the alphabet—namely, *u, d, s, c, b,* and *t.*

In the fields of zoology and botany, the letters of the alphabet are not used to represent the various categories of classification. However, an elaborate system based on the work Linnaeus is employed. All the flora and fauna ever observed have been classified according to species, genus, class, and order in a systematic logical and linear fashion based on principles that arose under the influence of alphabetic literacy. Linnaeus' scheme dates back to Aristotle—the first to systematically classify plants and animals.

In drawing the parallel between the various classification schemes used in science and the phonetic alphabet, we do not wish to suggest a naive causal relationship between these schemes and alphabetic literacy. Rather, we suggest that as scientists pursued their ideas in their particular fields, the alphabet served as a model for organization. The fact that they consistently use the letters of the alphabet to designate their categories is one hint of this influence. The fact that the linear classification schemes are a unique product of alphabetic cultures is another hint.

Preliterate and nonalphabetic literate cultures have means for categorizing information, but they do not use the same linear systematic rational systems used in modern science. The Chinese and preliterate cultures use analogy as a way to classify instead of the deductive logical techniques of Western science.

Once again we are not suggesting a causal link between the alphabet and techniques of modern science and deductive logic, but the correlation between the two is not an accident either. The alphabet and scientific thought provide an environment in which both are able to thrive and reinforce one another. Our study has revealed that the printing press played an important role in promoting the use of the alphabet, and hence created an environment in which the logical, analytic, rational techniques of modem science could evolve and thrive.

16

The Social and Cultural Impacts of the Printing Press

Just as the printing press changed the nature of science and technology, it also transformed the social, political, and economic institutions of Western civilization. Many of the social impacts of the printing press were the same as those of the alphabet, intensified by the way in which the printing press reinforced or enhanced the alphabet effect. This might explain the many similarities between the Renaissance and classical Greece. The humanism, individualism, artistic naturalism, capitalism, democracy, and nationalism of the Renaissance paralleled similar movements in ancient Greece. The Renaissance virtually replayed classical learning through the revival of Greek and Latin scholarship.

PRINT: THE TECHNOLOGY OF INDIVIDUALISM

One of the hallmarks of the Renaissance and the print revolution was a vibrant and active form of humanism and individualism similar to the one that accompanied the introduction of alphabetic literacy in ancient Greece. By allowing a greater dissemination of reading material and regularizing the format of textual material, the printing press had a stronger impact in promoting individualism than the handwritten alphabetic texts of the Middle Ages and the classical period (Eisenstein, 1979). "Print is the extreme phase of alphabet culture that detribalizes or decollectivizes man in the first instance. Print raises the visual features of alphabet to highest intensity of definition. Thus print carries the individuating power of the phonetic alphabet much further than manuscript cultures ever do" (McLuhan, 1962, p. 192). Also the printing press made available more texts from the classical period, which extolled individualism. The effects of the medium were reinforced by its contents.

The printing press permitted a new medium to come into existence that provided the opportunity for an individualistic expression of ideas and opinions and the emergence of the modern concept of an author. During the era of manuscript, learning was a collective activity in which each individual writer had to invest enormous amounts of energy strictly to preserve learning rather than to create new ideas. The lack of originality in the writers of the Middle Ages is beautifully illustrated in the following passage from the 13th-century Franciscan Saint Bonaventura:

> A man might write the works of others, adding and changing nothing, in which case he is simply called a scribe [scriptor]. Another writes the work of others with additions which are not his own; and he is called a compiler [compilator], another writes both others' work and his own, but with others' work in the principal place, adding his own for purposes of explanation; and he is called a commentator [commentator]. . . . Another writes both his own work and others' with his own work in the principal place, adding others for purposes of confirmation; and such a man should be called an author [auctor].

The most interesting aspect of this classification of writers is the omission of our modern notion of an author as one who creates totally new and original material. The reason for this omission is simple. The modern author did not emerge until after the introduction of print. The identity of the scribe, compiler, commentator, or author of a manuscript was, therefore, unimportant to the medieval reading public. The medieval student did not regard the "contents of a book as the expression of another man's personality and opinion" (Goldschmidt, 1965, p. 113). No attempt was made to identify the author or scribe of a medieval text or even its title. Manuscripts were referred to by the opening words of the text, following a tradition that dated back to the cuneiform clay tablets of Babylon.

With the advent of printing and the cheaper costs for paper, title pages emerged on which the author, title, and printer publisher of the book were all identified. With the possibility of new literary fame and financial gain, authors began to take pride in their literary output. The commercialization of publishing led to a new concept of literary property, in which the identity of the author became an important issue. "To copy and circulate another man's book might be regarded as a meritorious action in the age of manuscript; in the age of print such action results in lawsuit and damages" (Chaytor, 1945, p. 1). The concept of copyright to protect the literary property rights of the individual author further reinforced individualism. We see a partial return to the manuscript tradition with computer software in which the identity of the author is totally unimportant.

The printing press, together with the title page, gave rise to a notion of literary fame and individual achievement in letters; it also, as a medium of fixity, gave recognition to other feats of personal accomplishment. It was only after the advent of print that disputes arose regarding claims over individual achievement in terms of inventions, innovations, and discoveries. The rival claims of the Gutenberg and Koster camps, with respect to the invention of the printing press, was the first example of such disputes (Eisenstein, 1979).

The printing press, by making the production of textual material easier, broadened the kinds of topics and concerns to which authors addressed themselves. One of the new themes that emerged during the Italian Renaissance with writers such as Ficino, Pico, and Pomponazzi was the glorification of man and the dignity and freedom of the individual (Kristeller & Randall, 1948). The concerns of these early Renaissance humanists eventually evolved into the modern European liberal tradition, in which the rights of the individual are of prime importance.

The individualism that printing press and humanists promoted was reinforced by and gave support to other cultural innovations that characterized the Renaissance such as:

1. The use of vernacular language as a medium of literary expression;

2. An increase in the number of democratic institutions;

3. The Reformation, which extended democratic ideals from the secular domain to the spiritual one;

4. The system of capitalism in which free enterprise based on individual initiative replaced the restrictive trade practices of the Middle Ages; and

5. Increased opportunities for self-education and hence upward mobility and the emergence of the middle class.

UERNACULARS

One of the dramatic and direct results of the printing press in Europe was the establishment of several vernacular tongues as normative languages. "Typography arrested linguistic drift, enriched as well as standardized vernaculars, and paved the way for the more deliberate purification and codification of all major European languages" (Chaytor, 1945, p. 1). This development occurred only for those vernaculars for which a printed literature arose. "The Lithuanian, Latvian, Estonian, and Finnish languages might in the course of the sixteenth century have been absorbed by German, Polish, and Swedish, as were the languages of the Prussians, Pomeranians, and Courlanders, and other tribes before them, had they not been preserved in print" (Steinberg, 1955, pp. 121–122).

Steinberg provided a number of other examples where the printing press permitted the survival of the vernacular tongue of a national group with a small population. In the British Isles, the printing press ensured both the linguistic and political domination of English. However, Welsh and Irish Gaelic, which appeared in print in the late 16th century, have survived, whereas Cornish has disappeared. In the Iberian peninsula, Spanish and Portuguese have dominated politically, but Basque, first printed in 1545, and Catalan, one of the first languages to find itself in print in 1474, have both survived to this day and are enjoying a revival of nationalistic fervor.

The Germanic languages provide another example. Both Dutch and Swiss German, before the advent of print, were of equal status as other Germanic dialects. Because of the pioneering work of the Dutch in printing and publishing in their vernacular tongue, including the 1477 translation of the Old Testament at Delft, Dutch or Netherlands now has the status of a language distinct from German. However, "The Swiss edition of the New Testament followed Luther's (German] text closely, using only a few Alemannic words and phrases" (Steinberg, 1966, pp. 121–122). As a consequence, Swiss German has remained a dialect often looked down upon by those speaking High German.

The printing press and writing determined which of the many regional dialects of a family of languages would emerge as the national tongue. Because of political, economic, or religious factors, one of the regional dialects became the dialect of choice of the printers; as a result, it was the form of the language taught in the school and the language in which official documents were drafted. In other words, it became the national language. It also became the dialect that developed the richest vocabulary and the most elaborate syntax. "In England this happened to the upper-class London English dialect, in Germany, to High German (the German of the highlands to the south), in Italy to Tuscan" (Ong, 1982, pp. 106–107). To illustrate how rich a vocabulary develops when a dialect becomes a national language, Ong (1982) pointed out that *Webster's Third New International Dictionary* (1971) contained more than 450,000 entries compared with many oral dialects, which "get along with perhaps five thousand words or less."

The printing press also played a role in determining the national language of a number of Middle Eastern states. Syriac and Coptic were almost totally replaced by Arabic as a result of the conquest of their native speakers by Islam and because of the central role the Koran plays in these cultures. The absence of printing to fix these languages contributed to their demise.

By bringing the vernacular languages into print, the printing press created more activities for itself by dramatically increasing the number of potential readers and new authors. Not only did the absolute numbers increase, but the impact of the printed page on the individual reader was also greater because the visual cues of the printed words were reinforced by the daily aural impressions of the spoken language. The use of vernacular tongues in printed form reinforced and promoted many of the individualistic trends of the print era, such as the increased level of education, new democratic institutions, capitalism, the Reformation, and nationalism.

PRINT AND THE
BEGINNING OF MASS EDUCATION

Once vernacular texts were published, the exposure to print material no longer required a proficiency in a second language. The number of people who could read, and hence learn on their own, increased dramatically. It was only in the age of print that the notion of the self-educated man arose. The story of every self-educated man from Nicolo Tartaglia, born at Brescia in 1500, to Abraham Lincoln, born in Kentucky in 1809, is the same in that books provided their entry into the world of learning and eventually allowed them to make their own unique contributions.

Latin was dethroned as the universal language of educated men (Kohn, 1944). With the increasing number of books in vernacular tongues, particularly material of a learned nature, the traditional monopolies of knowledge by the Church and universities broke down. Both institutionally educated and self-educated individuals arose to successfully challenge these two monopolies of learning through the Reformation and the scientific revolution.

New patterns of education took advantage of the new medium. "The printed book was a new visual aid available to all students and it rendered the older education obsolete. The book was literally a teaching machine where the manuscript was a crude teaching tool only" (McLuhan, 1962, pp. 176–178). The new medium, with its visual bias and propensity to compartmentalize and specialize information, colored the new methods of education that arose partly due to the inspiration of Peter Ramus. Ramus spearheaded many of the curriculum reforms made by the 16th-century French academics who "were affiliated with scholar-printers and editors" (Eisenstein, 1979, p. 542). These reforms form the basic structure of today's modern educational curriculum.

The democratization of knowledge that the printed word inspired was not limited to the training of professionals at universities, which could accommodate only a small minority of the population. "It was the dissemination of literature through the new art of printing rather than the diffusion of education through the university lecture rooms, which brought to the masses of the people the consciousness of mental existence" (Putnam, 1962, p. 222).

One of the goals of the philosophers of the Enlightenment was a desire to bring learning within reach of artisans, as suggested by Floris: "Learning cannot be too common and the commoner the better. . . . Why but the vulgar should not know all" (Putnam, 1962, p. 362).

These aspirations of the Enlightenment were realized with the help of reasonably priced mass-produced books, which served as the backbone of the system of publicly supported schools and libraries that arose during the Industrial Revolution. The actual foundations of the public school system can be traced back to the Czech educator, John Amos Comenius, who outlined the principles of primary education that have been followed by teachers ever since. He published the *Orbis Sensualis Pictus* in 1654, the first picture book designed to teach children Latin (McLuhan, 1962).

THE PRINTING PRESS
AND THE RISE OF CAPITALISM

The printing press, use of vernaculars, and popularization of learning all contributed to the increased sale of books. Book printing and publishing contributed directly to the development of Western capitalism because it was one of the first industries that required a capital investment to procure the means of production. It was also one of the first enterprises in which speculation played a prominent role. Publishing involved the marketing of a mass-manufactured product. It was a highly competitive field, where price was dictated by the laws of supply and demand. The book, according to McLuhan, became a commodity.

> It created the price system. For until commodities are uniform and repeatable the price of an article is subject to haggle and adjustment. The uniformity and repeatability of the book . . . created modern markets and the price system. . . . Print was in itself a commodity, a new natural resource which also showed us how to tap all other kinds of resources including ourselves. (McLuhan, 1962, p. 238)

Print provided its users—both authors and readers—with a new organizing principle that applied with equal effectiveness to science, technology, and commerce and led to the Industrial Revolution and our present technology-based industrial system. The medium of the alphabet and printing press working in consortium provided a model for entrepreneurs and industrialists to create modern Western efficiency and manufacturing.

THE PRINTING PRESS
AND THE REFORMATION

The printing press helped bring about the Reformation. It contributed directly as a medium for the rapid and wide dissemination of information and opinions and indirectly by promoting the use of vernacular literature and the spirit of individualism. The translation of the Bible into vernacular languages removed the need for mediation through the Church.

Erasmus, together with the Basel printer Froben, published a Greek Testament in 1516 that "contributed more to the liberation of the human mind from the thraldom of the clergy," according to Pattison, "than all the uproar and rage of Luther's many pamphlets" (Innis, 1972, p. 144). In his introduction to this translation, Erasmus wrote: "I wish that every woman would read the Gospel and the Epistles of Paul . . . I wish these were translated into each and every language" (Harbison 1956, p. 101).

Part of Erasmus' dream came true, but at a price he could not have foreseen. The role that vernacular translations and the printing press would play was totally unknown to those first innocent churchmen who advocated their deployment in the service of God and his one true Church. In 1499, during that short period just after the first appearance of print and just before the first rumblings of the Reformation, the following passage was published in the *Chronicle of Cologne*: "The eternal God has out of his unfathomable wisdom brought into existence the laudable art, by which men now print books, and multiply them so greatly that every man may for himself read or hear read the way of salvation."

Within the short space of 18 years after the publication of that sentiment, Luther set in motion the greatest civil war and revolution that Christendom would ever experience when he posted his Ninety-five Theses on the church door in Wittenberg. The miscalculation by churchmen of the impact that printing would have on their religion serves as one of the classical examples of how difficult it is to understand the consequences of a new technology. The mechanism whereby print brought about the revolution and civil war that came to be known as the Reformation is complicated.

The ability of laymen to read the Bible directly in their own vernacular made them less dependent on the clergy. The spirit of humanism and individualism that print promoted also made those who were literate inclined to be more independent in forming their own opinions on spiritual and moral matters. "Prior to the printing-press, the responsibility [for individuals arriving at sound conclusions] had been left by the people with the 'spiritual advisers,' who were charged with the duty of doing the thinking for their flocks" (Putnam, 1962, p. 222). Books taught people to think for themselves, and this extended to religious matters. This practice had already begun in the Middle Ages with the scholastic philosophers such as Abelard. Publication of the Scriptures in the vernacular was followed by new interpretations and intensive controversies conducted in pamphlets and broadsheets that led directly to the establishment of Protestantism.

Although the internal organization of the Church was hierarchical and based on literary forms and codified law, the actual teaching provided to its parishioners was almost totally oral. Most of the mass in which the parishioner participated consisted of the recitation of oral formulae that they memorized and repeated frequently throughout the service. The flock was not encouraged to read for themselves. Whenever any use was made of written material, the congregation sat passively listening to the reading. The oral bias of the Church's services tended to reinforce the corporate tribal spirit of compliance to the authority of the storytellers or bards—namely, the priests. Just as it had never occurred to a member of tribal Greek society to challenge the ideas expressed by a bard reciting the epic poems of Homer, so the flock of the Catholic Church had remained passive over the centuries.

Before the advent of the universities, the Church had an almost total monopoly on the production and dissemination of written material.

Even after the founding of the universities, the Church exercised careful control of these institutions, tempering the activities of those like Abelard who championed ideas that challenged their authority. Just as the alphabet in Greece had encouraged the separation of religion and government, so the printing press encouraged a division between civil authority and faith. Alphabetic literacy and the press permitted faith to become an individual matter of conscience, rather than a slavish adherence to corporate authority. With the advent of printing and the spread of learning outside the Church and universities, control of literary activities could no longer be maintained. It did not take long for the literate to challenge the ideas of the oral-based Church, just as the educated and literate Greeks had challenged the ideas of Homer and Hesiod.

Once the challenge to the older oral order had begun, it spread like wildfire through the medium of the printing press. The lack of such a tool had limited the literary revolution of Plato and Aristotle and had permitted many of the tribal traditions of ancient Greece and Rome to survive even under Christianity. The analog of the Christian church, with its many "plastic" icons and the Greek and Roman temples, is clear. The Protestants reversed these tendencies and reverted to the strict iconoclasm of the Hebrews. Judaism was a far more literary religion than Christianity because of its scriptural obligation to read the law. Part of the Protestant revolution was the incorporation of Bible reading into the daily life of the family. As with the Hebrews, literacy became a religious tool for the Protestants. This helps explain why the Protestants returned to many of the practices of the Old Testament and took as much comfort in this work as in the New Testament.

The influence of alphabetic literacy and the printing press in bringing about the Reformation is a complicated one, but their role in its dissemination is straightforward. It has not been historically verified (Iserloh, 1968) that Luther, in fact, nailed his Ninety-five Theses to the door of the Castle Church in Wittenberg in 1517, as tradition teaches us, but it is certain that he used the printing press liberally to publish and publicize his ideas with lightning speed. "The theses . . . were said to be known throughout Germany in a fortnight and through Europe in a month" (Aston, 1968). Never before in the history of ideas had a challenge to authority been so rapidly and widely disseminated as Luther's crusade against the Church, thanks to the printing press. Luther acknowledged his debt to the press, describing it as "God's highest and extremest act of grace, whereby the business of the Gospel is driven forward."

It was through the Reformation that the power of the printing press as a medium of publicity and propaganda was revealed. The press had fomented international revolt against authority and totally transformed communication. In the 3 years after posting his Theses, Luther issued 30 publications, which sold in excess of 300,000 copies. "Luther was able to make exact, standardized and ineradicable impressions on the mind of Europe. For the first time in human history, a great reading public judged the validity of revolutionary ideas through a mass-medium which used the vernacular languages together with the arts of the journalist and the cartoonist" (Dickens, 1968, p. 51). Not only did Luther's publicity campaign set a precedent, but it was not equaled in magnitude until the advent of large-circulation newspapers and electronic media.

In exploring the relationship of the Renaissance and the printing press, we discovered that there had been other renascences before, but that print had served as the medium to establish the revival of learning on a global scale and a permanent basis. The relationship between the press and Reformation follows a similar pattern. There were other challenges to the authority of the Church before Luther, dating back to the very origins of the institution. Until the time of the printing press and the Renaissance, the conditions and logistics did not exist for a massive revolution on the scale of the Protestant Reformation.

Once the extent of the revolt had been properly gauged, the Church hit back aggressively against the Protestant uprising and launched the Counterreformation. One of the main targets of its counterattack was the printing press, which it hoped to control through censorship. The use of censorship began even before Luther's broadside attack at Wittenberg. Two years earlier, following the May 4, 1515, session of the Lateran Council, Pope Leo X issued a decree imposing censorship on all translations presumably because of the fear that inaccuracy would promote errors in faith and daily life. In fact, the Church probably wanted to prevent the further dissemination of vernacular versions of the Bible, which were obviously fueling the revolt. In 1520, papal and imperial edicts focused on the Lutheran tracts for censorship and prohibition. This eventually led to the institution of the papal Index and the prohibitions against Bible reading as well as Bible printing. This was tantamount to prohibiting reading and the use of the alphabet. The tool that had stimulated the development of monotheism—the alphabet—was perceived by the Church as a weapon attacking its moral foundation. It is little wonder that the Church rejected the concept of vernacular Bibles, preferring that all religious literature remain in Latin so that it could exercise greater control.

The Protestant churches encouraged Bible reading and the printing of vernacular editions. "In marked contrast to Catholic policy, vernacular Bibles, prayer books and catechisms were adopted by all reforming churches. Sooner or later, scriptural translations were officially authorized by all rulers who broke with Rome, and thus entered into the mainstream of national literary cultures in Protestant lands" (Eisenstein, 1979, pp. 348–349). Thus the Reformation and use of vernacular printing worked together to promote the spirit of nationalism.

I have argued that the publication of the Bible in vernacular tongues was one of the factors leading to the Reformation. Apropos of this hypothesis, it is interesting to note the following pattern among the national groups that adopted or rejected Protestantism. Those national groups whose mother tongue was one of the Romance languages, and hence closely related to Latin, remained Roman Catholic. These include the Italians, Spanish, Catalans, Portuguese, and French. Those national groups whose vernaculars were in no way related to Latin for the most part became Protestant, such as the Germans, Swiss, Dutch, English, Scots, Welsh, Danes, Norwegians, Swedes, Finns, Latvians, Estonians, and Czechs. There are some exceptions to the rule. The Irish, Polish, Lithuanians, Hungarians, and Austrians do not speak a Romance language, but remained Roman Catholic, and the French-speaking people of Switzerland became Protestant.

One possible explanation for the pattern is that of geographic proximity. Although not denying that geography might have contributed to the pattern, I argue that the following mechanism was also important. In those lands in which a Romance language was spoken, the need for a vernacular translation of the Bible was not as great because Latin bore some resemblance to the spoken language. In those cases, however, where the vernacular language did not resemble Latin at all, translations were an absolute necessity, and hence a greater percentage of the population made use of them. Vernacular translations contributed to the spirit of independence described earlier and, hence, might have contributed to the correlation of the Romance countries with Roman Catholicism and the non-Romance countries with Protestantism.

PRINT AND NATIONALISM

In the literate age, centralized control was achieved by the technique of divide and conquer. This model of fragmentation, Innis and McLuhan contended, was a by-product of alphabetic literacy and reinforced by the mechanical forms of industrialization that the printing press inspired.

> Political organizations determined to an important extent by the limitations of armed force and characterized by centralized power emphasized the capital and left their impression on cultural activity. They provided a shelter for the development of communication

facilities. Communication was subordinated to the demands of centralized power in religion and in political organization; it was
characterized by the use of the eye rather than the ear. The scribe
occupied a strategic position in centralized bureaucracies." (Innis,
1971, p. 135)

The pattern Innis described for literate society before the printing
press applied more to print-dominated cultures, particularly once the
Industrial Revolution commenced. It led to the creation of centralized
forms of commerce and governance in the form of nation-states, which
operated as both economic and political units.

The spirit of nationalism that engulfed Europe was reinforced by the
products manufactured by the printing press and the many fallouts of
this new technology, including the translation of the classical works into
vernaculars, establishment of vernacular literature and culture, the
Reformation, and the public education system. The printing press
played the central role in the rise of nationalism—first by releasing the
forces that generated the movement and then by providing the medium
whereby the movement took hold. This parallels the role it played in the
Reformation. "By the end of the sixteenth century the flexibility of the
alphabet and printing had contributed to the growth of diverse vernacular literatures and had provided a basis for divisive nationalism in
Europe" (Innis, 1972, p. 55). Through the promotion of the use of vernaculars, print gave rise to national languages and cultures through which
the aspirations of nationalism could be expressed and in which a national consciousness could emerge.

Many national literatures grew out of the vernacular translations of
the Bible, which lent them a new dignity (Kohn, 1955). Authors writing
in their native tongues—Chaucer, Dante, Luther, Montaigne,
Cervantes—were quietly building nations and national loyalties more
effectively than all the generals, kings, and statesmen of Europe. These
writers, and the printer publishers who disseminated their literary output, provided a medium for the expression of national sentiment and
identity. The relationship between this literature and the creation of new
loyalties based on ethnic identification once again illustrates McLuhan's
aphorism that "the medium is the message." In this case, the vernacular
language and printing press were the media and nationalism was the
message.

Another medium for the expression of nationalistic feelings was the
Protestant churches that came into existence during the Reformation.
These churches authorized vernacular versions of the Bible and hence
were organized along national lines (Eisenstein, 1979). These churches
opposed the authority of Rome and promoted local or national control
of religious and moral matters. The practice of the same religious belief,

which was identified uniquely with a people with a common language, reinforced their national identity.

The Reformed churches were not the only public institutions that reinforced nationalistic feelings. The school system, another by-product of the printing press, also inculcated the spirit of national uniformity in its attempt to create a homogeneous population of national citizens. Access to the education system was not universal, and only a small percentage of the population learned to read and write. It was precisely this population, however, that mounted the various campaigns for nationhood in Europe. "Nor is it at all certain that the 'masses' in any country have been directly responsible for the rise of modern nationalism. The movement appears to have gotten under way first among the 'intellectual' classes and to have received decisive impetus from support of the middle classes" (Hayes, 1931, p. 293). It was the middle class who became literate in their vernacular and who championed the Reformation and nationalism. The peasants were tied to their land and their mentality to their local district. Only the literate were in a position to appreciate that there were nationalities and languages other than their own.

PRINTING AND DEMOCRACY

The advent of the printing press contributed to the growth of the democratic spirit that the Italian humanists had promoted at the start of Renaissance. In addition to the Reformation and mass education, the printing press inspired the capitalistic and mercantile economic system that helped democratize economic opportunities. It also created the bourgeoisie, or middle class, which became the main pressure group for democratic reforms. The printing press also provided the medium through which those who campaigned for democratic institutions could rally support.

One of the impacts of alphabetic literacy in ancient Greece was the promotion of a spirit of democracy. The printing press had the same influence. However, because of the greater sense of uniformity that print inspired, there was an even greater emphasis in modern democracy on equality and uniform treatment before the law. The uniformity of the printed page was reinforced by the uniformity that the school system incorporated into its hidden curriculum and the common worship that a national church encouraged.

There emerged in this climate the idea of a uniform citizenry living in a national state united by a single language, mode of worship, and philosophy of government. The printing press and various institutions that sprang up around it promoted the notion of the "equal rights of individuals to determine the state and government to which they would belong" and the "equal rights of individual nations to self-determination" (McLuhan, 1962, p. 264). The Italian humanists' early notions of individual liberty evolved in this intellectual environment of nationalism and social uniformity into the modern ideas of parliamentary democracy based on an electoral system of equal representation and equality of treatment before the law. "Printing and improved communications strengthened a representative system in parliament" (Innis, 1972, p. 56). The battle cry of the French Revolution, "Liberty! Equality! Fraternity!", explicitly expressed these ideals. The American Declaration of Independence opens by expressing this sentiment as well: "We hold these truths to be self-evident, that all men are created equal."

The relationship between democracy and printing was embodied in the U.S. Bill of Rights, which guarantees freedom of the press (Innis, 1972). The printing press not only served as a stimulus to promote new democratic reforms, but it provided a mechanism for preserving past gains. The publication of the laws and regulations of a society protects the individual citizen from arbitrary treatment by the civil authorities. The Hammurabi code also owed its effectiveness to being published in the form of stelae in public places. The printing press did the same for modern legislation.

CONCLUSION

In exploring the social consequences of alphabetic literacy disseminated through the medium of print, a complicated pattern of effects, influences, spin-offs, and cross-impacts has emerged. No hard and fast direct causal links can be established between the advent of the printing press and vernacular literatures, universal education, individualism, the Reformation, modern democratic institutions, and capitalism. These modern innovations associated with print, however, can be said to have created a climate conducive to their mutual development. They interacted among themselves, reinforcing each other in a way not unlike the first innovations of alphabetic literacy—namely, the alphabet, codified law, monotheism, abstract science, deductive logic, and individualism. They formed an autocatalytic set of ideas.

17

The Alphabet in the Context of the Electric Age of Information

One of the consequences of print and the Industrial Revolution it inspired was the application of mechanical power to printing, which increased the speed and amount of information disseminated. The next step in the evolution of communications was the electrification of information, first in the form of the telegraph, loudspeaker, and radio, followed by the tape recorder, TV and computer. Electricity not only created new media, but transformed print media, altering the format of newspapers and changing the nature of book and journal publishing (Innis, 1971; McLuhan, 1964). Alphabetic literacy is still a major part of communications in the age of electric information, but its role has dramatically changed.

NEW INFORMATION PATTERNS EMERGE AT THE SPEED OF LIGHT

One of the major changes to occur with electric media—and one that will affect the use of the alphabet—has been the immediate and dramatic increase in the flow of information (McLuhan, 1964). Innis (1971), reflecting on an earlier transformation, noted the radical changes in cultural patterns that occurred with the speedup of information flow as stone and clay were replaced with papyrus and parchment. McLuhan (1964) showed that the changes created by electric information traveling at the speed of light were even more radical. Spatial separations were eliminated by the instantaneous communication of information. "Electric media do not just extend man's spatial powers of organization, they actually abolish the spatial dimension" (McLuhan, 1964, p. 255).

THE REVERSAL OF
MECHANICAL FORMS WITH ELECTRICITY

The electrification of information reversed many of the socioeconomic and cultural patterns of alphabetic writing, such as specialization, fragmentation, uniformity, mechanization, and centralization. Before the age of literacy, the thought patterns and social forms of tribal society were coherent, cohesive, and integrated. The printing press encouraged the emergence of classification, use of logic, separation of the knower from the knowledge central to scientific activity, and specialization of knowledge. Alphabetic writing promoted these developments in two ways—first, through its direct influence, and second, in a reinforced form through the printing press.

The written word not only affected the organization of knowledge, but also the organization of social, political, and economic institutions. The centralization of power; the creation of bureaucracies—whether political, military, or religious; the emergence of the industrial form of organization; and the assembly line, with its segmented specialization of tasks based on standardized interchangeable parts, are all consequences of the alphabet effect reinforced and enhanced by the printing press.

The mechanization and fragmentation of human experience and social forms reached its maximum during the Industrial Age just as electricity was being introduced in the 19th century. The application of electricity to machinery and the media of communications, with its instantaneous feedback and feed forward of information, began to reverse the mechanical forms of division, fragmentation, specialization, and centralization of an industrialized print-configured society. "The separation of function and the division of stages, spaces and tasks were characteristic of literate and visual society and of the Western world. These divisions tend to dissolve through the action of the instant and organic interrelations of electricity" (McLuhan, 1964, 247). The first electric medium to have this impact was the telegraph, which allowed the instantaneous transmission of news from the far corners of the earth. In an instant, the world was shrunk to the dimensions of a "global village" (McLuhan, 1964, p. 35).

Electricity not only affected social patterns, but those of work as well. Centralized patterns of organization, which generally characterize political and religious institutions, extended during the industrial age to forms of work, particularly in manufacturing and distribution. This centralization reversed with the introduction of electricity: "Electric information provides instant data access equally to all members of the organization regardless of their hierarchical positions. For the external action of an organization this fact of instant information spells total decentralization" (McLuhan, 1988, p. 67).

In electrically configured society, work no longer belonged exclusively to the realm of physical labor, but shifted from manufacturing material goods to processing information, which is a decentralized activity. Rather than holding a 9-to-5 job, individuals began to assume a role in their society that resembled the pattern prevalent during the Middle Ages. The boundaries between work and leisure began to disappear.

Electricity through its powers of integration affected the organization and pursuit of knowledge. The specialist, working exclusively in one field of study, no longer dominated learning. Generalists and multidisciplinary collaborations began to play an important role. The boundaries between science and the humanities began to dissolve. Innovation and new ideas in learning no longer belonged exclusively to a small number of centers of learning.

Electricity discouraged the centralization of other activities as well. World empires began to break apart, paradoxically enough, under the influence of instantaneous communication. Neither monopolies of knowledge nor those of power could withstand the all-inclusive and encompassing effects of electricity. Electrically configured information systems have the power to decentralize whether they operate in the political, economic, academic, or social sphere. "It is like the difference between a railway system and an electric grid: the one requires railheads, and big urban centers. Electric power equally available in the farmhouse and the Executive Suite, permits any place to be a center, and does not require large aggregations" (McLuhan, 1964, p. 36).

In the electric age of information, activity shifts from the manufacture of material goods to the processing of information, which is a decentralized activity. The mode of organization is like that of the electric circuit. No point along a circuit (or a circle) may be regarded as the center of the circuit because each point is as central as the next. For example, the telephone places us at the center of a worldwide network of information. Computers linked by telephone lines permit access to vast stores of knowledge from any point on Earth. The microelectronic revolution, which has greatly reduced the cost of electronic equipment and increased portability through miniaturization, enhances this trend toward decentralization. There is little point in going to a centralized office to use information equipment that one can operate just as easily at home. One can network with others by telephone or the Internet as easily from home as from the office.

SOCIETIES IMITATE THEIR TECHNOLOGY

McLuhan (1964) observed that industrial or mechanical society was fragmented and centralized and that this pattern reversed in the electric age of information to one of integration and decentralization, which retrieved certain aspects of the social organization of preliterate society. These observations were based on the following set of assumptions:

1. The dominant tools or technologies of a society create patterns of usage that infiltrate or penetrate the social structures of a society,

2. These patterns change those structures, and

3. The social structures come to imitate or replay the patterns by which these dominant technologies are organized.

"When a community develops some extension of itself, it tends to allow all other functions to be altered to accommodate that form" (McLuhan, 1964, p. 139). Consider the way in which cars have taken over our cities so that the pedestrian feels crowded out (McLuhan, 1964). The social structures that are changed by a technology tend to reproduce new technological innovations in the same mold, thus reinforcing the already existing pattern (McLuhan, 1964). There is an analogy here with Kuhn's (1972) notion that, once a new scientific theory scores a success, it serves as a paradigm for further scientific work, and every conceivable extension, articulation, and application of the original idea is developed. This process, which he called "normal science," also occurs with technology. A technological breakthrough serves as a paradigm that is extended, articulated, and applied in every conceivable way in a society.

The use of repeatable, fragmented, identical elements—the letters, which began with the introduction of the phonetic alphabet—is an example of such a paradigm. The extension of this idea resulted in the development of codified law, monotheism, abstract science, and deductive logic (McLuhan & Logan, 1977). The articulation of the alphabetic paradigm of the repeatability of fragmented identical items and the letters in the hardware realm of mechanics created the printing press, assembly line, mass production, and general organizing principle of the industrial age.

The evolution of this fragmented, specialist, linear, sequential mode of organization came to an end with the introduction of electricity and its application to information systems. Slowly the patterns of industrial organization and social interaction reversed themselves as electricity reconfigured social structures. This development continues with the penetration of microelectronics in the form of integrated circuits into organizational structures. It may lead to a greater integration and decentralization of social structures along with more of a shift to software and hybrid electronic systems.

In *The Third Wave*, Toffler (1980) discussed the possibility of being able to work at home by making use of an electronic workstation and increased communication with the outside world. This notion of an *electronic cottage* incorporates three major trends of economic life in the age of electric information: (a) the decentralization of economic activity, (b) the integration of work with home life and leisure activities, and (c) the replacement of a job with a role in society.

THE FUTURE OF THE ALPHABET
IN THE ELECTRIC INFORMATION AGE

To understand the role that alphabetic literacy plays in the electronic information age, we must understand that the form of print or book may remain unchanged. The information environment in which prints operates, however, may be vastly changed, and meaning and impact of the printed word may not be the same. Electronic-based information systems do not spell the end of print. Quite the contrary, they promote its use by radically altering its context and the role print plays in the overall information environment.

The book is and always will be a convenient medium in which to find and store information. However, the book may not necessarily be the child's first or only entry into the world of adventures and ideas as it has been in the past. In fact, that role is now played by TV and, as a consequence, young people are, according to McLuhan, "gray at the age of three." They know more about the facts of life and less about its mysteries than youngsters a generation ago.

The printed medium is no longer the principal source of information for adults either. Newspapers and magazines struggle to remain viable. The percentage of overall information disseminated by print compared with electric media constantly shrinks. This is a more relevant measure of the importance of print than the number of books sold—which, paradoxically, has increased.

The alphabet effect has not lost its power, but it has been diluted by the increased flow of electric information. It also has new functions. Electric media are dependent on the print medium for both their organization and content in the form of scripts. Even news shows depend heavily on newspapers and other print media for their story ideas despite that TV is the perfect medium for transmitting newsworthy events as they unfold.

The questions that must be addressed regarding the future of the alphabet in an electrically configured information environment are not of survival, but rather of market share. What kind of balance will be struck between the electric and print media? Two electronic media whose impact on literacy will be great, and therefore must be carefully examined, are TV and the computer.

TELEUISION

Despite that sales of books have steadily increased, the actual percentage of time that people spend reading, particularly as a leisure activity, has declined. One of the major reasons for this decline has been that TV has absorbed a major share of leisure time. In North America, viewers spend on the average 3 to 4 hours per day in front of the tube. It is not just the loss of time devoted to reading that has affected literacy, but the negative impacts that TV viewing has had on reading, particularly for school-children learning for the first time.

Brain-wave patterns, lateralization (left–right split) of the brain, and attention span are three factors, possibly related, that might explain some of the negative impacts that TV viewing has had on alphabetic literacy. Research in the field of neurophysiology and neurosurgery has resulted in empirical evidence for the lateralization and specialization of the two hemispheres of the brain. Although the notion that each of us possesses two different personalities is a bit overdone, there nevertheless exists solid evidence that each individual possesses two distinct modes or styles of cognitive activity associated with the activities of the left and right hemispheres of the brain.

The left-brain patterns of rationality, logic, linearity, sequence, mathematics, and analysis are characteristic of the literate mode of communications and have been reinforced by the phonetic alphabet, particularly in the print mode. The right-brain patterns of intuition, analogy, pattern recognition, nonlinearity, simultaneity, and holism are associated with both the oral and electric information modes of communication. Left-brain literary information patterns favor specialism, whereas the right-brain patterns of oral and electric information tend more toward a multi-disciplinary approach.

The lateralization of the brain provides a mechanism for under-standing how alphabetic literacy reinforces left-brain patterns and encourages the narrowness and tunnel vision of the specialist. Electric information breaks down the monopoly of print and encourages the right-brain activities of pattern recognition and environmental aware-ness of the generalist.

The alphabet created a lineal and visual environment of information products, which the printing press reinforced. These literary packages then became the models according to which socioeconomic structures were designed and organized, further reinforcing left-brain patterns. The conjecture that this form of organization can be associated with one of the lobes of the brain is consistent with the results of the Russian neu-rophysiologist A. R. Luria (1970):

> The mental process for writing a word entails still another special-ization: putting the letters in the proper sequence to form the word. Lashley discovered many years ago that sequential analysis involved a zone of the brain different from that employed for spatial analysis. In the course of our extensive studies we have located the region responsible for sequential analysis in the anterior regions of the left hemisphere.

Sequential analysis or linear thinking is not merely a figure of speech, but a bona fide activity of the brain, which Luria (1970) located in a specific place in the left hemisphere. According to our view, linear sequencing, which is crucial to logical, mathematical, and scientific thinking, is, stimulated by the use of the alphabet. Luria's findings now indicate the neurological mechanism whereby the phonetic alphabet, with its lineal structure, was able to create the conditions conducive to the development of Western science, technology, and rationality.

Alphabetic literacy reinforces left-brain patterns of cognition because of the linear, sequential way in which information is transmitted letter by letter. Electric information, in contrast, tends to be simultaneous in nature. Consider TV, where the 525 lines that constitute the video image are broadcast separately onto the cathode ray tube (CRT) screen. These 525 distinct lines are scanned and perceived separately. They are then simultaneously reassembled by each viewer using his or her own individual cognitive processes to re-create the original image in his or her own mind.

The processes of viewing TV and reading are completely different. The reader of alphabetic texts takes an active role in which he or she deciphers the visual signs and converts them into spoken language, which is heard in his or her mind. Beginning readers and those not proficient at the art must sound out each word they read to hear the spoken words. More experienced and efficient readers decipher the alphabetic code silently. The attention span of the reader is self-generated by his or her interest in the text.

Reading, however, requires the active participation and discipline of the user or else the communication link is broken. This is not the case with TV, where the viewer not only becomes a passive recipient of the information, but is also mesmerized by the video imagery. The addictive use of TV destroys the user's attention span and encourages other perceptual habits that have a negative impact on reading. This is accomplished solely through the perceptual processes that the user must undergo to watch TV and is largely independent of the medium's content.

Televised information, independent of the content, is sprayed on the CRT screen one line at a time in short bursts of 0.063 milliseconds that are refreshed 60 times per second. The viewer constructs an image by simultaneously adding each of the single-line images over a fraction of a second. This form of information delivery is totally unique and differs not only from textual systems such as the printed book, but also from other visual media such as photographs, slides, or moving pictures.

Although these effects are strictly a product of the medium and are independent of the programming, the characteristics of a medium influence the nature of its contents. The content of both oral speech and writing are words, but the way in which words are used and the patterns of sentence structure, differed significantly with the advent of writing. The content of literate communication is affected by the nature of the writing system and tends to imitate the medium. Writing styles in the electric age of information come to imitate electric media. The telegraph, for example, inspired newspaper headlines (McLuhan, 1964).

The content of TV is also influenced by the medium. The producers of TV programming have found that, to maintain viewers' attention, there must be a great deal of action. As a consequence, much greater use is made of cuts, dissolves, zooms, and scene changes in TV than in films. One hour of afternoon programming was monitored and found to consist of four 10-minute sequels of a soap opera and four 5-minute sequels of 30-second spot advertisements (Czernis & Logan, 1981). A typical scene in the soap opera lasted, on the average, 95 seconds. The change of scene and imagery in the 30-second advertisements was even more frantic. This hectic pace was not just a function of afternoon programming.

An analysis of the evening news revealed that the average length of a news item is 92 seconds, in which there are a number of different scene changes and cuts to and from interviewers and interviewees. [The observations reported here were made 20 years ago. The pace of changing images has actually increased in that time.] The pattern that emerges with TV is clear. A passive audience is continuously bombarded with short blips of information rendered in a fast-paced montage of changing images.

Is it any wonder that, after being exposed to hour after hour of TV, children will find reading, with its linear sequential repetition of the same 26 letters, boring?

> Television teaches the young child to "learn to learn" in a very special manner . . . before he has ever looked at a book. So the child learns to learn by quick looks. Later, if the child is in a society where reading is required, he conforms to the new "learn to learn" medium with the habits he has picked up earlier from TV. He tries to comprehend print via quick looks. It doesn't work. Learning to read is difficult, hard—and this comes as a surprise, an intolerable one in many cases. (Krugman, 1971)

BRAIN WAVES AND
THE ERGONOMICS OF READING

The problems that TV viewing creates for young readers go beyond attention span to the fundamental questions of brain function. In terms of left- and right-brain functions, it is obvious that reading requires and hence promotes left-brain processes of linearity, sequence, analysis, and rationality, whereas TV viewing requires and hence promotes a different pattern, probably that of the right-brain function of pattern recognition and formation. This would provide some explanation of why reading skills suffer among youngsters who are totally immersed in a TV environment.

H. E. Krugman (1971), who conducted a series of experiments at General Electric in which the brainwave patterns of TV viewers and print readers were measured and compared, provides an explanation of this phenomenon. The subjects were shown a series of TV advertisements and asked to read a number of printed advertisements while their brainwave patterns were monitored. Krugman found that, independent of the content of the TV programming, a distinct pattern of brainwaves emerged that was quite distinct from the patterns of those who were reading. "The basic electrical response of the brain is more to the media than to the content differences within the TV commercials" (Krugman, 1971, pp. 3–9). Krugman found that the response to print was active and consisted primarily of fast brainwaves, whereas the response to TV was passive and consisted primarily of slow brainwaves.

These results have a number of interesting implications. They illustrate McLuhan's aphorism that "the medium is the message" and show that the effects of a medium, at least at the neurological level of brainwaves, are independent of the content of the medium and vary from medium to medium. The results also have important implications for the future of the alphabet in the video environment. This is an extremely important issue because of the use of video displays by computers and, hence, the display of information on the World Wide Web (www)—a source of more and more information especially for students. If video displays independent of the content excite one set of brainwave patterns, which is completely different from that produced by reading, it is apparent that the extensive use of a CRT can result in stress. This explains why there is a growing tendency for users of the Web to print out the texts they retrieve and read the information on paper instead of directly from the monitor.

There have been a large number of reports of visual discomfort, headaches, muscle aches, nausea, and general fatigue. There have also been reports of abnormally high levels of miscarriages and/or birth defects among CRT users in certain offices. At first these were thought to be due to radiation, but measurements have failed to find evidence of harmful rays. Therefore, the problems that have been reported could be due to stress—the stress generated by attempting to use the left-brain patterns necessary for reading while utilizing a medium that promotes right-brain patterns instead.

As the use of computer systems with video displays continues to grow, the ergonomics of reading in this environment (i.e., the physical and mental effects on human beings) becomes an increasingly important issue. The work of Krugman (1971) has only begun to scratch the surface. Much more research is obviously needed, as well as an understanding of the effects of other display media such as light emitting diodes (LEDs), liquid crystals, and high-speed print terminals.

THE DOUBLE BIND OF COMMUNICATION

The computer, by combining left- and right-brain processes, might provide the way out of a paradox or double bind that the use of the alphabet in an electronic-information environment poses. In an article entitled "The Double Bind of Communication," McLuhan and I (Logan &

McLuhan, 1979) identified a paradox that arises out of his theory of communications. The use of the alphabet reinforced by the printing press created the dominance of left-brain patterns of thought and organization that have characterized science-based industrial society. One of the unfortunate side effects of this pattern of organization has been the tunnel vision of the specialist, which has contributed to a number of major global problems facing the world today, such as pollution, energy crisis, depletion of natural resources, overpopulation, and balance of nuclear terror. The advent of electric information systems brought with it new patterns of communication in which the right hemisphere began to reassert itself. The present-day concerns with environmental and ecological issues are in part due to this development. Unfortunately, some electric information systems, such as TV, have had a negative impact by destroying attention span and discouraging reading and other analytic skills associated with the left brain. Because human survival depends on our ability to manage and maintain the complex technological machinery we have created, the degradation of reading and other analytic skills could represent a serious problem.

We are caught in a double bind. Electric media are a mixed blessing. They encourage ecological patterns of thought and help us recognize the nature of our global village. Yet they discourage the development of reading and the concomitant analytic skills associated with them (Logan & McLuhan, 1979). Reading is a mixed blessing. Print encourages specialism and blinds us to the ecological patterns required for our survival. If our reading skills deteriorate, however, the capacity to maintain the complex technological infrastructure also vital to our survival will be impaired.

The unique challenge facing educators is to promote both sets of skills—the analytic ones associated with reading and the synthetic ones associated with computers and other forms of electronic information technology. There is no inherent conflict between print and electronic information or between left- and right-brain patterns of knowledge. The dynamic tension between these different ways of organizing information can be creative. A way to synthesize them must be found.

McLuhan and I first formulated the challenge of the double bind of communication 25 years ago, when the microcomputer revolution was just getting underway and the significance of its impact on education was not yet apparent. It is now clear that, because of its relatively low cost, compactness, and user friendliness, the microcomputer will continue to invade the classroom and make radical changes in the way alphabetic literacy and other skills are learned and subsequently utilized.

The microcomputer has been enthusiastically received by the majority of the school population, including normal, gifted, and slow students. With each of these groups, the computer has inspired positive attitudes toward all phases of learning and has promoted a good mix of skills. The microcomputer is the first technology introduced into classrooms at the grassroots level.

The microcomputer seems to promote new cognitive styles, in which the best of the analytic approach can be retained without the narrowness and tunnel vision of the specialist. The computer, by integrating both left- and right-brain processes, might lead to the solution of the dilemma of the double bind of communication. The computer can help the leaders of the future develop the analytic skills necessary to maintain the machinery of our science-based industrial economy while seeing the larger ecological patterns necessary for global survival. It could replace the present climate of confrontation between two opposing forces; one promoting the interests of industry and the other those of the environment. The computer system and operational research (or general systems) approach could become the metaphor or model by which industrial and environmental interests are balanced and integrated.

Let us examine the mechanism whereby the integration of left- and right-brain processes could take place and see what role the alphabet effect would play in the realization of this transformation. Just as the printing press enhanced the alphabet through uniformity and the ability to create multiple copies relatively cheaply, so too the computer steps up the intensity of alphabetic writing by making it more accessible and easily controllable through word-processing routines. The ability to easily assemble alphabetic texts—to automatically correct, edit, and manipulate them beginning at the first-grade level—reinforces a number of left-brain processes of analysis and rationality without requiring slavish conformity to the patterns of linearity and sequence. The ease with which blocks of text can be moved about in the larger composition promotes right-brain processes of pattern recognition and hence creates a new balance in the production of literary materials that belongs uniquely to the computer. It is somewhat paradoxical that it is the unique properties of the alphabet as a writing system that enables the computer to develop the right-brain features of pattern recognition and formation.

It is not an accident that the alphabetic writing systems were the first to find applications with the computer. This is because of the ease with which the individual, repeatable, and uniform letters of the alphabet can be manipulated and maneuvered. The alphabet as a coding scheme is totally compatible with the computer, which is another form of technology that codes information. The alphabet uses 26 bits (the letters) and the computer uses 2 bits (1 and 0). Special steps must be taken to use a nonalphabetic writing system like Chinese with the computer. The simplicity of using only the typewriterlike keyboard as the sole input device no longer works with Chinese characters consisting of two radicals. The need for computers might be one of the factors motivating the Chinese government to consider the alphabetization of Mandarin as well as the recent reforms and regularization of the spelling of Chinese places and names. Only an alphabetic script permits the easy manipulation and processing of textual material.

The only negative or down side to literary composition with computers is the use of the video environment to access text. Conflict of brainwave patterns arises when the left-brain process of reading is attempted in the video medium that favors right-brain patterns. Part of this difficulty can be obviated if extensive use is made of high-speed printers. The computer that is able to search and access great stores of information and then deliver the desired output on paper, using a fast printer, will obviously combine the best of left- and right-brain patterns of information handling.

This is the promise of computer technology—that the vitality of alphabetic literacy will be not only maintained, but also enhanced. The paradox of computers is that by stepping up the left-brain processes of linear sequencing to the speed of light new patterns emerge, such as cybernetics and ecological analysis. These right-brain processes, however, still retain many of the analytic properties of preelectric alphabetic literacy. It is also a reflection of the flexibility and durability of the alphabet that a machine designed primarily for numbers, as an automatic computing machine, should now emerge as a processor and handler of alphabetic texts (i.e., a word processor). This transformation of the computer, which we study in the next chapter, is another example of the ubiquity and potency of the alphabet effect.

18

The Alphabet in the Context of the Electronic Era of Knowledge

THE DYNAMIC NATURE OF LANGUAGE

To see the relationship between the phonetic alphabet and computing, it is necessary to explore the nature of language, communications, and informatics, which are intimately connected. In fact, alphabetic writing and computing are part of an evolutionary chain of languages (Logan, 2000).

Language, as we have seen throughout this book, is not merely the passive container or medium of human thought whose only function is to transmit and communicate our ideas and sentiments from one person to another. Language is, as McLuhan pointed out, a living vortex of power—that shapes and transforms our thinking. Language is both a system of communications and an informatic tool. Without verbal language, our mental life would be reduced to feelings, emotions, and processing our perceptions. Verbal language makes conceptualization, abstraction, planning, and reflection possible. Our ability to use verbal language is what differentiates us from the rest of the animal kingdom. Other animals are capable of communicating with each other, but the range of what they can express is limited to a small number (less than 50) of signals. In contrast, human verbal language is generative so there are an infinite number of possible messages or meanings that we are capable of composing and communicating.

Language is a dynamic living organism that is constantly growing and evolving. Not only does spoken language grow in terms of its increased vocabulary and new grammatical forms, but it also evolves into new forms of notated presentation and expression. In this first section of this chapter, we develop the hypothesis that speech, writing, mathematics, science, computing, and the Internet form an evolutionary chain of languages. Two of the languages—mathematics and writing—emerged at exactly the same point in time around 3100 B.C., followed approximately 1,000 years later by science. Two more languages have appeared in rapid succession in the past 50 years—namely, computing and the Internet, the fifth and sixth languages.

The idea that the alphabet and computing are part of an evolutionary chain of languages began as my attempt to understand how computers could best be used in the educational arena. My research, conducted at the Ontario Institute for Studies in Education (OISE) in Toronto, involved the classroom observation of the use of computers (Sullivan et al., 1986) and two theoretical studies (Logan, 1986b; Logan et al., 1983) conducted for the Ontario Ministry of Education. My work in computer applications in education was carried out against the backdrop of the research I had engaged in with Marshall McLuhan and that led to the alphabet effect. My approach to understanding computers in education was therefore strongly flavored by the communication theories of McLuhan and the notion that the computer is a medium of communication. My own work in theoretical physics, which heavily relied on computers, made me equally sensitive to the information-processing aspect of computers.

Therefore, at the outset of my study to understand the impact of computers on education, I regarded the computer as both a communication medium and tool for processing information. I reached the same conclusion regarding writing and alphabetic writing in particular. We have seen in earlier chapters how the phonetic alphabet, which is a communication medium, is also a tool for organizing information as it contributed to the development of codified law, abstract science, deductive logic, and place number system. Also the work of Schmandt–Besserat showed how the clay tokens originally designed for informatic purposes of keeping track of tributes evolved into the first system of written communication.

As a result of these considerations, I formulated the following two theses:

1. all forms of verbal language have both a communications and an informatics dimension that facilitates human thought (language = communications + informatics);

2. speech, writing, mathematics, science, computing, and the Internet form an chain of languages.

My insight that computing contained elements of both communication and informatics seemed to apply to all forms of language. The term *informatics* is generally used only within the context of computers. However, it is defined in Webster's as "the science of obtaining and transmitting information," and hence is not strictly limited to computers. Therefore, one can consider the informatics of the oral tradition or written texts as well as the informatics of mathematics and science.

THE SEMANTICS AND SYNTAX
OF THE SIX MODES OF LANGUAGE

The traditional view of linguists is that only the spoken form of language qualifies as a language. The written form of a language is merely a way to transcribe the spoken form of the language and cannot be considered as a language in its own right. Ferdinand de Saussure (1967), one of the founders of the field of linguistics, formulated the attitude of traditional linguistics toward writing when he wrote: "Language and writing are two different systems of signs; the latter only exists for the purpose of representing the former. . . . The subject matter of linguistics is not the connection between the written and spoken word, but only the latter, the spoken word is its subject." Leonard Bloomfield, (1933) another immensely influential linguist, reinforced de Saussure's position when he wrote: "Writing is not language, but merely a way of recording language by means of visible marks" (Bloomfield, 1933, p. 21).

The relationship between writing and language that de Saussure and Bloomfield posited is far too confining for understanding the implications of the alphabet effect for computing and the Internet and their impact on the future of communication, work, and education. Their definitions are restricted to a model in which the sole purpose of language is communication; they do not take into account the information-processing capabilities of language—a key consideration for understanding the role of computers in society. These traditional linguists are products of industrial age attitudes of assigning only a single task to any activity. The definitions of Bloomfield and de Saussure, however, have been re-evaluated by a modern generation of linguists from whom I draw inspiration. They view language from the perspective of informatics and, hence, understood the multitasking nature of language.

Michael Stubbs (1980) critiqued Bloomfield's definition of *writing* as follows: "Writing is not merely a record. . . . I know from personal experience that formulating ideas in written language changes those ideas and produces new ones." Smith (1982) agreed: "Ideas develop from interaction and dialogue . . . especially with one's own writing" (p. 204). Hertzler (1965) also concurred: "People often find that their thoughts are clarified and systematized, and that necessary qualifications and extensions appear, when they subject them to the more rigorous test of exactness and completeness demanded by the written form" (p. 444).

Although it is true that written language is derived from spoken language, it is useful to regard them as two separate language modes because they process information so differently. Arguments that support the notion that writing is a separate mode of language can also be made for mathematics, science, computing, and the Internet. These five additional modes of language each have unique strategies for communicating, storing, retrieving, organizing, and processing information. Therefore, I have extended the notion of those linguists who consider speech and writing as separate modes of language to claim that speech, writing, mathematics, science, computing, and the Internet are six separate modes of language that are distinct but interdependent. They form an evolutionary sequence in which the later modes are derived from and incorporate elements of the earlier modes of language. They form a nested set of languages in which the later forms contain the elements of the earlier forms.

I demonstrate that these six languages qualify as distinct forms of language based on criteria established by traditional linguists. I claim that each of these six forms of language possesses its own unique semantics and syntax (Logan, 2000). According to Paivio and Begg (1981), "semantics and syntax—meaning and grammatical patterning— are the indispensable core attributes of any human language" (p. 25). If writing, mathematics, science, computing, and the Internet are distinct modes of human language that deserve to be differentiated from speech, they must have distinct semantical and syntactical features above and beyond those of speech, which I set out to demonstrate.

The semantics of the written word are quite similar to those of the spoken word, although there are examples where a word used in oral language is not used in prose and vice versa. It is at the syntactical level that written language begins to more radically distinguish itself from speech. Punctuation serves a function beyond reproducing the natural pauses and reflections of speech; mainly it provides a syntactical structure to language that is quite different from that of speech. Writing encourages a formal structuring of language consisting of sentences, paragraphs, sections, and chapters largely absent in spoken language.

Analysis of the transcription of most oral discourse reveals that spoken language is not generally organized into grammatically correct sentences. In fact, the term *grammar* betrays its association with writing through its etymology. The Greek term for *letter* (as in letters of the alphabet) is *gramma*. In short, grammar was not formalized before writing, just as there was no such thing as spelling before writing and no uniform spelling before the printing press.

In addition to the formal distinctions between written and spoken language, there is also the empirical change of vocabulary and syntax that the storage features of writing encouraged. Within the semantic domain, one observes a marked increase in abstract words and terminology as a language acquires a written form. A comparison between the lexicography of Homer (as found in the transcriptions of his orally composed poems) and that of the ancient Greek philosophers and playwrights of the fifth and fourth centuries B.C. reveals the development of a new written vocabulary. The new lexicon of written words is rich in abstract terminology appearing in the Greek language for the first time, and older words take on additional new abstract meanings (Havelock, 1963). Within the syntactical domain, the major structural change with writing is the appearance of the prose system, which incorporates many more analytical features than the sentences constructed within the oral tradition.

In the language of mathematics, the semantical domain or lexicon consists of precisely defined notations for numbers such as 0, 1, 2, 100, 1/2, 0.4, and square root of 2; mathematical operations such as +, -, x, and ÷; and logical relationships such as >, <, and =. The other semantical elements unique to mathematics are its definitions and axioms, such as those found in geometry, number theory, and other logical systems. The semantic elements of the language of mathematics have unique and unambiguous meaning unlike spoken or written language.

The precision of the semantical conventions of mathematics also extends to the syntactical domain. The basic syntax of the language of mathematics is that of logic. Mathematical syntax, unlike that of spoken or written language, is totally unambiguous. The rules of grammar that govern speech and writing are subject to conflicting interpretations, whereas those of mathematics are not. The language of mathematics also introduces unique syntactical structures not found in natural languages, such as proofs, theorems, and lemmas.

The language of science includes the semantic elements of speech, writing, and mathematics, but it also introduces new semantic units unique unto itself. These include quantitative concepts like mass, force, velocity, mole; qualitative concepts like organic/inorganic, animate/inanimate, solid/liquid/gas, and intelligence; and theoretical concepts like inertia, entropy, valence, and natural selection. As is the case with the language of mathematics, the semantics of science is characterized by precise and unambiguous definitions, although much of the terminology employed corresponds to words that appear in everyday spoken language. In spoken English, *mass* can refer to either volume or weight. In physics, *mass* is precisely defined in terms of weight, but a careful distinction is made between *mass* and *weight*. An object's mass is universal, but its weight depends on what planet or gravitational field it finds itself. A traveler in outer space might experience weightlessness, but never masslessness.

As was the case with semantics, the syntax of science includes structures from speech, writing, and mathematics. Science also introduces its own syntactical elements, however. The three most important elements, the ones which in a sense define the nature of science, are: (a) scientific method, (b) classification of information or data (taxonomy), and (c) organization of knowledge such as the grouping of scientific laws to form a scientific theory. The centrality of the classificatory and organizational structures is due to the fact that *science* is defined as organized knowledge. The scientific method, with its elements of observation, generalization, hypothesizing, experimental testing, and verification, is the key element that defines the character of science. It is the scientific method that qualifies science as a distinctive language, rather than a carefully organized scholarly activity like history, which also makes use of organizational principles and other modes of language—namely, speech, writing, and mathematics.

The language of computing includes all of the semantical and syntactical elements of the four earlier modes of language. It also possesses its own semantical and syntactical elements by virtue of the activities of its programmers and end users. The semantics of the programming languages and preprogrammed software specify computer inputs and outputs. The syntactical structures of programming languages and software formalize the procedures for transforming inputs into outputs. These syntactical structures are basically unambiguous algorithms for ensuring the accuracy and reliability of the computer's output. The syntactical structures that arise in a programming language or relational database differ from the other language modes so that the user can take advantage of the computer's rapid information-processing speeds.

Although the Internet and the Web incorporate all of the semantical and syntactical elements of computing, they also include their own unique elements in both categories. Perhaps we should clarify the relationship between Web and the Internet. The Web is one of many different elements of the Internet, which include its e-mail facilities, listservs, chat rooms, ftp facilities, Telnet facilities, Web pages, Web sites, intranets, extranets, portal sites, and e-commerce sites.

The Internet has a number of unique syntactical elements. One of the unique syntactical elements of the sixth language is hypertext, which makes it possible to link all of Web sites and Web pages in cyberspace to form one huge global document. Another unique syntactical element is the Internet Protocol, which allows all of the computers connected to the Internet to form one huge Global Network and makes the Web, ftp, and telnet all possible. McLuhan's prediction of a *global village* has been realized. Still another unique syntactical element of the Internet is the search engine, which increases access to knowledge and information and hence provides an extra level of communication that the other forms of verbal language cannot match. The search engine also facilitates people finding each other, and hence contributes to the creation of a global knowledge community.

AN EVOLUTIONARY CHAIN OF LANGUAGES

Having established that speech, writing, math, science, computing, and the Internet may be considered distinct forms of language, one is entitled to ask, but why an evolutionary chain? I believe that a new language evolves in response to some form of information overload or chaos that arises when the informatic capacity of the previous set of languages can no longer cope with a new level of complexity. Each new language evolves from its predecessors as new information-processing needs emerge that the preceding languages cannot deal with effectively. The new language represents a bifurcation to a new level of order that was not possible with the previous set of languages. The new language retains vestiges of the previous languages from which it springs, but adds new elements specifically to deal with the information overload and chaos to which it is responding. Each new language eventually leads to an information explosion and a new set of challenges, which sets the stage for the next level of development and the emergence of still another form of language.

Mathematics and writing arose at exactly the same point in time around 3000 B.C. They were part of a notational system to record commercial transactions and emerged to deal with the information overload brought about by the rapid increase in the administration and trade of agricultural commodities in the city-states of Sumer. Writing and mathematics, the second and third languages after speech, immediately gave rise to the world's first formal schools to teach the new skills associated with these two languages. Schools required teachers who conducted scholarship and specialized study, which in turn generated a new information overload. The fourth language, science, emerged approximately

1,000 years later circa 2000 B.C. It represents an organized form of knowledge that brought a new level of order to the deluge of information generated by writing and math. Computing, the fifth language, emerged just 60 years ago out of the need to cope with the information overload created by science. The Internet, the sixth and most recent language in this chain, arose to deal with the information overlaod created by computing and the need to communicate the many messages generated by the fifth language—computing. The Internet arose by combining computing with telephony and hypertext markup language (HTML). In conclusion, each new language emerged as a bifurcation from the previous languages each time a new information overload developed.

ALPHABETIC LITERACY, COMPUTERS, EDUCATION, AND WORK

Computers and the Internet are having a positive impact on alphabetic literacy. Unlike TV, the effect of these media on literacy is positive. The place where computing is having its greatest effect on the use of the alphabet is in our educational systems and workplaces. The Gutenberg print revolution inspired a new form of education and commerce, in which printed text served as the principal focus of instruction and business communication. The educational goals and values of today's school system and the modus operandi of business are a product of that print mentality. We are currently in the midst of an electronic communications revolution that promises to create as much change as the printing press did over 500 years ago.

The computer is playing an increasingly important role in both scholastic and commercial communications. The computer will not replace the printed word, just as print did not replace handwriting or the spoken word. However, just as printing changed the role of manuscript and oral recitation, so the computer, which is also a medium for print, will transform print and the way it is used for learning and commerce. Computing and the Internet are also changing the relationships between teachers and pupils, as well as between workers and their colleagues and managers.

> Technological change continues at an accelerating rate, in the short term possibly compounding our economic and social difficulties and in the long term providing better solutions. The process of education will continue to be influenced by the explosive effects of microminiaturization on the technology of communication, and information storage and processing. (Ontario Ministry of Education, 1980)

Not only will the educational system be dramatically transformed to accommodate the computer, but the ways in which basic reading and writing skills are taught will also be totally revamped. The revolution has already begun; youngsters all across the globe are now using the computer to learn literacy skills. A similar revolution is taking place in the business world, which is transforming the nature of work, business communications, business relationships, and commerce.

MICROCOMPUTERS AND THE NINEFOLD ENHANCEMENT OF LEARNING IN SCHOOLS AND THE WORKPLACE

A steady invasion of microcomputers into our schools and workplaces for the past 20 years challenges us to evaluate the way we have organized these activities. The education system is particularly sensitive to the influence of communication media and, consequently, has been shaped by them over the centuries. The origins of schools and the formal classroom style of teaching can be traced to the need in Sumer some 5,000 years ago to train young people to use the medium of writing. Many aspects of school and classroom practice have changed surprisingly little since that time.

Alphabetic literacy played an important role in education because of the ease with which reading and writing with a phonetic alphabet can be learned and taught. In those instances, when the literate class opposed the reform of their writing system, as was the case with Egyptian hieroglyphics and classical Chinese, the motivation was the desire to keep the monopoly of knowledge that literacy imparted in the hands of a particular class. The scribal class realized that simplifying the writing system would erode the position of power that literacy conferred on them.

If the invention of writing was the impetus for starting schools and the alphabet for making it easier to acquire literacy, then the Gutenberg printing revolution represents another benchmark in the evolution of education. Low-cost printed material made possible the delivery of educational services to a mass audience. It inspired a system of schooling whose primary task was to teach children to function in the new print environment. Its goals and values, which came to be colored by a print mentality, still color today's schools.

We are now in the midst of a third major communication revolution—one created by electronic information devices. This revolution promises to have as profound an impact on society and education as the printing press had 500 years ago. Mainframe computers had only a minor effect on education and day-to-day practices in the workplace because of their high cost and subsequent lack of access. Microcomputers, in contrast, as a number of authors (Bitter & Camuse, 1984; Coburn, 1982; Papert, 1980; Pitschka, 1984; Taylor, 1980) have suggested, will be and are a source of revolutionary structural change in the modern education system and in the contemporary workplace. What is the basis of this thesis? Other media introduced into the business world and education system have had significant impacts, but they have not made truly revolutionary or structural changes. Certainly the telegraph, telephone, and electric lighting made significant changes in how business was conducted, but not enough to affect its hierarchical structures. The impact of these inventions on education was even less.

The mass media of radio, recordings, TV, and movies had a greater impact on education than on work, but they were not the radical change agents they had been touted to be. Educational TV is one of the more valuable forms of TV programming, but it has not had a lasting impact on education or been the source of any cognitive breakthroughs. Mainframe computers had little, if any, effect on education. Their effect in business has been significant from a quantitative point of view, but not from a qualitative one. They have allowed firms to expand the scope of their operations and automate a number of traditional business processes, but they have not changed the basic corporate hierarchical structure that has characterized companies since the beginning of capitalism and industrialism. What is different about the microcomputer and its power to effect structural change that distinguishes it from other media?

I respond to this question by postulating nine significant impacts microcomputers are having and suggest why they will have a profound and liberating effect on both work and learning:

1. The microcomputer is the first medium to successfully vie with TV for the attention of both adults and young people since the advent of commercial TV.

2. The microcomputer is a communication medium that is interactive and hence has the potential to promote exploration and discovery.

3. The microcomputer is a medium that promotes educational activity, especially continuous learning, and hence, can liberate untapped potential in students and workers.

4. The microcomputer is an ideal medium for delivering and promoting individualized learning and/or individualized work productivity.

5. The microcomputer and the Internet have the potential to promote a positive attitude toward learning and work and encourage a positive self-concept.

6. The microcomputer has the potential to profoundly change teaching patterns within the classroom, as well as the social interactions of pupils and teachers in schools and of staff and management in the workplace.

7. The microcomputer is the first educational technology to be introduced into schools at the grassroots level by teachers, parents, and students, and into the workplace by workers and middle managers rather than senior administrators.

8. The microcomputer is an ideal medium for the integration of the curriculum in the schools and the flow of work in the workplace.

9. The microcomputer can act as an agent of reform, challenging the notion that hierarchical control-and-command structures are the most efficient way to conduct business or that a formal school structure is the best setting for educating children.

Attention Span

The microcomputer is the first medium to successfully vie with TV for the attention of young people and adults alike. This is even more true of the Internet because it is graphical and video content. As a result there has been an increase in the interactivity with alphabetic texts and less attention paid to purely iconic media such as TV.

An Interactive Medium

The microcomputer is a medium of communication that is interactive and hence has the potential to promote exploration and discovery. The Internet increases the interactivity of microcomputers because of hypertext and the ease with which Web sites can be created that incorporate two-way communication and, hence, true interactivity. Television, in sharp contrast to the microcomputer, is a totally passive medium. Children watching its flickering mosaic images quickly become mesmerized. Commercial TV is mental junk food that leaves viewers' minds unnourished and inactive, as can be detected by the glazed look in the eyes of children watching TV. The microcomputer, in contrast, is a natural medium of exploration and discovery. Moreover, the microcomputer provides the user with a sense of control over both learning and the data or information contained within or generated with the computer.

The microcomputer is not the first interactive educational medium; the written word is certainly another example. Although the book is only a delivery vehicle, it engages the mind interactively because of the reader's need to decipher its message. Writing and reading entail the active coding and decoding of information from visual signs into spoken language and vice versa. Alphabetic writing also requires the active analysis of spoken words into their basic phonemes so that each phoneme can be coded by a letter of the alphabet. Writing has traditionally functioned as a medium for exploration and discovery for both schoolchildren and adults. Indeed the creative output of science and the humanities would not have been possible without this evocative medium.

The computer, like the phonetic alphabet, has also had an impact on stimulating the development of new ideas because it, too, is an interactive medium on two accounts: as a medium of communication for the written word, and as a data-processing device. The computer provides the user with an additional dimension of interactivity compared with writing—namely, the capacity to manipulate data through word processing, spread sheet, and database software. It is the most powerful research tool and stimulus to new ideas developed since the invention of the alphabet, numerical notations, and printing press. Like these media, its use will contribute to the further cognitive development of its users. The Internet enhances the interactivity of computing because of hypertext and the ability to navigate through a field of information.

An Educational Medium

The microcomputer and the Internet are media that promote educational activity, especially continuous learning, and hence can liberate untapped potential in students and workers by allowing its users to develop new cognitive skills as well as reinforce their literacy skills. In contrast, TV does not promote learning because it is basically a noninteractive medium that merely transmits information to passive viewers. Television informs, but it does not educate. Television viewers do not develop new cognitive skills as a result of using the medium. This helps explain why TV was such a disappointment as an educational medium. Information does not equal education; the ability to process information is an essential part of education, and TV does not promote this activity. Computing and the Internet allow their users to maintain their contact with the alphabet, whereas TV is a purely iconic medium. Print promotes educational activity because, in addition to informing its readers through its content, its use, unlike that of TV, requires that the individual possess certain cognitive skills to decode its content. The computer and Internet, like the printing press, provide media that increase access to alphabetic-based text and hence promote learning. Not only do these media provide additional access to alphabetic texts, but they do so in a way that is not dependent on institutions such as schools or libraries; hence, the learning they promote is both continuous and individualized.

Microcomputers encourage continuous learning in two ways: (a) they provide a medium for such learning, and (b) their presence in the workplace requires workers to engage in continuous learning just to keep up with the latest developments in technology. Before microcomputing continuous learning was engaged in by those who wished to advance their careers; today it is a necessity just to keep one's job.

Continuous and Individualized Learning

The computer and Internet are ideal media for delivering and promoting individualized and continuous learning. One of the advantages of microcomputers for individualized instruction is their ability to provide instant feedback without embarrassing the user if a mistake has been made. The use of microcomputers in education reminds us of the importance of individualized learning—not only with computers, but with other media as well. Individualized learning is not unique to computers. The book is also a medium that is conducive to individualized learning. Before the advent of printing, books were a precious hand-crafted commodity chained to tables and studied by individual students rather than a classroom of students all at once. Before printing, each student studied the manuscript most appropriate for his level of knowledge. The printing press and the mass production of textbooks changed the pattern of book usage in school. The self-taught person who does not attend school, but learns by reading books, continues to pursue an individualized style of learning.

The computer coupled with the Internet, an ideal source of learning material, provides both students and adults the opportunity for continuous learning outside the classroom. The Internet provides the opportunity to individualize learning because of the vast richness of its resources. Users follow their own individual paths on the Internet. They can bookmark their favorite sites so they can return to those places that pique their curiosity and where they have their best learning experiences. The fact that the Internet provides access to such a rich array of resources means that each individual student can find topics and information that appeals to his or her specific interests and needs.

The Affective Domain

The microcomputer and Internet have the potential to promote a positive attitude toward learning and work and encourage a positive self-
image. Microcomputers and Internet enjoy wide acceptance and enthusi-
astic responses from students and workers worldwide across a variety of
educational and work settings. This is not to suggest that every person
who uses a computer and/or surfs the Internet automatically enjoys his
or her learning or work. Computers are not a panacea, but they do provide a significant number of people with an alternative to print-based
learning and work environments. Another factor that motivates workers
who use computers is their belief in its importance for the advancement
of their careers. The computer also relieves much of the tedium of work
because it does repetitive tasks so easily. It also provides stimulation
and a constant source of challenge and hence makes people's work more
interesting.

Social and Learning Interactions

The microcomputer has the potential to profoundly change the social
interactions in our classrooms and workplaces. Because of its two-way
communication capability, the Internet also impacts on social interactions. One of the earliest fears surrounding the use of computers was the
concern that users would become antisocial automata—so transfixed by
their interactions with computers that they would lose interest in inter-
acting with their fellow classmates or coworkers. The intense social interaction and cooperation that surround computer use in both the classroom and workplace show that these fears were ungrounded, illustrating
once again that the effects of media are sometimes counterintuitive. The
microcomputer actually promotes cooperation and social interaction.
    The social interactions of computer users in schools or the office are
intense. Users are constantly conversing with one another, answering
one another's questions, and discussing what they are doing. Books do
not invite the same level of intense social interaction. There is something
intrinsically private about reading. Silence is requested in a library, but
not where computers are used. Mandatory silence would kill the social
interactions necessary for the successful use of computers. People use
books in public places such as trains or airports to achieve privacy; one
hesitates to interrupt someone who is reading or writing, but one feels
less compunction about talking to someone working at a computer.
    Peer teaching, the presence of experts, and the intense socialization
surrounding the use of computers all contribute to a completely different learning and management style among computer users. It is general-

ly recognized that the use of computers has helped flatten out hierarchical structures in business and led to a team-oriented rather than command-and-control style of management. Because of its capability for two-way communication, the Internet can also change the social interplay in either the classroom or the workplace. Computer users can make links outside the classroom. Meaningful learning experiences can develop with individuals in another city or country or company or department. The concept of the classroom without walls can expand right across the globe. The Internet also allows the network of co-learners and coaches to extend beyond the confines of an organization.

A Grass-Roots Movement

The microcomputer is the first technology introduced into the school system and workplace at the grass-roots level by teachers, pupils, workers, and middle managers rather than by senior administrators. The Internet was another tool that was introduced at the grassroots level. The grass-roots support of microcomputers and Internet were the key to their success. One of the important and interesting effects of the use of microcomputers coupled with the Internet is the autonomy it provides its users.

Integrating the Curriculumand Work Flow

The microcomputer is an ideal medium for the integration of the curriculum in the schools and the flow of work in the workplace. The Internet amplifies this capacity for integration but adds a second dimension of alignment. One of McLuhan's basic insights into the nature of electronic media was that they tend to encourage the integration of information rather than its fragmentation, as is the case with print.

The current school curriculum, a product of the print era, is organized into separate subjects that are, more often than not, taught independently. The spirit of specialism can be found throughout the education system from the primary grades to postgraduate studies. The arrival of the computer is reversing this trend. For McLuhan the integration of the curriculum is inevitable. "In education the conventional division of the curriculum into subjects is already as outdated as the medieval trivium and quadrivium after the Renaissance. Any subject taken in depth at once relates to other subjects." (McLuhan, 1964, p. 347)

The microcomputer and Internet provide media through which all the business processes of an organization can be integrated and aligned (i.e., working together pursuing the same objectives). Alignment involves collaboration and knowledge sharing, whereas integration only requires teamwork.

The Microcomputer as an Agent of Reform

The microcomputer and Internet acting in consort will become increasingly greater and greater agents of reform by challenging the notion that hierarchical control-and-command structures are the most efficient way to conduct a business or educate children. The microcomputer and Internet have already begun to change the nature of schooling and business because of the way the medium changes social structures wherever it is used and because it promotes interactivity and individualized continuous learning at the grass-roots level. The two media working together provides an environment that encourages peer-to-peer interaction and, hence, knowledge sharing, networking, and co-creation. As a result of these features, the user is provided with a tool and medium that make him or her more independent of their teachers or managers. The microcomputer and Internet make every person his or her own teacher and manager. The alphabet has traditionally had a democratizing effect. The same is true of computing and the Internet.

Learning how to read and use a computer both entail access to new stores of information and both promote new organizational skills. It is perhaps because of these parallels that the term *computer literacy* arose, describing a new skill in terms of an older one. Although the use of computers involves alphabetic literacy, the term *computer literacy* does not describe the new skill accurately. The skill of using numbers is not referred to as number literacy, but rather as *numeracy*. In a similar way, the skill of using a computer could be called *computeracy*.

Another reason for discouraging the use of the term *computer literacy* is that it conveys the erroneous conception that literacy—the use of the alphabet—and computeracy are basically the same. In terms of the lateralization of the brain, the skills associated with literacy are those of the left lobe, whereas the skills required for use of the computer require more of a mixture of left- and right-brain skills. It is this central fact that makes the computer such an important breakthrough in communications technology—the most significant since the invention of the movable type printing press and before that the phonetic alphabet.

AN EPILOGUE—THE EXTENDED MIND: THE ORIGIN, EVOLUTION, AND CHAOTICS OF HUMAN LANGUAGE, THOUGHT, AND COMMUNICATIONS

Shakespeare wrote that every exit is an entrance. I want to exit this book by sharing with readers some speculative ideas currently occupying me and which will form the basis of my next project. These ideas attempt to explain the origin and evolution of human language, thought, and communication by making use of complexity theory. They arise directly from my work on the alphabet effect, which began with McLuhan in 1977. Starting from the perspective that media are not merely passive conduits for carrying information or communicating ideas, but "living vortices of power creating hidden environments (and effects) that act abrasively and destructively on older forms of culture" (Innis, 1972, p. v, McLuhan's foreword), McLuhan and I (1977) discovered that the phonetic alphabet created an environment that led to a number of profound forms of human thought, including codified law, monotheism, abstract science, and deductive logic. This insight in turn led me to the notion that language is both communication and informatics, and that from spoken language there evolved a chain of notated forms of language— namely, writing, math, science, computing, and the Internet (Logan, 2000)—with each new form of language emerging to deal with the complexity due to some form of information overload that the previous forms of language generated.

These results leave us with the intriguing question of how the first form of human language—speech, emerges in the first place. This is the question I will address in the Extended Mind project. The development of language is the one characteristic of *Homo sapiens* that distinguishes it from all other species. All species communicate, as the behavior of bees, birds, and primates demonstrates. No other species, however, has created such a perfect tool for abstract thinking as human language. I believe that verbal language in the form of speech arose out of the need of prehuman hominids to conceptualize. The world of hominids became progressively more complex as they acquired the capability for tool making, controlling fire, social intelligence needed to live in large groups to share the advantages of fire, large-scale coordinated hunting, and mimetic communication or signaling through gestures, hand signals, body language, and nonverbal vocalization.

The chaos that emerged with this complexity gave rise to a new level of order in the form of spoken language, which represented in terms of Prigogene's theories of chaos and complexity a bifurcation from nonverbal to verbal language and communication. It also represented a bifurcation from percept-based thought to concept-based thought or conceptualization. I believe that all of the hominid skills iterated earlier—from tool making to mimetic communication—were percept based, and that the emergence of concepts in the form of words increased the chances for survival of those hominids that could verbalize their thoughts and hence conceptualize.

The first concepts were words that served as both metaphors and strange attractors for certain sets of percepts. The word *water* united all the experiences with water whether it was drunk, bathed in, or fell as rain. This transition from percept- to concept-based thinking and from nonverbal to verbal language also represented the transition or bifurcation from prehuman hominids to full blown-human beings, *Homo sapiens sapiens*. The hominid brain was basically a percept processor, but with language it bifurcated into the human mind that could conceptualize and process abstract information, react to situations ahead of time, and, hence, make plans. The mind is the brain plus language. This line of thinking justifies one of the basic assumptions of my work—namely, that language is more than just a communications system—it is also an informatics tool. It also ties in with Vygotsky's hypothesis that the evolution of speech is connected with the use and manufacture of tools and the growth of the braincase. "Biological evolution ties in with the growth of culture, since the use of language seems obviously associated with habitual tool use (limiting the use of gestures) and with increasing human intelligence" (Vygotsky, 1962).

The two principle uses of speech are for abstracting experience through conceptualization and communication. In preliterate societies, speech was the medium for social interactions and a tool for the coordination of activities that require cooperation, such as hunting or food gathering. Spoken language evolved more complex functions and was used in the cultural apparatus of a society to tell tales and sing songs. Eventually speech was used as a medium to record (or store) and retrieve cultural information in the form of poems, folktales, and folk songs. As stories became more complex, speech was used to organize the information stored in these formats. Organizational forms such as rhyme, rhythm, meter, and plot, in turn, became information tools that permitted larger amounts of data to be stored and successfully retrieved (Havelock, 1963).

Eventually, however, speech and the human capacity for memorization encountered limits as to how much data could be recorded in this manner. Writing systems and numerical notations emerged, which allowed the amount and type of data being stored to expand enormously. The invention of writing and mathematical notations also had a tremendous impact on the informatic capacity of human language and thought. Written records gave rise to new forms of classification, analysis, and other forms of information processing, especially with the invention of the phonetic alphabet. And this brings us back full circle to the alphabet effect. It is my hope with the Extended Mind project to fill in the details of the evolution I have sketched that leads from hominid tool making to the origins of speech and the human mind and from there to the emergence of the alphabet.

References

Ahn, P. Hi. (1997). The principles underlying the invention of the Korean alphabet. In Young-Key Kim-Renaud, (Ed.), *The Korean Alphabet*. Honolulu: University of Hawaii Press.

Albright, W. F. (1957). *From the Stone Age to Christianity* (2nd ed.). Garden City, NY: Doubleday.

Albright, W. F. (1966). *The Proto–Sinaitic incriptions and their development* (Harvard Theological Studies XXII). Cambridge, MA: Harvard University Press.

Arberry, A. J. (1964). *The Koran interpreted*. London: Oxford University Press.

Aston, M. (1968). *The Fifteenth century: The prospect of Europe*. London: Thames and Hudson.

Bayer, C. (1968). *A history of mathematics*.

Bellamy, J. A. (1989). The Arabic alphabet. In W. Senner (Ed.), *The origin of writing*. Lincoln and London: University of Nebraska Press.

Bernal, J. (1954). *Science in history*. London: Watts.

Bitter, G., & Camuse, R. (1984). *Using a microcomputer in the classroom*. Reston, VA: Reston Publishing Company.

Bloomfield, L. (1933). *Language*. New York: Holt.

Bloom, A. H. (1981). *The linguistic shaping of thought*. Hillsdale, NJ: Erlbaum.

Bohl, F. M. Th. (1946). *King Hammurabi of Babylon in the setting of his time*. Amsterdam: H. S. Paris.

Boman, T. (1960). *Hebrew thought compared with Greeks*. London: SCM Press.

Breasted, J. H. (1926). *The conquest of civilization*. New York: Harper and Row.

Bright, J. (1959). *A history of Israel*. Philadelphia: Westminster Press.

Buber, M. (1998). *Moses: The revelation and the covenant*. Atlantic Highlands, NJ: Humanities Press.

Buhler, C. (1961). *The fifteenth century book*. Philadelphia: University of Pennsylvania Press.

247

Burckhardt, J. (1883). *Die Kultur des Renaissance* [The Culture of Renaissance]. Berlin.

Carothers, J. C. (1959). Culture, psychiatry and the written word. *Psychiatry.*

Carpenter, R. (1933). The antiquity of the Greek alphabet. *American Journal of Archeology, 37,* 8–29.

Carpenter, R. (1938). The Greek alphabet again. *American Journal of Archeology, 42,* 58–69.

Chao, Y. R. (1976). *Aspects of Chinese sociolinguistics.* Stanford: Stanford University Press.

Chassant. (1864). *Dictionnaire des abbreviations latines et franfaises usitees dans les manuscrits.* Paris.

Chaytor, H. (1945). *From script to print.* Cambridge: Cambridge University Press.

Christianson, J. (1972, October 26). *Astronomy and printing.* Paper presented at 16th Century Studies conference, Concordia Seminary, St. Louis, MO.

Clodd, E. (1913). *The story of the alphabet.* New York: Appleton.

Coburn, P. et al., (1982). *Practical guide to computers in education.* Reading, MA: Addison-Wesley.

Cochrane, J. A. (1964). *Dr. Johnson's printer: The life of William Strahan.* London: Routledge and K. Pane.

Cottrell, L. (1965). *Quest for Sumer.* New York: Putnam.

Crombie, C. (1963). *Medieval and early modern science* (Vol. II). Cambridge, MA: Harvard University Press.

Cross, F. M. (1967). The origin and early evolution of the alphabet. *Eretz-Israel.*

Cross, F. M. (1980). Newly found inscriptions in old Canaanite and early Phoenician script. *Bulletin of the American School of Oriental Research, 238.*

Cross, F. M. (1989). The invention and the development of the alphabet. In W. Senner (Ed.), *The origin of writing.* Lincoln and London: University of Nebraska Press.

Czernis, L., & Logan, R. K. (1981). *Telidon as pure advertising: Implications for attention span.* Ottawa, Canada: Dept. of Communication Report.

Daly, L. W. (1967). *Contributions to a history of alphabetization.* Bruxelles: Latomus.

Dantzig, T. (1954). *Number: The language of science.* Garden City, NY: Doubleday.

Datta, B., & Singh, A. N. (1962). *History of hindu mathematics: A source book.* Bombay: Bombay Asia Publishing House.

Debus, A. (1978). *Man and nature in the Renaissance.* Cambridge: Cambridge University Press.

de Francis, J. (1989). *Visible speech: The diverse oneness of writing systems.* Honolulu: University of Hawaii Press.

de Saussure, F. (1967). *Grundfragen der allgemeinen Sprachwissenschaft* [basic questions of linguistics] (2nd ed.). Berlin: Springer Verlag.

de Solla Price, D. (1967, October 16). The book as a scientific instrument. *Science, 58,* 102–104.

Dickens, A. G. (1968). *Reformation and society in sixteenth century Europe.* New York: Harcourt Brace and World.

Diringer, D. (1948). *The alphabet.* New York.

Drake, S. (1970). Early science and the printed book: The spread of science beyond the universities. *Renaissance and Reformation, 6*(3), 43–53.

Driver, G. R. (1976). *Semitic writing from pictograph to alphabet.* London: Oxford University Press.

Dryer, J. (1890). *Tycho Brahe.* Edinburgh.

Easton, S. (1970). *The heritage of Western civilization to 1715.* New York: Holt, Rinehart & Winston.

Eberhard, W. (1957). The political function of astronomy in Han China. In J. Fairbank (Ed.), *Chinese thought and institutions.* Chicago: University of Chicago Press.

Ehrenberg, V. (1968). *From Solon to Socrates.* London: Methuen.

Eisenstein, E. L. (1979). *The printing press as an agent of change.* Cambridge: Cambridge University Press.

Elliott, R. W. V. (1959). *Runes: An introduction.* Manchester: Manchester University Press.

Escarra, J. (1936). *Le Droit Chinois.* Beijing.

Finkelstein, J. (1969). The laws of Ur-Nammu. In J. Pritchard (Ed.), *The ancient near east supplementary texts and pictures relating to the Old Testament.* Princeton, NJ: Princeton Univesity Press.

Fischer, H. G. (1989). The origin of Egyptian hieroglyphics. In W. Senner (Ed.), *The origin of writing.* Lincoln and London: University of Nebraska Press.

Flinders Petrie, W. M. (1906). *Researches in Sinai.* London: Murray.

Foucault, M. (1973). *The order of things.* New York: Vintage Books.

Fung, Y.-I. (1922). Why China has no science. *The International Journal of Ethics, 32.*

Gadd, C. J. (1965). *Hammurabi.* London: Cambridge University Press.

Gade, A. (1947). *The life of Tycho Brahe.* Princeton, NJ: Princeton University Press.

Gardiner, A. (1961). The Egyptian origin of the semitic alphabet. *Journal of Egyptian Archeology, 3,* 1–16.

Gelb, I. (1963). *A study of writing.* Chicago: University of Chicago Press.

Gibb, H. (1963). *Arabic literature.* Oxford: Clarendon Press.

Gibb, H., & Kramer, S. (unknown). Koran. In *Shorter Encyclopedia of Islam.* Leiden.

Giedion, S. (1969). *Mechanization takes command.* New York: Oxford University Press.

Goldschmidt, E. P. (1965). *Medieval texts and their first appearance in print.* Meisenheim: Hain.

Grimme, H. (1923). *Alterhebräische Inschriften von Sinai.* Hannover.

Hadas, M. (1950). *A history of Greek literature.* New York: Columbia University Press.

Hadas, M. (1952). *A history of Latin literature.* New York: Columbia University Press.

Hadas, M. (1954). *Ancilla to classical reading.* New York: Columbia University Press.

Hall, E., & Hall, M. (1975). *The fourth dimension in architecture.* Santa Fe, NM: Sunstone Press.

Hanson, C. (1998). *Language and logic in ancient China.* Bejing: Fa Hsing So.

Harbison, E. H. (1956). *Christian scholar in the age of the reformation.* New York: Scribner.

Harvey, F. D. (1978). Greeks and Romans learn to write. In E. Havelock & J. Herschbell (Eds.), *Communication arts in the ancient world.* New York: Hastings House.

Havelock, E. (1963). *Preface to Plato.* Oxford: Oxford University Press.

Havelock, E. (1971). *Prologue to Greek literacy.* Cincinnati: University of Cincinnati Press.

Havelock, E. (1976). *Origin of Western literacy.* Toronto: OISE Press.

Hayes, C. (1931). *Historical evolution of modern nationalism.* New York: R. R. Smith.

Hertzler, J. (1965). *A sociology of language.* New York: Cooper Square.

Hitti, P. (1961). *The Near East in history.* Princeton, NJ: Princeton University Press.

Hitti, P. (1964). *The Arabs.* Chicago: University of Chicago Press.

Hodgen, M. T. (1939) *Domesday water mills.* Antiquity XIII.

Innis, H. (1972). Empire and communication (2nd ed.). Toronto: University of Toronto Press.

Innis, H. (1971). *Bias of communication* (2nd ed.). Toronto: University of Toronto Press.

Iserloh, E. (1968). *The theses were not posted.* Boston: Beacon Press.

Kalgren, B. (1962). *Sound and symbol as Chinese.* Hong Kong: University of Hong Kong Press.

Kalgren, O. (1926). *Philology and ancient China.* Oslo.

Kapp, F. (1886). *Geschichte des Deutschen Buchhandels bis in das 17te Jahrhundert.* Leipzig.

Kaufman, Y. (1960). *The religion of Israel* (M. Greenberg, Trans.). Chicago: University of Chigago Press.

Keightley, D. N. (1989). *The origin of writing in China: Scripts and cultural contexts.* In W. Senner (Ed.), *The origin of writing.* Lincoln and London: University of Nebraska Press.

Kenyon, F. G. (1951). *Books and readers in ancient Greece and Rome.* Oxford: Clarendon Press.

Kepler, J. (1606). New star. In A. R. Lewis (Ed.), *Aspects of the Renaissance.* Austin: University of Texas Press.

Kim-Renaud, Y. K. (1997). Introduction. In Y. K. Kim-Renaud (Ed.), *The Korean alphabet*. Honolulu: University of Hawaii Press.

Kohn, H. (1944). *The idea of nationalism*. New York: MacMillan.

Kohn, H. (1955). *Nationalism: Its meaning and history*. New York: Macmillan.

Kramer, S. (1955). Lipit-Ishtar lawcode. In J. Pritchard (Ed.), *The ancient Near East texts relating to the Old Testament*. Princeton, NJ: Princeton University Press.

Kramer, S. (1956). *From the tablets of Sumer*. Indian Hill, CO: Falcon.

Kramer, S. (1959). *History begins at Sumer*. Garden City, NY: Doubleday Anchor Books.

Kramer, S. (1963). *The Sumerians*. Chicago: University of Chicago Press.

Kristeller, P., & Randall, J. (1948). *The Renaissance philosophy of man*. Chicago: University of Chicago

Krugman, H. E. (1971). Brain wave measures of media involvement. *Journal of Advertising Research, 2,* 1, 3–9.

Kuhn, T. S. (1957). *The Copernican revolution*. Cambridge, MA: Harvard University Press.

Kuhn, T. S. (1972). *The structure of scientific revolutions*. Chicago: University of Chicago Press.

Latourette, K. (1964). *The Chinese: Their history and culture*. New York: Macmillan Company.

Lehmann, R. P. (1989). Ogham: The ancient script of the celts. In W. Senner (Ed.), *The origin of writing*. Lincoln and London: University of Nebraska Press.

Levi-Strauss, C. (1960). *The savage mind*. London: Weidenfeld and Nicolson.

Logan, R. K. (1979). The mystery of the discovery of zero. *Etcetera, 36.*

Logan, R. K. (1982, March 1–2). Five technological breakthroughs. Cited at Telidon in the Total Information-Communications Environment Workshop, in *Proceedings of the DOC Workshop on Social Psychological Issues in Videotext Development*, University of Toronto.

Logan, R. K. (1986a). *The alphabet effect*. New York: William Morrow.

Logan, R. K. (1986b). *The use of computers in primary and junior science education: A guide for classroom teachers*, Consultants and Software Developers. Ontario Ministry of Education Report.

Logan, R. K. (2000). *The sixth language*. Toronto: Stoddart.

Logan, R., Padro, S., Miller, L., Ragsdale, R., Sullivan, E., Brine, J., Johnston, E. M., McKelvey, B., & Wideman, H. (1983). *Research questions on the impact of computers in the classroom* (Ont. Min. of Education. Ed. and Tech. Ser. ONO 4268).

Lounsbury, F. G. (1989). The ancient writing of middle America. In W. Senner (Ed.), *The origin of writing*. Lincoln and London: University of Nebraska Press.

Logan, R. K., McLuhan, H. M. (1979). Double bind of communications. *Human Futures.*

Luria, A. R. (1970). The functional organization of the brain. *Scientific American, 222*(3), 66–73.

Man, J. (2000). *Alpha beta: How our alphabet changed the Western world.* London: Headline Book Publishing.

Marmura, E. (1976). Arabic literature: A living heritage. In R. M. Savory (Ed.), *Introduction to Islamic civilization.* Cambridge, UK: Cambridge University Press.

Marshack, A. (1964). Tallies. *Science, 146,* 743.

McLean, G. F., & Aspell, P. J. (1971). *Ancient western philosophy.* New York: Appleton, Century, Crofts.

McLuhan, M. (1962). *The Gutenberg galaxy.* Toronto: University of Toronto Press.

McLuhan, M. (1964). *Understanding media.* New York: McGraw Hill.

McLuhan, M., & Logan, R. K. (1977). Alphabet, mother of invention. *Et Cetera, 34,* 373–383.

McLuhan, M., & McLuhan, E. (1988). *Laws of the media: The new science.* Toronto: University of Toronto Press.

Meek, T. (Unknown). The code of Hammurabi. In J. Pritchard (Ed.), *The ancient Near East texts relating to the Old Testament.* Princeton, NJ: Princeton University Press.

Mori, G. (1921). *Was hat Gutenberg erfunden?* Frankfurt.

Naveh, J. (1973). Some semitic epigraphical considerations on the antiquity of the Greek alphabet. *American Journal of Archeology, 77,* 1–8.

Naveh, J. (1982). *Early history of the alphabet.* Jerusalem: Magnes Press, Hebrew University.

Needham, J. (1956). *Science and civilization.* Cambridge: Cambridge University Press.

Needham, J. (1979). *The grand titration.* London: Allen and Unwin.

Neugebauer, O. (1952). *The exact sciences in antiquity.* Princeton, NJ: Princeton University Press.

Nicholson, R. (1969). *A literary history of the Arabs.* Cambridge, UK: Cambridge University Press.

Oauknin, M. (1999). *Mysteries of the alphabet.* New York: Abbeville Press.

Ong, W. J. (1982). *Orality and literacy.* London, New York: Methuen.

Ontario Ministry of Education. (1980). *Issues and directions.* Toronto: Ontario Ministry of Education

Oppenheim, L. (1964). *Ancient Mesopotamia.* Chicago: University of Chicago Press.

Paivio, A., & Begg, I. (1981). *Psychology of language.* Englewood Cliffs, NJ: Prentice-Hall.

Panofsky, E. (1972). *Renaissance and renascences in western art.* New York: Harper & Row.

Papert, S. (1980). *Mindstorms: Children, computers and powerful ideas.* New York: Basic Books.

Paton, W. R., & Hicks, E. L. (1891). *Inscriptions of Cos*. Oxford: Claredon Press.

Paul, H. (1890). Principles of the history of language (H. A. Strong, Trans.). London.

Pfeiffer, R. H. (1948). *Introduction to the Old Testament*. New York: Harper.

Pitschka, R. (1984). Little CAI in Hollister. In D. Peterson (Ed.), *The intelligent schoolhouse*. Reston, VA: Reston Publishing Company.

Pliny, the Elder. (1991). *Natural history*. London, New York: Penguin Books.

Putnam, G. (1962). *Books and their makers during the Middle Ages*. New York: Hillary House.

Rappaport, A. (1976). Private communication at a Club of Gnu seminar at New College, University of Toronto.

Reid, C. (1964). *From zero to infinity*. London: Routledge and Kegan Paul.

Robinson, C. E. (1948). *Hellas: A short history of ancient Greece*. Boston: Beacon Press.

Roux, G. (1980). *Ancient Iraq* (2nd ed.). Harmondsworth: Penguin.

Safadi, Y. H. (1978). *Islamic Callig*. Oxford: Oxford University Press.

Sansom, G. (1968). *An historical grammar of Japanese*. Oxford: Claredon Press.

Sarton, G. (1957). *Six wings*. Bloomington: Indiana University Press.

Savory, R. M. (1976). Law and traditional society. In R. M. Savory (Ed.), *Introduction to Islamic civilization*. Cambridge, UK: Cambridge University Press.

Schmandt-Besserat, D. (1978). The earliest precursor of writing. *Scientific American, 238*.

Schmandt-Besserat, D. (1979). An archaic recording system in the Uruk-Jemdet Nasr period. *American Journal of Archeology, 83*.

Schmandt-Besserat, D. (1980). The envelopes that bear the first writing. *Technology and Culture, 21*(3).

Schmandt-Besserat, D. (1981a). Decipherment of the earliest tablets. *Science, 211*(3), 283–285.

Schmandt-Besserat, D. (1981b). From tokens to tablets: A re-evaluation of the so-called numerical tablets. *Visible Language, 15*(4), 321–344.

Schmandt-Besserat, D. (1982a). How writing came about. *Zeitschrift fur Papyrologie und Epigraphik, 47*.

Schmandt-Besserat, D. (1982b). The emergence of recording. *American Anthropologist, 84*, 872–876.

Schmandt-Besserat, D. (1983, Spring). Tokens and counting. *Biblical Archeologist*, 117–120.

Schmandt-Besserat, D. (1984a). Before numerals. *Visible Language, 18*.

Schmandt-Besserat, D. (1984b). The use of clay before pottery in the Zagros. *Expedition, 16*(2).

Schmandt-Besserat, D. (1985). Clay symbols for data storage in the VIII Millennium B.C. In M. Puglisi (Ed.), *Studi di Palentologia in onore di Salvatore*. La Spaienza: Universita di Roma.

Schmandt-Besserat, D. (1986a). An ancient token system: The precursors to numerals and writing. *Archeology, 39*(6).

Schmandt-Besserat, D. (1986b). The origins of writing. *Written Communication, 13.*

Schmandt-Besserat, D. (1986c). Tokens at Susa. *Oriens Antiquus, 25*(1–2).

Schmandt-Besserat, D. (1987). *Oneness, twoness, threeness. The sciences.* New York: Academy of Sciences.

Schmandt-Besserat, D. (1988a). Quantification and social structure. In D. R. Maines & C. J. Couch (Eds.), *Communication and social structure.* Springfield, IL: C.C. Thomas.

Schmandt-Besserat, D. (1988b). Tokens at Uruk. *Bagdader Mitteilungen, 19.*

Schmandt-Besserat, D. (1992). *Before writing: Vol. 1. From counting to cuneiform.* Houston: University of Texas Press.

Shlain, L. (1998). *The alphabet and the goddess.* New York: Viking.

Smith, F. (1982). *Writing and the writer.* New York: Holt, Rinehart & Winston.

Speises. (1960). In E. Meyers (Ed.), *Education in the perspective of history.* New York: Harper.

Sprengling, M. (1931). *The alphabet: Its rise and development from the Sinai incriptions.* Chicago: University of Chicago Press.

Srinivasiengar, C. N. (1967). *The history of Ancient Indian mathematics.* Calcutta: Calcutta World Press.

Steinberg, S. (1955). *Five hundred years of printing.* Middlesex, UK: Penguin Books.

Strauss, G. (1965). A sixteenth century encyclopedia. In C. H. Carter (Ed.), *From the Renaissance to the counter-reformation.* New York: Random House.

Stroud, R. S. (1989). The art of writing in Ancient Greece. In W. Senner (Ed.), *The origin of writing.* Lincoln and London: University of Nebraska Press.

Stubbs, M. (1980). *Language and literacy.* London: Routledge & Kegan Paul.

Sullivan, E., Olson, P., Watson, N., Bors, D., Wideman, H., Zimmerman, J. & Logan, R. K. (1986). *The development of policy and research projections for computers in education: A comparative ethnography.* (Project No. 499-83-0017). Study funded by Social Science and Humanities Research Council of Canada and carried out at Ontario Institute for Studies in Education, Toronto.

Taylor, R.P., (Ed.). (1980). *The computer in the school: Tutor, tool, tutee.* New York: Columbia University, Teachers College Press.

Toffler, A. (1980). *The third wave.* New York: William Morrow.

Toffler, A. (1990). *Powershift.* New York: Bantam.

Usher, A. (1954). *A history of mechanical inventions.* Cambridge, MA: Howard University Press.

Van der Waerden, B. (1954). *Science awakening.* Groningen: P. Noordhoff.

Ventris, M., & Chadwick, J. (1973). *Documents in Mycenaean Greek* (2nd ed.). Cambridge: Cambridge University Press.

Vygotsky, L. (1962). *Thought and language.* Cambridge, MA: MIT Press.

Wallace, R. (1989). The origin and development of the Latin alphabet. In W. Senner (Ed.), *The origin of writing.* Lincoln and London: University of Nebraska Press.

Webster, T. B. L. (1960). *From Mycenea to Homer.* London.

Welland, J. (1972). *By the waters of Babylon.* London.

White, L. (1940). Technology and invention in the Middle Ages. *Speculum, 15.*

White, L. (1962). *Social change and medieval technology.* Oxford: Oxford University Press.

White, L. (1968). *Machina ex deo.* Cambridge, MA: Howard University Press.

Wickens, G. M. (1976). The Middle East as world centre of science and medicine. In R. M. Savory (Ed.), *Introduction to islamic civilization.* Cambridge, UK: Cambridge University Press.

Yi, K.-M. (1975). Language and writing systems in traditional Korea. In P. H. Lee (Ed.), *The traditional culture and society of Korea: Art and literature* (Occasional Papers of the Center for Korean Studies, 4, 15–32). Honolulu: University of Hawaii.

Author Index

257

Subject Index

CPSIA information can be obtained at www.ICGtesting.com
Printed in the USA
LVOW07*1626300116

472139LV00003B/6/P